Inclusive Research with People
with Learning Disabilities

of related interest

Women with Intellectual Disabilities
Finding a Place in the World
Edited by Rannveig Traustadottir and Kelley Johnson
ISBN 1 85302 846 0

Sexuality and Women with Learning Disabilities
Michelle McCarthy
ISBN 1 85302 730 8

Advocacy and Learning Disability
Edited by Barry Gray and Robin Jackson
ISBN 1 85302 942 4

Quality of Life and Disability
An Approach for Community Practitioners
Roy Brown and Ivan Brown
ISBN 1 84310 005 3

Helping People with a Learning Disability Explore Choice
Eve and Neil Jackson, illustrated by Tim Baker
ISBN 1 85302 694 8

Helping People with a Learning Disability Explore Relationships
Eve and Neil Jackson, illustrated by Tim Baker
ISBN 1 85302 688 3

Ethical Practice and the Abuse of Power in Social Responsibility
Leave No Stone Unturned
Edited by Helen Payne and Brian Littlechild
ISBN 1 85302 743 X

User Involvement and Participation in Social Care
Research Informing Practice
Edited by Hazel Kemshall and Rosemary Littlechild
ISBN 1 85302 777 4

Inclusive Research with People with Learning Disabilities

Past, Present and Futures

Jan Walmsley and Kelley Johnson

Jessica Kingsley Publishers
London and New York

First published in the United Kingdom in 2003
by Jessica Kingsley Publishers Ltd
116 Pentonville Road
London N1 9JB, England
and
29 West 35th Street, 10th fl.
New York, NY 10001-2299, USA

www.jkp.com

Library of Congress Cataloging in Publication Data

A CIP catalog record for this book is available from the Library of Congress

British Library Cataloguing in Publication Data

A CIP catalogue record for this book is available from the British Library

ISBN 1 84310 061 4

Printed and Bound in Great Britain by
Athenaeum Press, Gateshead, Tyne and Wear

Contents

Acknowledgements   7

Introduction: Reputable? Helpful?...and Inclusive?   9

PART 1: DESCRIBING THE PAST   21

1   Of Shoes and Ships and Sealing Wax and...
Inclusive Research: Or Where Did It All Start?   23

2   Normalizing, Emancipating and Making a Stand   44

3   Inclusive Research in Learning Disability: Beginnings   61

4   Knowing the Elephant   79

PART 2: EXPLORING THE RESEARCH PROCESS   93

5   Nothing About Us Without Us: *Good Times Bad Times*   95

6   Living Safer Sexual Lives: Making Research Work   109

7   What Matters to People with Learning Disabilities?   126

8   Managing Inclusive Research   146

9   Who Uses it and How?   164

10   What Has Been Achieved?   183

PART 3: BEYOND RHETORIC TO NEW REALITIES   189

11   Beyond Rhetoric...   191

12   ...To New Realities   207

Conclusion: Why Do It?   220

References   224

Subject index   244

Author index   253

Acknowledgements

We would like to thank most sincerely many people with whom we have worked over the years on 'inclusive research' projects. It is invidious to single out individuals, but Jan would particularly like to thank her long standing friend and colleague, Dorothy Atkinson, and, though she may not thank her for mentioning it, Simone Aspis, whose challenges to us 'non disabled' researchers over the years have really kept her on her toes. She would also like to record her thanks to Ian Davies, Nigel Lott and Karen Spencer (plus Neil Morris) of Central England People First, and to Kathleen Franklin and colleagues at Milton Keynes People First.

Kelley would particularly like to thank Marian Pitts for her assistance in reading and commenting on the manuscript, Ria Strong and Janice Slattery for their contributions to the book and Lynne Hillier, Lyn Harrison and Patsie Frawley for their contributions to the thinking which underlies the chapter on Living Safer Sexual Lives.

We would like also to thank most sincerely Jane, Jim, Kate, Spen and Sam for living with us, and for offering the warmth, support and forbearance without which books like this never get written!

Introduction

Reputable? Helpful?...
And Inclusive?

In social research you are usually either disreputable or unhelpful.

(Marris and Rein 1969, p.14)

This book is about inclusive research as it has developed in the learning disability field in the past two decades. We will be spending a lot of time explaining and debating what is inclusive research in the course of the book, but for the moment we will define it as research in which people with learning disabilities are active participants, not only as subjects but also as initiators, doers, writers and disseminators of research.

Many researchers struggle to resolve the tension that exists between research which is academically rigorous, acceptable to funding organizations and publishable, and research which is of use to the people who are subject to it, which is relevant to their needs and can inform and promote needed social change. A resolution of this tension is probably not possible. Rather it is met anew with each study and involves a continual process of balancing and compromise. It is a 'big ask' to be both reputable and helpful – and it is not enough.

The quotation itself encapsulates some of the dilemmas that have led us to write this book. A certain degree of reputability is necessary. Without it future research will not be funded and there will be a lack of trust in the work itself. Yet being reputable alone can mean books, reports and articles left on dusty shelves, unread, untouched and of little use to those about whom they are written. To be helpful sounds worthy and practical. But helpfulness can be a problematic way of perceiving both the research process and those who are involved in it. In inclusive research particularly, it can mean researchers positioned as the helpers – strong and powerful and with knowledge and skills. Those with whom researchers work are positioned as the experts, but experts who need help, who are powerless and needy.

This is not the way we want to see ourselves or those around us. Rather we view the research situation as a microcosm of the wider community. For people with learning disabilities that community is often unfriendly and excluding. Within this smaller world of research many researchers, as the book shows, have tried to create more equitable structures and relationships. Researchers have tried to move beyond being reputable and helpful by transforming the nature of the research process itself to one which changes radically the nature of the power relations in research, the ways in which it is done and its outcomes. In doing this they have moved towards an approach which in this book we have called inclusive research.

Defining inclusive research

Essentially this book seeks to explore the many meanings attached to inclusive research with a particular emphasis on how it has been used by and with people with learning disabilities. The brief definition of inclusive research that we give here provides an orientation to the book rather than a final definition. Inclusive research as used here embraces a range of research approaches that traditionally have been termed 'participatory', 'action' or 'emancipatory' (Freire 1970c; Reason 1998). Such research involves people who may otherwise be seen as subjects for the research as instigators of ideas, research designers, interviewers, data analysts, authors, disseminators and users. Each of these forms of research has specific meanings for those who espouse it; each is privileged territory for certain groups of researchers. It is for these reasons that we have decided to use the term inclusive research.

The term inclusive research also has the advantage of being less cumbersome and more readily explained to people unfamiliar with the nuances of academic debate – including people with learning disabilities.

The issues of what makes inclusive research, how it is done and what its implications are, are contentious for all those involved in it. This book has been written in part to address the meanings of inclusive research and to explore some of these issues.

There are good reasons for attempting this now. The move to what we have called inclusive research with people with learning disabilities gained pace in the 1990s until there were literally hundreds of studies which owed some inspiration to the ideas of inclusive research, in the UK (primarily), but also in Australia, New Zealand, Canada, Ireland and, to a lesser extent, the USA and some parts of continental western Europe. This proliferation of studies, while very welcome, also demonstrated a certain lack of clarity and some limitations, which to us as inclusive researchers ourselves seemed to need some exploration and clarification. Hence the decision to write this as an attempt to clarify and suggest future direction.

Why this book?

The book was inspired by a long discussion as we (the authors) walked around a lake on an early spring day. It continued over a long pub lunch that followed the walk. We talked about the excitements and frustrations of undertaking inclusive research and of our growing unease about some aspects of it. Since then we have had numerous discussions together and with other researchers to reflect on these issues. It is out of these discussions, and from experience of trying to do inclusive research over many years, that this book has been shaped.

Our preliminary discussions revealed that the ideas informing the book had been slowly developing within each of us over the long period of our work as researchers with people with learning disabilities. We were both in at the beginning of research approaches in the UK, and to a lesser extent in Australia, which sought to challenge long-held assumptions that people with learning disabilities had nothing to say that was of value to researchers. They were, at best, passive beneficiaries of well-intentioned academics who argued for improved services (see, for example, Bayley 1973) and, at worst, dehumanized objects whose actions were observed and counted with no recognition of their humanity (Lyons and Heaton Ward 1955; Tredgold 1947). We would regard ourselves, and be regarded by many in the field, as activists who pioneered involvement and inclusion in a number of ways. We have written this book not only because we believe it is time to record, review and celebrate what has been achieved (a great deal), but also because we are troubled by a certain stifling of debate about the real difficulties of including people with learning disabilities in research. We believe it is time to challenge certain orthodoxies and assumptions in order to clarify what inclusive research is and how and where it can be applied.

First, the celebration: as we will show, inclusive research with people with learning disabilities has a relatively short history. Although one can point to a few examples of life histories or autobiographies which date from the 1970s or earlier (Bogdan and Taylor 1976, 1982; Deacon 1974), we would place the beginnings of the inclusive research era no earlier than the late 1980s. The late 1980s saw a modest exploration of methodologies which sought to enable people with learning disabilities to have a voice in research publications, particularly in the UK (Atkinson 1986; Flynn 1989; Jahoda, Markova and Cattermole 1989b).

Know Me As I Am: An Anthology of Prose, Poetry and Art by People with Learning Difficulties (Atkinson and Williams 1990) was the first major mainstream publication which claims to represent the authentic voices of people with learning disabilities. The authors themselves acknowledge that it appeared at the outset (in 1987) as a risky enterprise. Would people have anything more to offer than a banal description of uneventful lives? Would it be their own stories, or would other people, intermediaries, actually take over? In the event, a rich vein of thoughts, experiences, personal histories and political perspectives was revealed, drawing on the work of over 200 contributors across the UK, and the book has come to be seen as marking a paradigm shift (Booth and Booth 1994). Since then, numerous projects have been initiated and completed that draw people with learning disabilities into research in ways which would have been unimaginable in the mid-twentieth century. Such projects have been seen as part of an emerging social movement in which people take up new roles that confound previous assumptions and cast those with learning disabilities in a fresh light, as significant and influential actors (Bersani 1998). Part of our aim in this book is to review these remarkable developments and their significance, and to celebrate what has been achieved in a number of different western countries in only a little over a decade.

Inclusion is not just an issue of abstract celebration. Its importance in relation to marginalized groups, particularly people with learning disabilities, has been acknowledged by those who provide funding for social research in both the UK and Australia.

Some philanthropic trusts and government departments in both our countries now have the inclusion of participants in the research process as a criterion by which research submissions are judged. For example, in England the Department of Health Learning Disability Research Initiative, launched in 2000, set one of the five criteria for judging the worth of the bids as 'involvement of users and carers' – formal recognition that inclusion is central, not just an optional extra. People with learning disabilities joined the commissioners of research in selecting those to be funded. The Stegley Foundation in Australia has included the need for prospective projects to demonstrate partnerships and participation by users in its criteria for the selection of funded projects. It is therefore of increasing pragmatic importance to those involved in funded research that they understand the shifting nature of inclusive research and its implications for their work.

In preparing this book we were conscious that it is not only about research. Many of the contested issues about inclusive research mirror fundamental debates about social inclusion, about the involvement of users and carers in developing and evaluating services, about the nature of citizenship and how it can encompass and accommodate difference, and about the use of power by different groups within our society. Although we have used research as the focus of this book because that is what we know most about, we believe it will make a significant contribution to these broader debates about the inclusion of people with learning disabilities and other marginalized groups in the twenty-first century.

Although most of the case studies included in this book involve research with people with learning disabilities, we have also had experience in working with other people who historically have been silenced and marginalized, and who are demanding inclusion and involvement in ways unimaginable only 20 years ago. For example, Kelley Johnson has worked with women on low incomes on health matters and with women from linguistically and culturally diverse backgrounds on gambling issues in Australia (Brown *et al.* 1998; Brown, Johnson and Wyn 2001; Gridley *et al*, 1998; Moore, Gridley and Johnson. 2000). Jan Walmsley began to include people with head injuries in her work following her daughter's experience of a serious road traffic accident in 1998.

Finally, this book has been written to discuss and explore some of the dilemmas and difficulties we have experienced in working inclusively with people with learning disabilities. To suggest that inclusive research is easy, always positive and fulfilling for all parties would be a fairy tale: yet sometimes accounts of it suggest a happy-ever-after process and ending. We believe that there are real difficulties in undertaking inclusive research for the researcher as well as for people with learning disabilities. Sometimes we have felt as if research must bear the burden of the injustices which people with learning disabilities experience in the rest of society. It then behoves us as researchers to provide a model in our work which will change the surrounding social structures and processes. At times this has been a difficult and even unachievable goal. Sometimes we have felt silenced, disempowered and devalued as we have tried to ensure the centrality of people with learning disabilities in the research design and process. Sometimes we have felt frustrated by the difficulties of theorizing within an inclusive context. None of these concerns are insurmountable, but in the current environment of inclusive research they remain unsaid. We hope in this book to begin to take discussion of inclusive research into new areas and open up possibilities hitherto unexplored.

Who the book is for

The readership for the book is broader than researchers and those working specifically with people with learning disabilities. We believe that readers will find it useful if their work involves listening to service users, and taking their views into account in designing and delivering services, as a commissioner or as a manager of health and social care services or a teacher working in integrated schools. Intending or practising professionals in the human services who expect to engage with people from marginalized groups in their work, either as a student or as a practitioner, will also find it helpful. People will find it at the very least thought provoking if their work involves them in soliciting the views and experiences of marginalized people of all types.

This is not a 'how to do' manual, but we hope that by drawing together in one place a comprehensive range of examples of inclusive research, those embarking on projects which seek to involve people with learning disabilities, whether in evaluating or planning services or in major research projects, will find it of practical use.

Why are people with learning disabilities not part of the target audience?

Although both of us have co-written extensively with people with learning disabilities (Johnson *et al.* 2002c; Millear with Johnson 2000; Slattery with Johnson 2000; Walmsley with Downer 1997), co-edited books by women with learning disabilities (Atkinson *et al.* 2000) and been involved in innovative projects which have included people with learning disabilities in education (Johnson *et al.* 2000b; Open University 1996), we have not included them as co-writers in this book or as likely readers, at least in this form.

The reason they are not included is because we feel we need space to air arguments and debates before attempting to 'translate' them into accessible formats. Indeed, one of the frustrations of being involved in inclusive research in our experience is that the need to translate research questions and findings has in itself been a barrier to clarifying and theorizing, and that this has inhibited the vigorous growth of inclusive methodologies. We argue in the book that this has prevented the sort of high level theorizing that characterizes women's studies, disability studies and black and ethnic studies. We chose, on this occasion, to permit ourselves the liberty of extensive exploration *before* attempting to make the ideas accessible.

In adopting this position and in raising questions about some of the assumptions underpinning inclusive research, we admit to a considerable sense of discomfort, even disloyalty, to people we have worked with over many years, some of whom we count as friends as well as professional colleagues. Even writing a book such as this as non-disabled academics flies in the face of some current orthodoxies in learning disabilities research which say 'Nothing about us without us' (see, for example, Aspis 2000; Harrison *et al.* 2002). We anticipate considerable criticism. However, we would argue that failure to grapple honestly with some of the questions underlying the struggles we and others have in pursuing inclusive research actually limits its impact and effectiveness, and risks marginalizing it to just a handful of committed researchers. It is as if some researchers are being left to work in inclusive ways, leaving others to carry on regardless. The principles upon which inclusive research is based are as follows:

- that research must address issues which really matter to people with learning disabilities, and which ultimately leads to improved lives for them

- that it must access and represent their views and experiences

- that people with learning disabilities need to be treated with respect by the research community.

They are just too important to be left entangled in a marsh of political correctness. Furthermore, we would argue that the future development of inclusive research requires us to reflect critically and honestly on the contradictions inherent in current practice and assumptions so that it can move forward, untrammelled by unhelpful dogmatizing. As Riddell, Wilkinson and Baron (1998, pp.81–2) comment: 'Current models ...suggest that the pulls either to the trivial or to the professionally stage managed are hard to resist!'

We believe that a frank and open debate about some of the difficulties of undertaking this kind of research, as well as its advantages, will assist in developing methodologies and approaches which offer a middle way between trivializing and puppeteering. This book offers both an analysis and a first step towards breaking out of current orthodoxies.

We intend and indeed have already begun to translate some of the ideas here into plain English and key messages. We believe that all researchers have a duty to make their findings accessible to people with learning disabilities, if only after the work is complete.

Key questions

In framing this book we constructed a list of the issues that we had encountered in our practice as inclusive researchers, and which we felt we had been unable to discuss for fear of being seen as undermining the enterprise. Rather melodramatically we termed them 'questions we dared not ask':

1. How far has inclusive research been influenced by particular research perspectives and the broader social context?

2. To what extent did inclusive research arise from the concerns of people with learning disabilities?

3. What is the place of people with learning disabilities in initiating research?

4. How do we as researchers avoid the continuation of the 'othering' experienced by many people with learning disabilities in research?

5. What are the barriers to people with learning disabilities in research?

6. Can and should we manipulate the environment to the extent that people with learning disabilities can be meaningfully included in all stages and aspects of research?

7. How can the interests of all parties in the research process be safeguarded?

8. How valid is it to assume that researchers with learning disabilities are better able to access and represent the views and experiences of other people with learning disabilities than professional researchers?

9. Are there boundaries to the researcher's role – and if so who should set them?

10. Should (non-disabled) researchers have a distinctive voice?

11. Do existing research methods stereotype people with learning disabilities?

12. Should the researcher be cast in the role of advocate?

These are questions we return to throughout the book. Underlying them are some more fundamental questions about the nature of learning disabilities and the nature of research which we hope will be clarified by the discussion.

How the book is organized

The book is organized in three parts. Part 1, 'Describing the Past', provides an analysis of the nature and origins of participatory (or inclusive) research methodologies in the social sciences. Essentially it addresses the first two of our questions:

- How far has inclusive research been influenced by particular research perspectives and the broader social context?

- To what extent did inclusive research arise from the concerns of people with learning disabilities?

Chapter 1 explores the origins of this kind of research in feminist, participatory, emancipatory and action research traditions. In Chapter 2 we consider how far it has been influenced by normalization/social role valorization, by the social model of disability and its associated research idea, emancipatory research, and by the growth of self advocacy. In Chapter 3 we define inclusive research and describe how and when researchers began to adopt participatory methods in work with people with learning disabilities. In Chapter 4 we stop and reflect upon the dilemmas we have been airing in Part 1.

Part 2, 'Exploring the Research Process', opens with two case studies (Chapters 5 and 6) in which each author describes and analyses in detail one inclusive research project in which she has been involved.

The rest of Part 2 reviews the work done to date which can be termed inclusive, roughly according to the chronology of research projects. Part 2 is concerned with the practice issues of inclusive research and discusses questions two to ten. For example, Chapter 7, 'What Matters to People with Learning Disabilities?', is concerned with the initiation of the research and the extent to which people with learning disabilities determine what is researched. It links to the third, forth and fifth of our questions:

- What is the place of people with learning disabilities in initiating research?

- How do we as researchers avoid the continuation of the 'othering' experienced by many people with learning disabilities in research?

- What are the barriers to people with learning disabilities in research?

Chapter 8, 'Managing Inclusive Research', analyses how research methodologies are developed and who does what in the research process. In it we address the sixth question:

- Can and should we manipulate the environment to the extent that people with learning disabilities can be meaningfully included in all stages and aspects of research?

Chapter 9, 'Who Uses It and How?', is essentially about who owns the outputs of research and the extent to which people with learning disabilities can control the ways in which research is used, relating to the last three questions:

- Should (non-disabled) researchers have a distinctive voice?

- Do existing research methods stereotype people with learning disabilities?

- Should the researcher be cast in the role of advocate?

In Part 3, 'Beyond Rhetoric to New Realities', we move away from the questions to examine ways of moving on the inclusive research agenda. We end the book by considering the implications for work in a wide range of contexts, both in terms of research and in terms of user involvement.

We see this book as a contribution to open discussion and debate about issues relating to research with people with learning disabilities. More broadly we hope that it will lead to discussions about the nature of inclusion within the community and to new ideas about how to create more just and equitable processes and structures. We have found the book challenging and sometimes anxiety-creating to write. We hope that it will have a similar effect on our readers. Airing discomfort is one way of moving forward and seeking change.

A note on terminology

Terminology in this field is never straightforward. We have adopted the term 'people with learning disabilities' in the book, as it is the 'official' UK term. 'People with learning difficulties' is preferred by the UK self advocacy movement, while 'intellectual disabilities' is more common in Australasia. These terms, along with some others like the US 'mental retardation', will appear in quotations.

We quote our own work extensively in the book, and, rather than adhere to the formal conventions, indicate that it is our own work that is referred to by using our initials in brackets. The term 'we' is used to refer to ourselves, the authors.

PART 1

Describing the Past

Part 1 of this book focuses on discussion of the first two questions posed in the Introduction:

- How has inclusive research been influenced by particular research perspectives and the broader social context?

- To what extent did inclusive research arise from the concerns of people with learning disabilities?

To answer these questions we seek to trace the origins of what we have called inclusive research. This involves an account of how this kind of research developed broadly from qualitative research, particularly action, participatory, emancipatory and feminist research, and how it has been adapted to work with people with learning disabilities. We then go on to explore the way in which inclusive research has been informed by developments in the way disabled people are viewed by those around them, and by moves by disabled people (sometimes including people with learning disabilities) to wrest control of the agenda from non-disabled people.

CHAPTER 1

Of Shoes and Ships and Sealing Wax and…Inclusive Research

Or Where Did It All Start?

'The time has come,' the Walrus said,
'To talk of many things:
Of shoes – and ships – and sealing wax –
Of cabbages – and kings –
And why the sea is boiling hot –
And whether pigs have wings.'

(Lewis Carroll, *Through the Looking-Glass* [1872] 1990)

The wide-ranging discussion proposed by the walrus and the carpenter was designed to camouflage their real purpose: eating the ill-fated oysters. But wide-ranging discussions can serve to clarify activities as well as obscure them. As we began to talk about the nature of inclusive research in our practice it became clear that to understand it we needed to broaden the discussion to help us understand what has influenced this quite extraordinary set of developments in learning disability research. We realized that our views of inclusive research must have come from somewhere. Ideas do not exist in a vacuum. We were aware that our own ideas had evolved over time and had been influenced by particular theories and perspectives on research and also by wider social changes and so we have included examples of our own early work for consideration and analysis. For example, one of us (JW) can recall a moment, circa 1991, when we began to ask: 'Why are people with learning disabilities not on the list of people for whom higher education is an option?' Whether it was to do with our own limitations as teachers or the inherent limitations of the people carrying the label remains a nagging question.

This chapter is concerned primarily with the first of the ten questions posed in the Introduction:

- How far has inclusive research been influenced by particular research perspectives and the broader social context?

In answering the question we have identified a range of different perspectives which have established principles on which inclusive research with people with learning disabilities appears to be based.

Research does not occur in a social vacuum. Wider social changes over the past 20 years which have affected the way academic disciplines and research are viewed have also had an impact on the practice of inclusive research. This chapter describes these changes briefly and then shows how some of the issues are reflected in an early example of our work with people with learning disabilities.

The search for answers to our question led to an exploration of key developments in research over the past 50 years. In particular we traced many of the ideas of inclusive research to participatory action research (particularly emancipatory research), feminist research, and to developments in qualitative research more generally. In reviewing the literature about these approaches to research we became aware of the many common elements they share. We have also become aware of the difficulties in separating out how each perspective has influenced the others. To develop an intensive discussion or review of each of these areas is far beyond the scope of the present chapter. Rather we have provided a short introduction to each of these methodologies and have then identified key principles and practices in these approaches which have informed the practice of inclusive research.

Of shoes and ships

Participatory research! Action research! Emancipatory research! Feminist research! Postcolonialism! All of these research approaches are contested, ambiguous and have multiple meanings. Discussing them together is indeed like conversing about shoes and ships. They are often

the source of heated dispute and angst among the researchers who practise them. The origins of each of these approaches to research can be
traced in part to the concerns following the Second World War about
the rights of groups who were marginalized, the need to protect such
rights and to define a place for research in developing concerns about
social justice (Freire 1970a; Lewin 1946; Oakley 2000; Russell 1946).
The trend was fuelled by the break-up of the colonial empires, both trig-
gered by and leading to critiques of research which assumes a Euro-
centric perspective of the world. These developments also arose out of
critiques of positivist research, which was seen as dehumanizing and
which failed to take account of the need for acknowledgement of class,
ethnic, gender and cultural differences among researchers and those
with whom they worked (Oakley 2000). Qualitative research, participatory action research (PAR) and feminist research offered the promise of
'brave new' paths in which research participants would find different
roles and work towards a more just society, whilst postcolonial perspectives opened up minds to the major limitations of simplistic modernist
ideas about 'progress':

> They [colonizers] talk to me about progress, about achievements,
> diseases cured, improved standards of living. *I* am talking about
> societies drained of their essence, cultures trampled underfoot,
> institutions undermined, lands confiscated, religions smashed,
> magnificent artistic creations destroyed, extraordinary *possibilities*
> wiped out. (Cesaire 1972, pp.23–4, quoted in Plummer 2001)

Researchers face a huge challenge if they are to show that research does
not need to be like that.

Qualitative research

While qualitative research may be defined differently by individuals at
different times and by different practitioners, it does have some generally agreed on characteristics:

> Qualitative research is multimethod in focus, involving an inter-
> pretive, naturalistic approach to its subject matter. This means that
> qualitative researchers study things in their natural settings,
> attempting to make sense of, or interpret phenomena in terms of the

meanings people bring to them. Qualitative research involves the studied use and collection of a variety of empirical materials – case study, personal experience, introspective, life story, interview, observational, historical, interactional, and visual texts – that describe routine and problematic moments and meanings in individuals' lives. (Denzin and Lincoln 1998, p.3)

Underlying such an approach is a view of the world and of knowledge which is seen as different from the traditional positivist approach. The latter focused on the capacity of research to allow prediction and control in a world which can be objectively known. Some theorists now see this as a failed endeavour in the social sciences because it was framed on a 'simplistic and reductionist view of research with people and their cultures' (Lather 1991). In contrast, qualitative researchers constitute the world as one which is complex, multi-faceted and largely socially constructed. Such research seeks to understand and interpret how the world is seen by others. It attempts to answer the question: 'What is going on here?' Some researchers would also ask: 'What is my role in this?' (Brechin and Sidell 2000). This kind of research focuses on a more holistic approach and on the voices of those who are 'subject' to it.

The distinction between a positivist approach to research which finds expression in an experimental and quantitative methodology and qualitative research has led to heated debate between researchers and a polarity which has seen different directions taken by those who see themselves as qualitative and those who see themselves as quantitative. The history of this polarity and the need for a reconciliation of the different approaches has been explored only recently (Oakley 2000). The divide remains.

Feminist research

Like qualitative research, feminist research covers a wide range of different methods and approaches. Fundamentally it developed from an awareness that much positivist research had been gender biased and was undertaken only from the perspective of 'bourgeois, white men's experiences' leading to 'partial and even perverse understandings of social life' (Harding 1987, p.7). In contrast, feminist research has a strong liberationist emphasis which finds expression in attempts to remedy social injustices experienced by women and to provide them with a voice for their concerns which must be exemplified in the process of the research as well as in its outcomes (Oakley 2000). In doing this it reflects the wider political framework of feminism which has been defined as 'the struggle to end sexist oppression. Its aim is not to benefit solely any specific group of women, any particular race or class of women. It does not privilege women over men' (hooks 2000, p.28).

While it may be relatively easy in the abstract to make the link between feminist research and this ideology, feminist researchers have been forced to confront difficulties that exist in practice. For example, just because the researcher and the participants in research are women does not mean that differences in class, culture, education and power will be obliterated. Gradually feminist researchers have come to realize that even when working from best feminist principles the researcher may be continuing the oppression of groups of women both by the kind of research undertaken and by the groups which are not included in the research (Gluck and Patai 1991; Spelman 1988).

Participatory action research

Participatory action research (PAR) has been variously defined and conceptualized by those who practise it. Defined conservatively as action research, Rapoport describes it as follows:

> A type of applied social research differing from other varieties *in the immediacy* of the researcher's involvement in the action process… [It] aims to contribute both to the practical concerns of people in an immediate problematic situation and to the goals of social science by joint collaboration with a mutually acceptable ethical framework. (Rapoport 1970, in Foster 1972, p.532)

For many researchers the focus of action research is a highly political one which includes the active participation of all stakeholders in the research process. For example, Kaplan and Alsup perceive it as including: 'active and democratic community participation, non-traditional power relations, use of critical theory, emergent design, praxis, a focus on empowerment, and science as a tool for change' (1995, p.41).

Such research involves participants in all stages, from defining the problem to disseminating results. At the far end of the participatory action research continuum is emancipatory research in which all participants are involved in a process designed specifically to heighten political awareness and to lead to radical social change (Freire 1970a, 1970b, 1970c; Park 1993). Emancipatory research has come to be closely associated with the disabled people's movement in the UK, a point explored further in Chapter 2. However, as we shall discover, the conceptualization of such an approach is much easier in the abstract than in its implementation.

Summing up

This brief orientation to different research approaches which have informed the development of inclusive research does not reveal the differences which can exist between the ways they are practised by different researchers. It also suggests misleadingly clear distinctions between these forms of research. In practice, as we shall describe later in the book, the boundaries are often blurred and shifting. Further, while there are many variations in the ways qualitative, feminist and participatory action research are formulated, they do have fundamental principles in common and it is these which we believe have informed practice in inclusive research.

And sealing wax

Each of the perspectives to research discussed in the previous section is constantly changing and adding to its repertoire and to its underlying assumptions. Yet there are some common principles or elements which seal them together. We believe that these underpin the work in which we have been involved with people with learning disabilities. This section of the chapter outlines these key principles.

Commitment to social change

Each of these methodological approaches embraces in some form a commitment to structural social change designed to create a more just and equitable society.

While the definition of qualitative research offered earlier in this chapter does not mention the possibility of social change as an inherent part of the work of such research, for many qualitative researchers it is an important goal. Because qualitative research seeks to identify the way the world is viewed by those participating in it, researchers are often motivated in the process of the research to make the world a fairer and more just place. For example, the case study shown in Box 1.1 reveals how qualitative research (in this case undertaken by KJ) can be regarded as a tool for social change.

Box 1.1 A qualitative study of institutional closure

The questions

- How have the policies of community living affected the lives of people with learning difficulties who live in institutions?
- What is life like for women living in a locked unit in an institution?
- How are they seen by staff and by themselves?
- What is the impact of institutional closure on these women and those working with them?

Answering these questions led to a four-year project which explored the impact of the closure of a large institution for people with learning difficulties on a group of women who lived in a locked unit at the institution. They had been labelled as having learning difficulties and as having 'challenging behaviours'.

Searching for answers

To answer my research questions I was involved in a number of different research activities over the 20 months I spent with the women living and working in the locked unit. These included:

- Hundreds of hours in the locked unit, talking with residents and staff and helping with day-to-day tasks.

- Three interviews with each staff member in the unit and interviews with the families and advocates of the women.

- Three interviews with each of the people managing the closure of the institution.

- Attendance at management meetings during the closure of the institution.

- Analysis of the women's files.

- Participation in and observation of the meetings held with the women and their families during the closure of the institution to establish preferences for their future living arrangements.

- Participation in and observation of meetings held by professionals who made the final decisions about where the women would live.

Findings

My work provided a rich description of the lives of the women living and working in the locked unit and assisted in understanding the ways in which institutional life shaped the behaviour and subjectivity of the women. It also demonstrated the problematic nature of labels like 'challenging behaviour' or indeed learning difficulties when applied to individuals. The study revealed how institutional closure was influenced by two different ways of thinking: rights and management. By doing this it sought to make the process of institutional closure fairer by proposing changes to the process.
(Gomm and Davies 1999)

For feminist researchers the issues around social change have particular importance since they see themselves as directly involved in the liberation which would result from social change arising from their research (for examples of feminist research with a particular focus on social change see Benmayor 1991; Gluck 1991; Gluck and Patai 1991).

Social change is integral to much of the work of participatory action researchers. From its beginnings action research was used to influence changes in policy and practice in relation to marginalized groups (Baddou 1946; Krech 1946; Lewin 1946), to bridge the gap between the 'man of action and the man of research [sic]' (Krech 1946, p.4) and as a way of addressing major social concerns (Carr and Kemmis 1983; Lewin 1946).

While the permutations of action research are now many, its focus on change remains. Some writers focus particularly on action research as a means of changing professional practices of workers in relation to their work with 'marginalized' or excluded groups (Cosier and Glennie 1994; Traylen 1994; Treleaven 1994). Others are concerned with self-reflective management practices (Greenwood and Levin 1998; Zuber-Skerritt 1996). One of the major themes in participatory action research has been the effort to change the wider society (Brydon-Miller 1993; Jackson 1993; McTaggart 1997; Swantz and Vainio-Mattila 1988). However, whatever the emphasis, the underlying principle which guides much of this research is the need to ensure that research itself prompts change, usually though not always in the direction of increased social justice. For example Maguire (1987) comments:

> [Participatory] research is a way for researchers and oppressed people to join in solidarity to take collective action, both short and long term, for radical social change. Locally determined and controlled action is a planned consequence of inquiry. (Maguire 1987, p.29)

Park makes even more explicit the nature of participatory research in relation to social change:

> The explicit aim of participatory research is to bring about a more just society in which no groups or classes of people suffer from the deprivation of life's essentials, such as food, clothing, shelter, and health and in which all enjoy basic human freedoms and rights. (Park 1993, p.2)

Therefore participatory action research involves a responsibility on the part of the researcher and participants to ensure that it is used to positive effect in the society or the organization in which it is undertaken.

Social change is a contested term. As researchers we bring to it our own experiences, values and expectations. We may differ in our conceptions of what it means as may participants in the research process. But a commitment to social change and social justice is often interpreted as meaning that the means must be commensurate with the ends – that the research process itself should be liberating for those taking part in it.

Empowering participants

Not all qualitative research is concerned with empowering those who take part in it. The definition which we offered early in this chapter makes no mention of the need for empowerment. Yet the ways in which it suggests that qualitative research is done – case studies, interviews, stories – suggests an approach in which increasing power for the participants may be part of the process. Many feminist and action researchers are more definite about their agendas in relation to empowerment. For example, Oakley (1979), in a study of what it means to become a mother, challenged the positivist views about 'objectivity' of the researcher as the women she interviewed began to ask questions and demand answers about their experiences. In particular, she argued that the women's point of view had as much validity as that of the experts who were more often approached for their opinions on the subject.

Participatory action researchers have a commitment not only to ensuring that the outcomes of the research promote social change, but that the process itself reflects a more just and fair society in microcosm. It is in fact a contradiction in terms to think of participatory action research that does not have this agenda as an integral part of its approach. Such research is designed to break down the barriers between researcher and other participants in the research and to empower the participants not only to develop skills in research during its process but to take political and social action on the basis of what they have learned. Examples of such research include consumer evaluation of acute psychiatric hospital practice (Wadsworth 1994; Wadsworth and Epstein 1996a, 1996b) and work with Aboriginal groups in Canada (Horton 1993) and in Australia (Colin and Garrow 1999).

Box 1.2, 'Having a Real Say', was one of my (KJ's) earlier approaches to working with people with learning disabilities. It had a strong emphasis on empowering people to manage their own service and to have the power to make more day-to-day decisions about their lives.

Box 1.2 Having a real say

Consumer participation at AMIDA

In 1987 AMIDA, an organization which provided housing and support for people with mild 'intellectual disabilities' in Melbourne, Australia, undertook 12-month action research:

- to empower people with learning disabilities within AMIDA
- to develop their skills in relation to decision making within the organization
- to establish an independent advisory panel to advise government on housing issues for people with learning disabilities.

A consumer participation worker was appointed to work alongside me, the researcher, and, unusually, an ongoing independent action research evaluation was undertaken. None of the people employed on the project were people with learning disabilities. In true action research style we evaluated the strategies as they were implemented, recommended changes to them and then evaluated these as they were put into practice (O'Brien and Johnson 1987, 1988). By the end of the project:

- The numbers of people with learning disabilities had increased on the management committee so that they had a majority (endorsed in the revised constitution).
- President, secretary and co-treasurer roles were filled by people with learning disabilities.
- Meetings were more accessible and framed around the interests and needs of people with learning disabilities.
- Support and training (including clear complaints mechanisms) were in place for people with learning disabilities and staff.

- People's consciousness had been raised about consumer participation and management.

We learned:

- Not all people with learning disabilities wanted to be involved in the management of the organization.

- The needs of people with learning disabilities were not very different to those of other participants in community organizations, for example, people on low incomes (Benn 1981; Liffman 1978).

- Organizational change was an extremely important part of the project. Without these changes efforts to increase the participation of people with learning disabilities were tokenistic and actively resisted by staff.

- Some people with learning disabilities were highly skilled but these skills were not used in the organization.

- Staff had begun the project and remained influential in its development.

AMIDA remains a radical organization run by people with disabilities although its emphasis has now changed to housing advocacy. (Kelley Johnson)

Our expectations in Having a Real Say were high. After all we were working with a radical organization. There was hope that people with learning disabilities would be able to manage their own organization and that we would develop strategies which would assist other groups to do the same. In fact there was considerable resistance from staff (though not explicit) to the increasing role of people with learning disabilities in management. We found, for example, that decisions began to be made by staff in meetings separate from the management committee meeting. This kind of resistance to empowerment of people is one that has been found in other literature (see, for example, Wadsworth and Epstein 1996a, 1996b).

Our research and that of others suggest that empowerment is interpreted in a variety of ways. The means may be viewed as being as important as the ends. It can be interpreted as people gaining power through the research process to take on other issues in their lives. Sometimes it is seen as empowerment in terms of learning specific research skills. There is also sometimes (though often with less emphasis) a view that empowerment may mean the results of the research can be used by the people concerned to change society. Later in this book we will examine the implications of these different ways of viewing empowerment, particularly the tension between ends and means.

Such a hope of promoting empowerment is also present in much feminist research, summed up in the credo: 'research by for and about women' (Gluck and Patai 1991, p.2). In such research it is anticipated that women involved in the process will be empowered in other areas of their lives as well as in doing research. However the situation is not as simple as the credo suggests. Feminist researchers have gradually become aware that even when empowerment is the focus of their research they may in fact reinforce the disempowerment of some women. Differences in culture, class and the aims of the research itself can undermine what was seen as a fundamental common interest and trust between women researchers and 'others' involved in the research (Oakley 2000; Patai 1991).

Focusing on the individual

Viewing individuals in the context of their lives has been one of the important characteristics of qualitative research. This has been contrasted with a positivist approach in which fragmentation of the individual and the culture have occurred in order for isolated variables to be studied free from contamination of other lived issues (Daly 1996). Rather than being viewed from afar through a scientific research lens, people are individualized, speak for themselves, emerge as rounded and often complex human beings. The forms of data gathering described in the definition of qualitative research offered earlier in this chapter suggest a focus on lived experience: stories, documentary analysis and semi or unstructured interviews are all designed to assist understanding of individual viewpoints, attitudes and lives. However this emphasis in qualitative research has also come under criticism on the grounds that it can lead to an invasion of the individual's life and is a further development in the surveillance of the person (Armstrong 1983). The concentration on naturalistic settings or the world of the individuals and on their characteristics can lead to a stress on difference between individuals rather than, as in positivist research, on the commonalities between groups. It may mitigate against social change because the individual differences are perceived to outweigh the common interests.

The need to undertake research which respects a woman's unique experience and which seeks to give this a voice is found in much feminist research. Perhaps it explains the attraction of using autobiography and biography for many feminist writers (Gluck and Patai 1991) for these forms of research enable women to work together in depth. However, the concerns of the individual are also important to feminist researchers who are not concerned with developing individual biographies. For example, both Roberts (1981), in a study of women and their relationships with general practitioners, and Oakley (1981), in a discussion of interviewing women, are concerned to focus on the importance of the individual experience of the women in their studies, and on their credibility as informants. This was seen not only as important in empowering women but also as a crucial element in data collection since it brought into the open issues which might otherwise have remained hidden. The black feminist, bell hooks, also emphasizes the importance of such life stories: '[we] radical black women need to tell our stories: we cannot document our experiences enough' (hooks 1992).

In Plummer's (2001) book *Documents of Life*, which reviews such approaches, he notes that such stories can constitute 'resistance texts' (p.182). One of the criticisms of using biographical methods is that they may lead to a focus on the individual at the expense of social change and result in soundbites which illuminate no more than one person's opinion. However, this need not be so. The example in Box 1.3 suggests that an individual story, like a good case study, may open up important questions about societal discrimination and injustice.

Box 1.3 From individual experience to societal discrimination

Amanda Millear is a strong self advocate for people with learning disabilities who has worked with advocacy organizations for about 20 years. In the early 1990s she undertook leadership training with the Scouts and was keen to become a group leader. However when her training was complete she was told that she could not become a leader because of her disability. Amanda took the case to the Human Rights and Equal Opportunity Commission in Australia, a national body to safeguard the rights of citizens against discrimination. The case went on for 39 months. It was confusing and often upsetting for Amanda. At its conclusion the Scouts agreed to a settlement. However some years later only some of the conditions of the settlement have been met and it is clear that loopholes have allowed the Scouts to ignore some of them.

Amanda's life history was much more than the account of her discrimination case. However she saw this as the focus of her autobiography because she believed it was important that people use the Disability Discrimination Act in order to obtain their rights. Her story was not just an individual account but opened up questions for her and her co-writer such as the following:

- How successful is the anti-discrimination legislation in protecting the rights of those who use it – even when they win their cases?
- Why do cases take so long to be heard?
- How can people with learning disabilities get the best support when they are involved in discrimination cases?
- What other mechanisms or means may be possible to ensure that discrimination does not arise for people with learning disabilities?

These issues are not individual ones; they are social or structural issues. However they arise from a consideration of the individual story. (This account is based on Millear with Johnson 2000.)

It is hard to imagine participatory action research not having a strong focus on the individual. After all it is concerned with empowerment and with the participants taking up the challenge for social change. Such involvement by individuals or by a group of participants is seen as a challenge to the researcher (Maguire 1993; Wadsworth 1994) and can also be a means to ensure that the research is useful in facilitating wider social change.

Emancipatory research

A recent development of PAR in a context of particular relevance to this book has been the espousal of emancipatory research by disabled people. Oliver (1992) and Zarb (1992) argued for research to be under the control of and in the interests of disabled people. Emancipatory research is seen as having a key role in identifying those social structures and processes which create disabling barriers, and in eradicating those that exist (Finkelstein 1999; Priestley 1999). This is a topic we address in more detail in Chapter 2, where we consider particular developments in disability studies which have influenced inclusive research. Here though, it is worth noting that a number of disabled scholars have rejected the emphasis on the individual which characterizes PAR as 'a return to the old casebook approach' (Finkelstein 1996), and argue for true emancipation to focus on the common interests of disabled people. It is a position that has been challenged as ignoring difference amongst disabled people, and tending to privilege white males (Vernon 1996, for example). The debate has continued, as we write.

Reflecting on the research

Much qualitative research demands self-reflection from the researcher. Although it is not included within the definition of such research given earlier in the chapter, we would argue that a recognition of the researcher's attitudes and values is integral. Participant observation, interviews, case studies and a focus on the meanings which people bring to their worlds necessarily require a degree of self-consciousness in the researcher about their own beliefs and values. The degree to which these are shared during the research or in its publication vary with the researcher.

The issue of the position of the researcher in relation to their research and the need for them to clearly state this has been particularly important in feminist research which has been critical of positivist social science for its failure to consider the importance of gender in research or to recognize the influence which the characteristics and interests of the researcher may have on the research process and results (Fine and Gordon 1992; Harding 1987; Oakley 1981, 2000).

The importance of self-reflection is also part of the ideological underpinning of both feminist and participatory action research which stress the importance of the researcher 'standing with' those involved in the research and of breaking down barriers between self and others. It is easy to say this but researchers have found it much more difficult to do in practice. Traustadottir (2001), in an account of an Icelandic study of the social discrimination confronted by marginalized women (lesbians, women with learning disabilities and women from culturally and linguistically diverse backgrounds in Iceland), struggles to tease out the highly complex and different issues which define her in relation to the women with whom she works. She concludes:

> In doing our research and writing our findings we always make decisions about whose story should be told, and whose left out. In doing this we are constructing and reconstructing reality. Our production of knowledge serves to legitimate some views and experiences while challenging others. I have become increasingly aware of the power of the researcher in creating knowledge about our social worlds, and the peoples who inhabit these worlds. If we are self reflective in our research we will be less likely to run the risk of uncritically reproducing Othering or oppressions. (Traustadottir 2001, p.26)

Fine (1998) explores the way in which much qualitative research has continued a discourse of 'colonizing the other', speaking for and about those with whom we research. In a message of hope she suggests a way in which such colonizing may be disrupted: through the works produced by those who are 'othered', by a dissection of the nature of the way self and other are constructed by elites and by the interweaving of research and social action. Imaginative ways of writing have resulted from these concerns, such as Pat Caplan's life story of Mohammed, a Tanzanian villager. The book opens with a discussion between Caplan and Mohammed as to how the story should be written, how it will be told and who will read it. In the book Mohammed and Caplan take turns in being narrators, with some sections consisting of a dialogue between them (Caplan 1977). All of these messages demand a self-consciousness on the part of the researcher and a capacity to consider and to express their dilemmas and concerns at being part of the research process. An instance of the role of self-reflection is shown in Box 1.4.

Box 1.4 The researcher subject to the research

In the study of institutional closure described in Box 1.1, I (KJ) spent 20 months in a locked unit with a group of women who had been labelled as having learning disabilities and challenging behaviours. The importance of the position of the researcher and of self reflection became very apparent in this work. The quotation below summarizes some of the reasons for this:

> There are many voices in this study, but inevitably they are all heard through my voice. For this reason, if for no other, it was important that I become 'subject' to my own research. The questions I asked, the observations I made, the knowledge and information I gained from others were constructed and interpreted by me as researcher (Shakespeare, Atkinson and French 1993; Steier 1992). Further, examining my own emotional reactions to situations and exploring some of the unconscious means I used to defend myself against the stress of the women's world enabled me to hypothesise about some of the reactions of others in this situation. This was particularly so in interpreting the reactions of the women during the closure process, for they were often not able to articulate their concerns verbally. An examination of my own reactions acted as a signpost to their possible responses (Sinason 1992). (Johnson 1998, see also Johnson and McIntyre 2001)

Not included in this quote was the effect on me as a researcher as I came to identify with some of the issues which the women confronted and to take on a role as advocate with the authorities.

As shown in Box 1.4, the issues of reflection in relation to research are complex. In part they may be a result of concern about the validity of research which does not take into account the impact of the researcher. They may also be seen as an integral part of the research process and data collection and may be an expression of a political and ideological commitment to stand with other participants in the research. There is also an ethical dimension. Researcher reflexivity can be a major safeguard against abuse and exploitation of research participants (Walmsley 1995).

Translating principles into practice

The principles which we have described briefly above underlie much of qualitative, feminist and participatory action research and have important implications for how research is undertaken. In summary such an approach would involve the following characteristics:

- Those involved in the research have a commitment to social change arising from it. There may be a commonly shared definition of what this constitutes among the people involved in it at the commencement of the research process or this may evolve as the work continues.

- There is a commitment to taking people's words seriously, to believing them as credible respondents with their own understandings, without a need for triangulation or other checks.

- The research is undertaken with the aims of empowering those involved in it. This may involve empowerment in terms of consciousness raising and preparedness for action resulting from the findings of the research and designed to achieve social change. It may also involve empowerment in terms of learning new skills through doing the research itself.

- Research is holistic in nature, concerned not to fragment the individual, but rather to focus on freeing their voices and enabling a consideration of lived experience, taking into account the broader context of lives.

- The research involves self-reflection by all those taking part. In particular however the researcher would reflect on their position in relation to others involved. At a minimal level such self-reflection is focused on the need to make explicit the values, beliefs and relevant characteristics of the researcher (e.g. culture, class, gender) and how these may influence the research. Beyond this, the importance of voice, whose story is being told, and for whose benefit, looms large.

The translation of principles into practice is always difficult. As we considered the practice implications of these particular principles, some of the ethical dilemmas which we and others have confronted as researchers became clearer. Integral to these underlying principles are (often unstated) political and ideological positions which pose fundamental and sometimes paradoxical conceptual, practice and ethical issues. Chapter 4 examines these in detail as they affect research with people with learning disabilities.

Conclusion

We began this chapter with the question:

- How has inclusive research been influenced by particular research perspectives and the broader social context?

We propose that inclusive research in learning disability is part of a wider movement which has transformed some parts of the social sciences over the past 40 years. It has reflected wider societal concerns about the rights of marginalized groups and political and ideological positions held by citizens not concerned with social research. These positions have not only impacted on the way results of some social research are used, but they have also framed and shaped the foundations of this research and the way it is implemented.

Regarding the second question, about where inclusive research came from, while we might like to believe that those who have been subject to research have led the charge to a more socially responsible, useful and empowering form of research, overall this does not seem to be the case. Rather the movement for change has most frequently come from shifts and changes among researchers and theoreticians. Only slowly, and some would argue partially (Beresford 2000a), as marginalized groups became more empowered and stronger have they begun to challenge the way research is conducted with them. The movement to feminist research began largely with white women academics, the movement to participatory action research with white men academics and qualitative research began from academics' discontent with perceived limitations of prevailing positivist methods. The concerns of marginalized groups have only slowly been heard and there are limits to which their demands are being implemented:

> Service users are demanding that social policy goes beyond seeing them as a data source... Service users and their organizations can and want to offer their own analyses, interpretations and plans for action. (Beresford 2000a, p.508)

This quotation summarizes beautifully a key issue – merely accessing the views or voices of the disadvantaged is not enough. True change, it is argued, is achieved when they take control of the action, whether in research or in social policy.

The following two chapters examine in some detail how inclusive research found its way from mainstream research endeavours to research with people with learning disabilities.

CHAPTER 2

Normalizing, Emancipating and Making a Stand

In this chapter we look at the competing philosophical influences on inclusive research with people with learning disabilities arising specifically from the disability context. The chapter builds on the previous one by demonstrating that inclusive research in learning disability took the specific form it currently has because of some developments which arose from analyses of the situation of people with learning disabilities and disabilities, and the political movements which gave rise to them. These include particularly normalization/social role valorization, the social model of disability and the growth of self advocacy. We propose that normalization created the conditions for inclusion, while not in practice paying much attention to accessing people's views directly. The social model of disability, particularly as reflected in a focus on emancipatory research, raised the stakes for learning disability researchers who aspired to work in inclusive ways. Self advocacy enabled more genuine inclusion – but also led to challenges to the comfortable role many researchers had assumed for themselves as sympathetic allies of people with learning disabilities.

Normalization/social role valorization: paving the way

To understand the context of inclusive research, we need to go back in time to ask why interest in accessing the views of people with learning disabilities grew in the mid-twentieth century. One can discern a broad move to listening to voices of marginalized groups in research, a development which accompanied civil rights movements such as anti-racism and feminism (see Chapter 1). In learning disability one can identify a very specific influence, that of normalization/social role valorization, which came to underpin UK and Australian social policy during the 1970s and 1980s and to be highly influential in shaping the research agenda.

Normalization is a set of ideas, or a theory, with applied and practical outcomes. It originated in Denmark and Sweden in the late 1950s, but was later reformulated and recast in North America during the 1970s and 1980s. This means there are two main strands of normalization: the original Scandinavian version and the recast North American version.

The ideas underpinning the Scandinavian model are largely attributed to Bank-Mikkelson in Denmark (1969, 1980) and Nirje (1980) in Sweden. The principle of normalization was defined by Bank-Mikkelson as 'letting the mentally handicapped obtain an existence as close to normal as possible' (1969). According to Emerson (1992), this formulation of normalization defined equality in ways which could be pursued in segregated settings – it did not require integration in mainstream society.

The North American reworking was largely the work of Wolf Wolfensberger. He initially formulated normalization thus:

> The utilization of means which are as culturally normative as possible, in order to establish and/or maintain personal behaviours and characteristics which are as culturally normative as possible. (Wolfensberger 1972, p.28)

Two subsequent emphases are discernible. The image of disadvantaged people was argued to be vital – positive imagery would assist people in being accepted in mainstream society (Wolfensberger 1980). 'Valued social roles' rather than culturally normative practices came to be the leading edge idea. If people could occupy such socially valued roles then their image would be enhanced (Wolfensberger and Thomas 1983; Wolfensberger and Tullman 1982).

These ideas came to be very influential both in policy and in research. The influence of normalization ideas can be clearly seen in the three principles of the All Wales Strategy (AWS), the most sustained attempt in the UK to develop a coherent approach to service provision for people with learning disabilities:

> People with a mental handicap have a right to ordinary patterns of life within the community

> People with a mental handicap have a right to be treated as individuals

> People with a mental handicap have a right to additional help from the communities in which they live in order to enable them to develop their maximum potential as individuals. (Welsh Office 1983, quoted in Felce and Grant 1998, p.xii)

In Australia, the principles of the Victorian legislation (Intellectually Disabled Persons Services Act 1986) were underpinned by normalization ideas. The Act stated among other things:

> (d) The needs of intellectually disabled persons are best met when the conditions of their everyday life are the same as, or as close as possible to, norms and patterns which are valued in the general community.

> (e) Services should promote maximum physical and social integration through the participation of intellectually disabled persons in the life of the community. (Victorian Government 1986, section v)

This Act, which is the only one worldwide to focus specifically on the needs of people with intellectual disabilities (Cooper and Vernon 1996), has had a profound influence in shaping services and the inclusion of people with learning disabilities in their communities.

In research terms, Chappell (1992) argues that normalization/social role valorization spawned a wealth of literature featuring applied research which set out to investigate and evaluate the quality of services (see, for example, Blunden 1988; Evans *et al.* 1987; Humphreys, Evans and Todd 1987; Mansell *et al.* 1987). In Australia it had an influence on research undertaken in the late 1980s around crime and intellectual disability (Johnson *et al.* 1987; Osman 1986), participation (O'Brien and Johnson 1987) and advocacy (Nicholls and Andrew 1990). In the USA its values underpinned the movement to close large institutions, and studies of community integration were shaped by normalization/

social role valorization principles (see, for example, Taylor, Bogdan and Lutfiyya 1995; Wolfensberger 1972).

Normalization delivered much of value. However, it has been criticized. Unlike anti-racism, feminism, or disability rights, normalization was a philosophy which was created and sustained by non-disabled people. At the time it was invented that is hardly surprising. As we will show in Chapter 3, the voices of people with learning disabilities were almost totally absent from the published literature or the media. It has, however, continued to be the property of non-disabled people. Few disabled people have gone on record as supporting it and a number have challenged it forcibly (French 1999; Oliver 1994). Moreover, the voices of the disadvantaged are notably absent from leading publications, even quite recent ones (see, for example, Race 1999).

Normalization also focused heavily on the quality of services. PASS and PASSING, tools to evaluate service quality from a normalization perspective, were two of the most potent means of spreading normalization ideas. There can have been few leading figures in learning disability services in the 1980s who avoided PASS workshops. Much research inspired by normalization subsequently has taken services as its focus – the audience is service providers who are expected to learn from positive exemplars of community-based provision – the Wells Road service (Ward 1989), NIMROD (Felce and Grant 1998). This has meant that more subtle issues like self-identity, or more structural issues like poverty or the social construction of disability, tend not to be explored in research inspired by normalization. As Chappell writes: 'It neglects issues outside the narrow world of service provision' (1999, p.105).

Normalization made service providers a major target. It was premised on the view that their attitudes would have to change in order to ensure people's rights to an ordinary life and high quality services. Thus it offered non-disabled people a continuing and central role in the lives of people with learning disabilities.

Normalization is essentially values based. Its supporters see social norms as 'homogenous and easily identifiable' (Chappell 1999, p.106). Normalization principles can be used as a yardstick for what is valued, thus sidestepping the significance of gathering individuals' views. At the same time, with its emphasis on positive images, it required change on the part of people with learning disabilities and other devalued groups to facilitate their integration (or assimilation) into mainstream society.

By implication, normalization devalued association with other people with learning disabilities because of its emphasis on association with 'valued' others – people without disabilities (see King's Fund 1988). This, notes Chappell (1992), inhibited the development of a collective identity amongst people with learning disabilities. For if people are discouraged from associating with other disabled people in favour of integration with 'valued' others, then their opportunities to develop shared understandings of oppression are limited.

Normalization and inclusive research

Although normalization has been justly criticized, we argue that it paved the way not only for more inclusive policies, but also for more inclusive research. We discuss how this happened below. However, although we argue that normalization paved the way for more inclusive research, normalization-inspired research per se is not inclusive. Normalization may have helped to create the conditions in which people with learning disabilities could speak up, but often they did not (Atkinson 2001, p.18). Normalization itself did not seek people's views; rather it assumed knowledge of them (Chappell 1992). People were portrayed as victims, a category of people who were devalued, without individuality, gender, ethnic origin or class. The drive was a reversal of devaluation, the principle means an improvement in services, and the engagement of the energies of 'valued people'.

However, one can attribute to normalization a role in making inclusive research possible and a continuing influence. At one level, the mere encouragement to see people with learning disabilities as human beings deserving of ordinary patterns of living encouraged others to view them as potential contributors to research. The more integrationist policies of hospital closure, rights to school education, etc. influenced by normalization have meant that people with learning disabilities are more available to researchers and probably have more interesting stories to tell, certainly as far as policy makers are concerned. Certainly the experiences of deinstitutionalization and community living have been major areas where researchers have tried to get inside the experience from a user's point of view (Atkinson 1986; Flynn 1989; Johnson 1998; Potts and Fido 1991; Wilkinson 1989).

At a more sophisticated level, involvement in research has been seen as offering a 'valued social role' in itself; one on which Atkinson and Williams (1990) commented as a positive outcome of their work with contributors to their seminal anthology of work by people with learning disabilities, *Know Me As I Am* (discussed in detail in Chapter 3). We would argue that much inclusive research, including our own, has been at least in part motivated by this idea. This goes beyond the concept of people with learning disabilities as respondents. Being a researcher offers even more in terms of valued social roles – conference goer, the one who asks rather than answers the questions, presence at prestigious academic events, having one's name in print.

In the UK, furthermore, the emphasis in normalization/social role valorization on the importance of citizen advocacy as the duty of ordinary people to work for people with learning disabilities has, we would argue, given researchers an unambiguous place in the lives of people with learning disabilities.

If the citizen advocate's duty is to 'bring their partner's gifts and concerns into the circles of ordinary community life' (Butler, Carr and Sullivan 1988, quoted in Atkinson 2001), then the researcher who wants to help people with learning disabilities can do just that by promoting their inclusion in research.

This association with the role of advocate also works at the level of content – and links to the tenet of normalization which argues for positive imagery. If the researcher/advocate is discharging his or her duty well, then their work is promoting a positive image of people with learning disabilities. The debt to citizen advocacy principles is explicitly acknowledged by Tim and Wendy Booth in relation to their research project on parents with learning disabilities:

> Our obligations to the parents [with learning difficulties] always came before the interests of the research whenever the two appeared to move in different directions. (Booth and Booth 1994, p.24)

In adopting this principle, they acknowledge a debt to both self and citizen advocacy. The association can be fruitfully developed further into the issue of the researcher's own voice. A central precept of citizen advocacy is that it demands substituted judgement: 'The role of the advocate is to help the partner express their point of view, not to judge whether it represents the "right" choice' (Simons 1993, p.36).

Should this be the inclusive researcher's role also? The extent to which the researcher/advocate's privileged knowledge, as an expert or indeed as possessor of information which the respondent or co-researcher has not made public, is allowable in inclusive research remains an uncomfortable area, as indeed it is in the practice of advocacy as we show in discussing the development of the genre (Chapter 3).

The disabled people's movement and emancipatory research

The social model of disability is the creation of the disabled people's movement. Rather than focusing on the individual's limitations, the social model sees disablement as inherent in society. The barriers to participation, inclusion and full citizenship by people with impairments are many and complex. At the simplest level, this translates into the need for ramps and hearing loops to overcome physical barriers in the built environment. At a more complex level, social model theorists have found barriers in the way paid work is structured (Oliver 1990), the pre-eminence given in societal values to youth, beauty and physical perfection (Hevey 1992), and the close association between impairment and evil in much western literature, like Long John Silver, Captain Hook, etc. (Keith 2001).

It follows from this model that research should shift from the 'problems' created by impairment to changing society in order to increase disabled people's opportunities for full inclusion. The influence of the social model of disability on the way inclusive research in learning disability has developed began to be evident from the early 1990s onwards. In particular, ideas about emancipatory research (Zarb 1992) appear to have filtered into learning disability, leading some researchers struggling to go beyond participation in trying to meet more stringent demands of emancipatory research; that the researchers are the expert servants of disabled people who must put their knowledge and skills at the disposal of their research subjects, for them to use in whatever ways they choose (Oliver 1992, p.111).

This formulation goes beyond the participatory paradigm and transforms the long-standing role of the sympathetic ally into something more akin to an expert advisor.

Although it now seems self-evident that people with learning disabilities are disabled, in social model terms, by societal barriers, I have argued elsewhere (Walmsley 2001) that this was not inevitable. The 1959 and 1983 Mental Health Acts, for example, legislated for people with mental impairments, both people with mental health problems and people with learning disabilities, as they would now be termed. People with physical disabilities had their own legislation – the Chronically Sick and Disabled Persons Act 1976 being the best known. The adoption of the term 'learning disability' by the UK Department of Health from the mid-1990s has apparently hastened an alignment of the interests of people with learning disabilities to the disabled people's movement. Whereas the term 'mental handicap' semantically aligned the 'problem' with mental illness, the term 'learning disability' made a clear statement that it belonged with disability more generally.

In Australia, under the 1959 Mental Health Act in Victoria, a process of increasing differentiation occurred. No longer were people with intellectual disabilities included with 'the poor, those with psychiatric illness or other marginalised groups' (Johnson and Tait 2003, in press). The gradual differentiation of people with intellectual disabilities from others is reflected in the Intellectually Disabled Persons Services Act 1986. The term intellectual disability removed the stigmatizing label of mental deficiency or mental retardation. Again there is the semantic link with disability in the term 'intellectual disability'.

Linguistic changes both reflect and encourage a tendency to see learning (or intellectual) disability as a fit subject for disability studies and at the very end of the twentieth century scholars (Chappell, Goodley and Lawthorn 2001) began to wrestle with the application of the social model to self advocacy and to inclusive research.

In research terms, the association with the social model of disability increased the demands on those who aspired to conduct inclusive research with people with learning disabilities, because in the emancipatory model power and control need to be in the hands of disabled people. This raised the stakes considerably in terms of what some learning disability researchers began to demand of themselves and their work. The type of research characteristic of normalization-inspired models – that the research should demonstrate ways in which a 'normal life' could be promoted – was not enough. Somehow, the researcher was expected to find ways of giving control to people with learning disabilities and being accountable to them.

However, the applicability of models derived from the disabled people's movement to people with learning disabilities deserves more attention than it has had to date (Walmsley 2001). The connections between the disabled people's movement and people with learning disabilities have not been straightforward or comfortable. The emphasis on embodiment in disability studies has led to a focus on people with physical disabilities and has excluded theorizing about people with learning disabilities (Chappell 1997). There are many instances of people with intellectual disabilities being added as an afterthought within publications by disabled people. Of the 31 contributors to Campbell and Oliver's *Disability Politics* (1996), only one identifies herself as a person with learning disabilities, while at the 1996 conference to mark ten years of the journal *Disability and Society* there were no speakers with learning disabilities. Simone Aspis, an advocate with learning disabilities, comments that disabled people have been as active in excluding her as have non-disabled researchers (2000). Nor have these exclusions been restricted to publications in the UK. In the USA accounts of the lives of women with disabilities have excluded women with learning disabilities (Saxton and Howe 1988).

The impact of the arguments about emancipatory research, which came into prominence with the publication of a special issue of the journal *Disability, Handicap and Society* on disability research in 1992, began to filter into learning disability research in the UK. As early as 1994, I (JW) considered what such a project might look like:

> Perhaps a group of parents with learning disabilities getting together, deciding that they wanted to find out why people like them were having such a hard time, raising some money, employing interviewers or doing it themselves, supervising the production of the report and

finding someone to publish it. It is almost impossible to visualize such a scenario given the way things are at present; yet it is such a vision that application of the social model of disability can create. (Walmsley 1994, p.157)

The nagging sense that learning disability research should move towards a more emancipatory approach has become evident subsequently. Townsley (1998, p.78) cites emancipatory research principles in arguing for research to be made accessible: 'The field of disability research is currently making efforts to move towards a more emancipatory approach where the involvement of disabled researchers and consultants is central to the success of any research project.'

Rodgers (1999) published a reflective piece on the extent to which her work with women on health issues met the demands of emancipatory research and, whilst she concluded that it did not, indicated by her title 'Trying to Get it Right' that it should have done!

One of our purposes in writing this book has been to explore the influence of emancipatory research principles on learning disability. Partly because the disabled people's movement has not embraced issues relating to learning disability (or indeed mental health problems) seriously (Beresford 2000), a number of assumptions made about emancipatory research have not been examined in the light of the particular situation experienced by people with learning disabilities.

For example, the belief that access is vital, something subscribed to by all inclusive learning disability researchers (Townsley 1998), is less pressing in the disability field where it can safely be assumed that at least some physically disabled people can access complex theory. Physically impaired academics like Vic Finkelstein and Mike Oliver do not need plain text versions, Makaton symbols or illustrated reports to be able to understand research in the way most people with learning disabilities do (although they do sometimes need mechanical aids such as Braille versions, hearing loops, enlarged print, etc.). Similarly, the assumption that ideally disabled people should carry out some research themselves is one that is more readily applied in the context of physical disability than it is for people with learning disabilities. At least some physically disabled people have access to higher education, the traditional training ground for researchers, far more readily than do people with learning disabilities. Even the ability to access research funds is easier for organizations of disabled people (though not as easy as it should be perhaps) than it is for people with learning disabilities who are likely to need human support in discovering what sources of funding are available, in completing a literature review and in filling in the forms.

Physically impaired scholars have the luxury of debating whether narrative research, the focus on individual experience, is a valid focus for research (Finkelstein 1996). However, if this position were adopted in learning disability, most of what has yet been published would not be permissible. The autobiography, life history and ethnographic traditions have led the field in inclusive learning disability research; there is little else other than service evaluations.

Our point is that the parallels between people with physical impairments and people with learning disabilities are striking – but differences are also considerable. The equivalent to Braille, guide dogs, ramps, etc. is not technological but human. For most research, people with learning disabilities need the assistance of non-disabled allies – and they are less amenable to control than technology. To date, a wholesale migration to emancipatory research has been considered but not implemented. Whether it could or should be are key issues we seek to discuss.

Self advocacy

There can be no doubt that self advocacy has played an important role in enabling inclusive research. Without self advocacy there would be no possibility of organized groups to work on research projects. Without self advocacy there could be little prospect of people with learning disabilities collectively defining their own research questions. If researchers are to be accountable to organizations of people with learning disabilities, then self advocacy groups are vital. Without self advocacy, the level of sophistication of the potential contributions to research, either as respondents or as researchers, would be that much less organized and consistent. Self advocacy is the particular form that speaking up and out has taken in learning disability. The very nomenclature, self rather than citizen advocacy, distances it from normalization while at the same time acknowledging its parenthood. Indeed some, including

Wolfensberger, regard citizen advocacy as an essential prerequisite for self advocacy:

> A severely limited person learns self advocacy best within the undemanding shelter, protection, love and friendship of a citizen advocacy relationship, because these processes are especially apt to bring the person towards growth and independence. (Wolfensberger, quoted in Williams and Schoultz 1982, p.93)

Few self advocates would accept this paternalistic view now. People First (Open University 1996) says that self advocacy is:

• Speaking for yourself.

• Standing up for your rights.

• Being independent.

• Taking responsibility for yourself.

A similar view of the role of self advocacy is taken by Reinforce, a self advocacy organization in Victoria which describes itself as: 'A group that helps promote the rights of people with a disability' (Hiscoe 2002, personal communication). Self advocacy is both an individual and a group activity. At the individual level it promotes having a voice, an identity and a sense of rights and responsibilities. At a group level it represents the collective voice of people with learning disabilities, people joining together to thrash out political positions and to fight for their interests. Although it has been a patchy process, it can also be about people with learning disabilities learning to take a pride in difference rather than denial of difference, as normalization implies (Walmsley with Downer 1997). This sense of group solidarity and pride has been relatively slow to develop. Some leading self advocates appear to remain uneasy about their labels. The People First slogan, 'Label jars not people', appears to owe as much to denial of difference as it does to pride in identity. Joyce Kershaw is quoted by Goodley (2001) as saying:

> Learning disabilities – I don't like that, disability makes you believe that we are in wheelchairs and we can't do anything for ourselves when we can. We've got jobs now, we've got paid jobs. (Goodley 2001, p.217)

There is little sign, to date, of a Pride movement where the derogatory labels of the past are reclaimed and used with defiance, as has happened with other marginalized groups (Mairs 1986). Despite its current limitations, Goodley (1998) argues that self advocacy potentially provides participants with a collective voice, a framework for resistance, and that it is founded on an assumption of competence.

Great claims have been made for self advocacy. Hank Bersani junior, for example, regards it as a new social movement in which members go beyond their typical social roles, which represents ideological change and which involves the emergence of a new dimension of identity 'often drawing on a characteristic formerly seen as a weakness' (1998, p.59).

> A major activity of the disability right movement has been the development of a positive identity and group consciousness. This can be seen in the specific successes of the self advocacy movement. Organisations now insist on 'People First Language' and refuse to accept what they call the 'r' word (retarded). This is clear evidence of action and success in escaping the role of victim... The idea that people with disabilities are 'people first' represents a radical ideological change. What was once a weakness (a cognitive impairment that required supervision and control by others) is now a strength (greater identity with others in oppressed lives that professionals will never understand). (Bersani 1998, p.60)

Bersani is not someone with learning disabilities. Theorizing by people with learning disabilities rarely finds its way into print. As such it continues to be the role of the non-disabled ally. One exception is Simone Aspis, a UK self advocate who has gained a considerable reputation as a theorist of self advocacy. Aspis has written a critique of the way self advocacy has developed, particularly in the UK. She is suspicious of the way self advocacy is boiled down to a series of precepts – particularly the focus on meetings and how to conduct them. There is a danger, she argues, of self advocates developing a naive view of power as residing in the attitudes of a particular individual, rather than as part of the very fabric of social structures. She also sees self advocacy as becoming part of the service structure, in the light of continuing demands upon service providers to demonstrate that they are consulting 'users'. She argues that self advocacy is becoming 'a tool to find out what people want of a service rather than to challenge the philosophy of services and system that creates them and their inherent limitations' (Aspis 1997, p.653).

For other self advocates, however, self advocacy offers the possibility of power not only in relation to research but also in fundamentally changing society and in challenging discriminatory practices (Tuttleby with Johnson 2000). It is not easy to write about self advocacy just because few self advocates have the means to develop arguments in the standard way academics do. Print is a medium to which they gain access through others, rather than as authors in their own right. Writing about self advocacy overall tends to become adulatory. Bersani's chapter is a good example, though few have been as bold as he in making such elaborate claims.

This is an issue which also clouds inclusive research. In terms of research, self advocacy is important 'because it has paralleled and to some extent made possible the development of inclusive research and history' (Atkinson 2001, p.33). It has grown alongside research studies which seek to represent the views of people with learning disabilities (Walmsley 1995). Atkinson argues that this has been a two-way process:

> On the one hand it could be argued that self advocacy influenced researchers by demonstrating not only that people with learning disabilities wanted to 'speak up' but also that they could do so. On the other hand it seemed likely that self advocates influenced the people who were involved in it, showing them the value of research and giving them the confidence to take part. (Atkinson 2001, p.34)

Self advocates have written their own autobiographies (Barron 2000); engaged researchers to assist them in writing their life stories (for example, Andrews with Rolph 2000; Cooper 1997; Tuttleby with Johnson 2000); have initiated research of their own (for example, Reinforce 1992; Williams 1999); have worked in partnership as co-researchers (March et al. 1997; Rolph 2000); have co-written papers (Souza with Ramcharan 1997; Walmsley with Downer 1997); have bid for research funds of their own (Central England People First 2000); and have been commissioned to undertake service evaluations (Whittaker 1997).

However, self advocacy has not touched equally the lives of different groups of people with learning disabilities. Most people with learning disabilities who are active in research have been relatively able, a lot are male, most are white. Jackie Downer, herself a black self advocate, argues that a lot more needs to be done to include people with severe and profound learning disabilities by self advocates themselves (Walmsley with Downer 1997).

There is a danger that self advocacy provides for those people who are able, sometimes with encouragement, literally to gain a 'voice'. For those people who cannot speak, finding a voice is both literally and metaphorically far more challenging.

Most recently, some self advocates have challenged the role of non-disabled people in research on learning disability, inspired, one might suggest, by the arguments developed in the disability movement. This critique is best articulated by Simone Aspis. In an important paper she sets out her argument, informed by the principles of the disabled people's movement:

> The key area to address is who has the power to set the hypothesis, gather the evidence, interpret the experiences, make recommendations and define the political, physical and practical context. Social research is very important as a tool to influence social change and how this is carried out. Many of the government policies are based on social research findings. It is not surprising that a lot of government policies are confusing and ill-thought out in relation to disabled people with learning difficulties. This is because there are too many different researchers jumping on the bandwagon of learning disability research which includes providing their own interpretations and solutions to our individual and collective experiences. (Aspis 2000, p.3)

Aspis argues that much of the involvement of self advocates in research to date has been tokenistic:

> When disabled people with learning difficulties [sic] are included in research projects or as authors it's usually the 'tame' ones who are chosen. I am known to challenge, and I suspect people find me difficult to work with because I shake their assumptions and make life uncomfortable, so they tend to choose other people. (Aspis 2000, p.2)

In terms of this book, this is a crucial issue. If the research in which self advocates have been involved is indeed tokenistic, if their power is subject to the goodwill of non-disabled allies, then the whole enterprise is suspect.

Summary

In this chapter we have explored three major influences on inclusive research in learning disability – normalization/social role valorization, the social model of disability/emancipatory research, and self advocacy. We would propose that each has shaped the development of inclusive research and that between them they have helped us frame the 'questions we dare not ask'.

Normalization/social role valorization opened the way for research which took people with learning disabilities seriously as potential respondents with its emphasis on the importance of according people valued social roles, and the emphasis it places on the duty of non-disabled people to work for the interests of devalued people, particularly as advocates. Although in many ways inimical to inclusive research, with its assumption that normalization principles could be used as a proxy for the views of people with learning disabilities, and its exclusive interest in services as the means to improving the quality of people's lives, in practice it appears to have been a potent influence on non-disabled people working in the inclusive research field. In particular, in the UK some ideas drawn from the precepts of citizen advocacy have been significant: the research as presenting positive images of people with learning disabilities, showing them in valued social roles; the researcher as someone who represents the views of people with learning disabilities, whether or not they agree with them; in sum, the researcher as advocate.

The ideas developed by disabled people about emancipatory research, have also had an impact. The challenge posed by emancipatory research removes the comfortable position of researchers in the normalization tradition – as allies. Instead, researchers are expected to put their skills at the disposal of disabled people and the research should, at all stages, be controlled by disabled people and accountable not just to individuals, but also to organizations of disabled people. Ideas developed by disabled people about the importance of research being a tool for social change, about the need for disabled people to control the agenda, processes and outcomes, and about the necessity of accountability to organizations of disabled people, have been taken up, initially by non-disabled allies (Rodgers 1999; Townsley 1998; Walmsley 1994), and subsequently by some people with learning disabilities (Aspis 2000). Our position has been that there has been a failure to examine critically the ideals of emancipatory research in the light of the particular context of people with learning disabilities. This is partly due to the failure of the disabled people's movement to take on the issues of people with learning disabilities. Thus the application of emancipatory or social model theory to this group has not been attempted by disabled people. It has also, we would suggest, been partly the failure of non-disabled allies to assist people with learning disabilities in working through the implications of emancipatory research for themselves.

Finally, self advocacy has been of vital importance in enabling people to find a voice, to develop a collective position and to recognize the value which research may have for them. Many researchers have worked successfully with individual self advocates and with groups to undertake participatory research, and insights into the perspectives of people with learning disabilities have been gained. Some have expressed reservations about tokenism; others about the potential of relatively able self advocates to represent issues relating to people with more severe learning disabilities. Most recently, some individual self advocates and one or two groups have begun to question the role of the non-disabled allies and their right to do research in topics which are seen to be the rightful property of self advocates – the history of the movement – even with participation by other people with learning disabilities.

CHAPTER 3

Inclusive Research
in Learning Disability

Beginnings

Chapter 3 is concerned with the second of the questions posed in the Introduction to this book:

- To what extent did inclusive research arise from the concerns of people with learning disabilities?

In this chapter we review the origins of inclusive research in learning disability. In particular we trace how the research methodologies and influences discussed in Chapters 1 and 2 shaped its early development. First, we examine in more detail what is actually meant by inclusive research with people with learning disabilities and establish some criteria by which such research can be identified. Second, we look at the beginnings of inclusive research starting with the earliest examples of research in which people with learning disabilities are quoted verbatim, particularly the work of Robert Edgerton (Edgerton 1967; Edgerton and Bercovici 1976; Edgerton, Bollinger and Herr 1984). We end with the publication of *Know Me As I Am* (Atkinson and Williams 1990), the first major publication which embodied many of the principles of inclusive research and foreshadowed both the potential and the dilemmas.

Defining inclusive research

As mentioned in the Introduction, we define inclusive research as research which includes or involves people with learning disabilities as more than just subjects of research. They are actors, people whose views are directly represented in the published findings in their own words but – and this is important – they are also researchers playing an active role as instigators, interviewers, data analysts or authors. As Beresford (2000a) notes, it is not enough to be mere data sources.

In effect, inclusive research as a term covers two major disability research traditions, participatory and emancipatory research. We described participatory research in Chapter 1. It is research where a sympathetic ally works alongside people with learning disabilities to do research where people with learning disabilities participate actively. Chappell (2000), drawing on the work of Cocks and Cockram (1995), states that participatory research has the following characteristics:

- The research problem may be identified by disabled people or non-disabled researchers who then bring it to the attention of non-disabled people.

- Disabled people and researchers work together to achieve a collective analysis of the research problem.

- Alliances are formed between disabled people, researchers and other experts although these alliances must be under the control of and primarily in the interests of disabled people. (Chappell 2000, pp.38–9)

These characteristics in essence restate the principles established in Chapter 1 which unite qualitative, feminist and participatory research with one exception. Chappell does not include any categories relating to subjectivity or objectivity. However, other authors state unequivocally that the researcher should abandon 'objectivity' and be 'on the side of' disabled people (see Barnes 1996; Williams 2002). An additional principle which we believe should be added is one of accessibility. This is particularly (though not exclusively) important in the context of learning disability research. If people cannot understand the research, then they cannot meaningfully participate (Townsley 1998). Thus to Chappell's list we would add:

- The researcher is on the side of disabled people.
- The research must be accessible to some people with learning disabilities.

However, as shown in Chapter 2, disabled activists have argued that participatory research remains under the control of people without disabilities (French and Swain 1997) and that it is emancipatory research, where disabled people control the process and the resources, which truly promises to deliver social change. Chappell again provides a helpful set of categories. Emancipatory research (after Zarb 1992) is characterized in the following ways:

- Research should be used as a tool for improving the lives of disabled people.
- There should be opportunities for disabled people to be researchers.
- Researchers must adopt a reflexive stance regarding their work.
- The democratic organizations of disabled people should act as commissioners and funders of research.
- Researchers should be accountable to the democratic organizations of disabled people. (Chappell 2000, p.38)

There has been a great deal of debate over the pros and cons of these two approaches (see Atkinson 2001; Chappell 1997) and this book will add to those discussions. However, for the sake of our definition of inclusive research we propose a set of categories which can cover both participatory and emancipatory research in the learning disability context. In our view if a piece of research is to be viewed as 'inclusive' (either participatory or emancipatory) it must exhibit the characteristics shown in Box 3.1.

The categories in Box 3.1 are not unproblematic, as will be shown. It will be important to bear them in mind as the review of what has been achieved so far in the learning disability field unfolds.

Box 3.1 Definition of inclusive research

- The research problem must be one that is owned (not necessarily initiated) by disabled people.

- It should further the interests of disabled people; non-disabled researchers should be on the side of people with learning disabilities.

- It should be collaborative – people with learning disabilities should be involved in the process of doing the research.

- People with learning disabilities should be able to exert some control over process and outcomes.

- The research question, process and reports must be accessible to people with learning disabilities.

Where does inclusive research come from?

Here we look at the beginnings of inclusive research methodologies in learning disability.

Traditional research in learning disability: the empiricist model

Inclusive research with people with learning disabilities has had a relatively short history, dating from the late 1980s. Richards (1984) could find only five studies in the previous 20 years which had featured people with learning disabilities, even as respondents. The dominant paradigm of research in learning disability was (and some might argue still is) positivist and often rooted in a medical model of learning disability which sees it as an unalterable condition; the researcher's task being to describe and analyse the behaviour or characteristics of the people so labelled. Kiernan characterizes 'traditional' research as very much 'on' rather than 'with' people:

> The behaviour of human beings and human organizations are seen as equivalent to other 'natural' phenomena, to be studied through reliable objective measures, by detached researchers, in the development and testing of theories of behaviour.

In the traditional model 'participation' of subjects is strictly limited. The researcher decides on the research question, develops and employs what are felt to be suitable measures, analyses the ensuing data, and interprets the results in terms of the original hypothesis... The subjects of research studies are therefore almost entirely passive in the research process. (Kiernan 1999, p.43)

This kind of research is still very prevalent in the research journals. An example is shown in Box 3.2. The research abstract is consistent with Kiernan's view of traditional research.

Box 3.2 Analysis of expenditures and outcomes of residential alternatives for persons with developmental disabilities

Expenditures, staffing and outcomes were examined for 116 adults with severe or profound mental retardation who moved from state institutions in Minnesota to various community living settings and a comparison group of 71 people who remained institutionalized. Outcome variables included community access, social activities, community inclusion, family relationships and choice. Comparison of participants' personal characteristics revealed no difference between groups but several differences emerged when the community sample was grouped by residence size or public versus private ownership. Where necessary, covariance analysis was used to adjust for these preexisting differences. Community residences were less costly and had more favorable staffing and uniformly better outcomes than the institutions. Few outcome differences were evident between community residents when compared by residence size or service ownership. (Stancliffe and Lakin 1998)

Traditional research: qualitative studies

It was not only people working in a positivist tradition who ignored the perspectives of people with learning disabilities. Research into the nature and experience of families caring for children or adults with learning disabilities undertaken in the 1970s and 1980s illustrates how the perspectives of people with learning disabilities were sidelined. A number of UK-based researchers were influenced by the move away from institutions to 'community care' which inevitably made the capacity of families to care for people with learning disabilities a significant policy issue.

The (largely qualitative) studies which emerged in this era are characterized by a focus on the plight of families (particularly women) and on the construction of their disabled offspring as burdens: 'The burden goes on, moreover, potentially for ever' (Abbott and Sapsford 1989, p.74). None of the researchers in this vein (including Abbott and Sapsford 1987; Ayer and Alaszewski 1984; Baldwin and Glendinning 1983; Bayley 1973) saw it as necessary to present the perspectives of people with learning disabilities in their research. It was the mothers, not the people with learning disabilities, whose interests were paramount: 'Services should be designed around the needs of mothers, not those of professionals' (Ayer and Alaszewski 1984, p.235).

This focus on the carers rather than the cared for became, in the 1990s, a criticism of prevailing research into caring launched by academics speaking for the interests of the 'dependants' in the equation, inspired by the social model of disability (Morris 1993; Walmsley 1993). This is not to argue that families do not deserve consideration – they do – but to illustrate the extent to which the views and perspectives of people with learning disabilities were disregarded by qualitative researchers in the mid-1980s.

The sympathetic researcher

In his review, Kiernan (1999) does not single out the role of the sympathetic ally or advocate (Chappell, Goodley and Lawthorn 2001; Walmsley 2001). However, since at least the late 1960s and probably before there has been a long tradition of non-disabled 'experts' taking up the cause of people with learning disabilities and speaking for them. As Mittler put it:

> People with learning disabilities have not lacked advocates who have been prepared to speak out against abuse and for human rights and better services. Courageous individuals have always been ready to make a public protest about inhuman or degrading conditions to

which people with learning disabilities have been – and still are – subject. (Mittler 1996, p.3)

In the chapter he cites individuals – Peggy Jay, Ann Shearer, Richard Crossman, Barbara Castle, Wolf Wolfensberger – as examples of such people. This tradition continues into the twenty-first century, increasingly alongside efforts to work *with* rather than speak out *for* people with learning disabilities. Chappell (2000) notes this ally role as a constant in the changes over the past 30 years, and defends it. However, all methods, whether the sympathetic ally, the qualitative or the positivist researcher, had until fairly recently the effect of excluding the voice of people with learning disabilities. Atkinson and Walmsley (1999) describe the apparent silence of people with learning disabilities prior to the late twentieth century as 'lost voices':

> In this century, the voices of people with learning disabilities have remained lost as other voices remained in the ascendant. From the turn of the century until the 1930s, the influential voices were those of the eugenicists, or people sympathetic to their cause. The link was made or claimed by the eugenists between 'mental deficiency', as it was then known, and the various social ills of the time. At the same time, and in later years, other voices became dominant; the voices of the doctors, as the medical model came into vogue… The mental defective became 'the other'; different, inferior and silent. (Atkinson and Walmsley 1999, p.204)

Later in the paper they note that as attitudes changed from fear to pity the person with a learning disability became subject to being represented by their parents, or through the parents' eyes, sometimes as a justification for institutional care, sometimes as a justification for refusing institutional care. The person's own voice remained 'lost'.

Early voices of people with learning disabilities

The earliest instances of self-representation by people with learning disabilities in print were autobiographies (Deacon 1974; Hunt 1967), a genre which has continued to be represented in the field (Cooper 1997; Slattery with Johnson 2000).

Other pre-1980s examples of research where the words of people with learning disabilities are central are from the USA. They include *Inside Out*, Robert Bogdan and Steven Taylor's (1982) life history of Ed Rhodes, a man with mental retardation, and Robert Edgerton's celebrated ethnographic studies of patients released from the Pacific State Institution, California, between the mid-1960s and mid-1980s (Edgerton 1967; Edgerton and Bercovici 1976; Edgerton, Bollinger and Herr 1984). Although both Bogdan and Taylor and Edgerton present people with learning disabilities as rounded human beings, often in their own words, we do not see their work as inclusive, largely because the authorial voice of the researcher is not modified by any influence from the people researched.

Bogdan and Taylor's work can be seen as part of the tradition of the Chicago school of ethnographic research in which researchers portray the lives of the underdog, people usually denied a voice in publications (Plummer 1983). They are described as being the product of a collaboration between the 'subject' and the author. However, there is no discussion of the degree of control the 'subject' exercises in the final product. Bogdan and Taylor state:

> People who are labeled retarded have their own understandings about themselves, their situations and their experiences. These understandings are often different from those of professionals. (Bogdan and Taylor 1989, p.168)

This view has become increasingly influential in inclusive research and a touchstone for a number of authors in the late twentieth century.

Both Edgerton and, arguably, Bogdan and Taylor were influenced by Goffman's (1963) concept of 'stigma' – a term used to describe negative qualities attributed to certain social identities by others in the society. Thus the problem is to be found not in the individual but in negative attitudes found in society. People who are different will be treated differently and come to regard themselves as inferior – leading to efforts to 'pass' as normal or unstigmatized individuals. Edgerton identified 'stigma' in the individuals he studied and observed 'passing' behaviour, particularly the acquisition of a benefactor who would help the former patient learn the techniques necessary to negotiate everyday life on the outside. The 'subjects' were given no opportunity to debate this conclusion. Gerber (1990) is critical of Edgerton for his 'uneasy combination of empathy and acceptance of mental retardation as an unalterable condition' (p.3) which, he says, denied people a voice to speak authoritatively about their own situation. According to this argument Edgerton's findings might have led him to undermine the original diagnosis of mental retardation, rather than see the behaviour he observed as stratagems designed to resist the stigma. Bogdan and Taylor, by contrast, used Ed's story to question the whole concept of mental retardation:

> Our research suggests, however, that the concept of mental retardation is not just less than useful, it is actually seriously misleading. (Bogdan and Taylor 1989, p.76)

In drawing this conclusion, Bogdan and Taylor added their voices to those of a number of mid-twentieth century sociologists who questioned mental retardation (learning disability) as a construct. For example, Mercer, a US sociologist, wrote: 'It follows that a person may be mentally retarded in one system and not mentally retarded in another. He may change his social role by changing his social group' (Mercer 1973, p.23).

These debates on the nature of learning disability/mental retardation have a bearing on the whole issue of inclusive research. For if learning disability is a social construction rather than an innate condition, then changing the environment and the social relations of research should indeed be able to liberate people with learning disabilities to be active participants in research, and other aspects of life from which they have been traditionally excluded. This view has clearly influenced the inclusive research agenda which has been premised upon the potential to alter the environment to facilitate the involvement of people with learning disabilities – a position, we will argue, which is not fully tenable.

The 1980s' glimmerings of change

The work of some sociologists in the USA did not immediately make a major impact on mainstream traditional learning disability research elsewhere. It continued much as Kiernan (1999) described above –

pathologized individuals whose plight needed ameliorating (perhaps) through 'scientific' research. The voices and opinions of those individuals were disregarded. However, gradually change began to happen and the focus of research began to shift to a concern with the lives and voices of people with learning disabilities.

During the 1980s it is possible to discern a shift on the part of some researchers to taking the point of view of people with learning disabilities seriously. This coincided with the growth of the self advocacy movement, initially in the USA, and with several significant publications including *We Can Speak for Ourselves* (Williams and Shoultz 1982) which described people with learning disabilities as service evaluators. Some of the ideas developed in the USA began to be imported to the UK and Australia during the 1970s. In the UK a couple of conference reports were published by the Campaign for the Mentally Handicapped (CMH) which 'gave a voice' to people with learning disabilities. In Australia the advocacy movement began to gain force in the late 1980s with the establishment of self-advocacy organisations such as Reinforce. People with learning disabilities started to make their concerns and complaints heard in public forums and on reference groups for some research (Johnson, Topp and Andrew 1987), but little consistent research was undertaken which reflected their concerns.

Gradually however the scene began to change. The way was paved by the work of Sigelman *et al.* (1981), the first (to our knowledge) methodological paper on involving people with learning disabilities as respondents. The focus of the discussion was how to ask questions which did not produce compliance. People with learning disabilities were seen in this research as people who had 'deficient cognitive, verbal and social skills' who were so eager to please the researcher that they would answer yes unless great care was taken in framing the questions. Although its assumptions were rooted in a medical deficit model of learning disability, the fact that eminent US scholars were taking people with learning disabilities seriously as potential respondents was in many respects seismic. The impact was soon felt in the UK and elsewhere. In the UK two well-known studies into the way people adjusted to and experienced community life (Atkinson 1986; Flynn 1989) used testimony from people with learning disabilities as one of several methods of data collection. Both cited Sigelman *et al.*'s work. Although neither researcher expected at the outset that this aspect would yield significant and reliable data, in practice the words of the disabled respondents became the centrepiece of subsequent publications. Both women went on to publish methodological papers exploring issues including research design, where and how to interview, and anticipated areas of difficulty (Atkinson 1989; Flynn 1986). This methodological work was marked by a further refinement. 'Problems' encountered in the research were not necessarily in the respondents so much as in the relationship between researcher and researched. Atkinson in particular reflected upon the respondents' perceptions of the researcher and how that might influence the findings:

> Alice Wise (in an aside to her social worker): 'She's very nice, isn't she. I thought she'd be strict and horrible.'

> Edward Hayes (in an aside to his social worker): 'She must be very important, asking us all these questions'. (Atkinson 1989, p.69)

Furthermore, Atkinson noted that many people welcomed her visit – there were few occasions when such an interest was taken.

In Australia qualitative studies which included people with learning disabilities as informants and members of reference groups were beginning to be developed (Johnson *et al.* 1987; O'Brien and Johnson 1988). In a large study of people with learning disabilities as victims of crime, Johnson *et al.* used focus groups and individual interviews to find out how people with learning disabilities experienced crime, the law and the courts. In this project self advocates were represented on the reference group. The researchers used self-reflection through journals and peer discussions to look at difficulties experienced in the methodology. These issues were to become important themes of future participative work. The perceptions of the researcher and associated dangers that research interviews would recreate in people's minds experiences of being assessed and tested and the potential for people to (mis)interpret the researcher's interest as that of a friend, with consequent expectations of longer term relationships, have consistently resurfaced in the participatory research literature.

Although the UK studies were methodologically the most sophisti-cated and arguably influential in the development of inclusion of people with learning disabilities in research, a number of other UK studies of that era began to feature the perspectives of people with learning disabilities as central. Some of these focused very specifically on how people viewed and experienced services. A series of projects sponsored by the Scottish Home and Health Department on independent living (Markova, Jahoda and Cattermole 1988), adult training centres (Jahoda, Markova and Cattermole 1989a) and hospital life (Cattermole, Jahoda and Markova 1988) explored how people with learning disabilities perceived life. The authors used direct quotations from the respondents as major data sources, arguing how important it was to get inside the different perspectives of professionals and service users.

More abstract subjects began to be explored using qualitative interviews with people with learning disabilities – stigma and self-concept (Jahoda, Markova and Cattermole 1989b); the meaning of adulthood (Walmsley 1989, 1991); and self-identity (Aull Davies and Jenkins 1997). Overall, this body of work suggested that self-identification as a group labelled as people with learning disabilities was low. Indeed some evidence from these papers suggests a deliberate self-distancing from other people with learning disabilities. 'Gwen', for example, whom I (JW) interviewed in the adulthood project, denied having learning disabilities, claiming instead that her bad leg was the reason for her place in an adult training centre (Walmsley 1991). Aull Davies and Jenkins also noted that 'the majority...do not comprehend the terms most commonly associated with their primary social identity' (1997, p.8); that is they did not apply the term 'mental handicap' or 'learning difficulty' to themselves.

How far did this body of research qualify as 'inclusive'? Reading back on our own work of that time we note with interest that 'empowerment', allowing the respondents to 'set the agenda', was on our agendas (O'Brien and Johnson 1988; Walmsley 1991). This was explicitly drawn from feminist and action research, summed up in three questions:

Who frames the research and how?

What relationship is established between the researcher and the respondent?

Who analyses the data and how? (Walmsley 1989, p.23)

However imperfectly achieved, these were beginning to be seen as legitimate, nay desirable, research questions. They were to become overriding imperatives in the following decade. Not only this but means were
being sought to ensure that people were enabled to reflect upon and influence the process and outcomes of the research (Walmsley 1991).
Nevertheless, the low level of group consciousness was clearly an inhib-
iting factor in empowering people to ask questions, at least about learning disability.

Know Me As I Am: revealing potential and dilemmas

The decade ended with the publication in the UK of *Know Me As I Am:
An Anthology of Prose, Poetry and Art by People with Learning Difficulties*
(Atkinson and Williams 1990). This was by far the most ambitious piece
of work yet attempted to include the 'voices' of people with learning
disabilities, and in many ways it embodied the principles of inclusive research. It also highlights some of the continuing dilemmas and for this
reason we examine it in some detail.

Know Me As I Am began to reveal both the potential of inclusive research, and some of its central dilemmas. In terms of potential, the editors emphasized the importance of understanding the world from the
point of view of someone with learning disabilities: 'It challenges our
assumptions and stereotypes, even when we think we have none' (p.7).
They also emphasized the importance of the work for the contributors:

> Being a published author or contributor is a valued social role...We
> know that this social recognition is highly valued. (Atkinson and
> Williams 1990, p.236)

Box 3.3 *Know Me As I Am*

Know Me As I Am was a conscious attempt to make the 'voices' of people with learning disabilities a centrepiece of an undergraduate course about learning disability, Changing Perspectives, produced by the UK Open University. It was edited by two women academics: Dorothy Atkinson, already with a considerable reputation as a qualitative researcher who had pioneered interviews with people with learning disabilities (see above); and Fiona Williams, a social theorist who brought a strong commitment to feminism and anti-racism. It proved a potent partnership. I (JW) was part of the team which produced the course and was therefore privy to some of the debates which accompanied the book's creation.

It is an example of a genre which has continued to flourish, life histories by people with learning disabilities, in this instance drawn from across the UK. The editors write:

> This book is unusual. It is, as far as we know, unique in its breadth and scope. It is a collection of life stories, but a very distinctive collection. The people whose lives are portrayed are people with learning difficulties. And the material compiled and presented here is theirs: their lives and their words, pictures, photographs and poems. (Atkinson and Williams 1990, p.5)

This idea is clearly associated with Wolfensberger's formulation of social role valorization. In the previous chapter we noted the proposition that the move to inclusive research owes a great deal to the encouragement which social role valorization gives to the promotion of valued social roles for people with learning disabilities, and this is a good example. Being involved in research is a 'valued social role', which sometimes appears to become an end in itself.

How far does *Know Me As I Am* 'qualify' as inclusive, according to our definition in Box 3.1? Examining this project against each of our criteria reveals that it met most of them at least to some extent.

The research problem may be identified by disabled people or non-disabled researchers who then bring it to the attention of non-disabled people

Although the idea came from academia, there are signs that it was adopted with enthusiasm by contributors. The contributions vary from quite simple statements to sophisticated and lengthy life stories. Doreen Cocklin wrote:

> This is the first time anything I have said has been written down.
>
> I don't know what to say.
>
> But I like what I see. It's good how it comes out. Nice!
>
> I like that. That's all right. (Atkinson and Williams 1990)

Disabled people and researchers work together to achieve a collective analysis of the research problem

Self-evidently people with learning disabilities were collaborators – it was the stories and pictures they generated that were the 'data'. There certainly were genuine attempts to offer people with learning disabilities some control over the process. An editorial group was assembled to assist in selecting material and resolving some dilemmas. These were all people with learning disabilities, not drawn from the contributors, but with a distinct role. Some of their advice is quoted in the conclusion:

> Question: Sometimes people make spelling mistakes, but at other times they use words in an unusual way – what should we do? Correct everything? Leave everything?
>
> Answer: Correct the spelling mistakes but keep the unusual words because they make the stories more interesting. (Atkinson and Williams 1990, p.230)

This advice was followed.

Contributors were given the opportunity to approve or correct their stories before publication and offered the option of using their full names or only their first names. They were paid, both in cash and with a copy of the final publication. There is also evidence of reflexivity, both on the part of the editors, who kept diaries of their visits to potential contributors, and the intermediaries who assisted people to collect the stories. The editors admit to doubts both about the viability of the overall project and about some of the processes. The following are two of several diary extracts quoted:

> The ward was fairly grim. Some ambulant, but severely handicapped men sat or wandered in the dining space. In the office was a container full of toothbrushes! (Are they doled out?) The attitudes were grimmer. Permission? To speak to us? (Atkinson and Williams 1990, p.232)

> A wet Monday in South London. Tired and distinctly jaded. Three hours by car from Milton Keynes and a full five minutes to negotiate reception... I walked into the room and was greeted by the tutor. The students were working on computers.

> This was a third hand contact who thought we were producing a book for teachers. She hadn't told the class I was coming. Her suggestion was that I drifted round the room chatting to people as I went, sort of Princess Di style. That didn't seem right. (Atkinson and Williams 1990, p.233)

Alliances are formed between disabled people, researchers and other experts although these alliances must be under the control of and primarily in the interests of disabled people.

The question of promoting the interests and 'being on the side of' people with learning disabilities is addressed in some depth. This is formulated as promotion versus acceptance. The editors acknowledge that they were motivated by a desire to promote 'positive images' (p.234). They argue, however, that an anthology which merely focused on 'achievements' would miss the point. Some of the drawings submitted were 'childlike' and there was some concern that publishing such material would diminish the contributors. Again, the influence of social role valorization (see Chapter 2) is evident. Yet some of the childlike drawings, and some at first sight very slight contributions were included, partly on the advice of the advisory group. The editors argue that these represent major accomplishments for their originators and deserved incorporation.

The research question, process and reports must be accessible to people with learning disabilities

Most contributions probably are accessible to many people with learning disabilities with support. Care was taken to ensure the design of the book was high quality and it is liberally illustrated. There are no easy-to-read versions and by the standards of the twenty-first century the layout looks dense and rather muddled. What is perhaps more significant is that the introduction and conclusion are not accessible to people without a reasonable level of literacy. In research terms, these are the sections which cover further theorizing and methodological innovation and they are not immediately open to people with learning disabilities.

Now to the dilemmas. Some of the frustrations and tensions of inclusive research are already evident. The editors, often through communication with intermediaries, knew that some stories masked 'a great deal of pain and suffering' (p.235), but made a conscious decision not to tell 'the story behind the story' (p.235). Victimhood was avoided by and large – in the process the survivor message may have been overstated. Some potentially important information was deliberately omitted. In life history research like this, the researcher may often know more than they can tell. The category learning difficulty was problematic and, like most qualitative researchers, the editors took a broad church view. They acknowledge that this risks diminishing the very specific problems experienced by people with severe and profound difficulties.

Compromises were also made about the power of people with learning disabilities over some major decisions. As an 'insider', I (JW) can recall the debate over the title. The advisory group was presented with a selection of five titles, and chose one. In the end, the editors chose another. There were no repercussions.

Finally, undoubtedly the careers of the editors were furthered by the publication of the anthology, far more than those of the majority of the contributors – an ethical dilemma underlying almost all inclusive research.

Overall, *Know Me As I Am* fulfils many of the criteria we set for inclusive research. Where it did not are areas where genuine difficulties and dilemmas exist in inclusive research and exploration of these is the rationale for this book, and the 'questions we dare not ask'.

Conclusion

Looking back, it is startling to observe how much changed in five short years, 1985 to 1989. My (JW's) initial contact with mental handicap, as it was then termed, was with the Open University teaching package *Patterns for Living* (Walmsley 1989). Although essentially life-story based, there was very little in the package which was directly quoted from people with learning disabilities. Their names were changed, their voices muted, their visual representations were artists' line drawings. By 1990, a dramatic change is discernible and enabling people to represent themselves became, for some, at least, a pressing imperative. Yet it is clear that even in this change the initiative and the processes themselves were devised by researchers and academics who were influenced by normalization/social role valorization, the rights movements and the movement towards qualitative research. The research being undertaken in a movement towards inclusive research was seen to be in the interests of people with learning disabilities but did not necessarily reflect their interests or motivations. Moreover the dilemmas and ethical difficulties which accompany efforts to promote inclusive research had also begun to emerge: questions about ownership, the extent to which the non-disabled researcher has a distinctive voice, the degree to which everyone with learning disabilities can be included, the difficult tightrope between representing people with learning disabilities honestly and being on their side, the dangers of stereotyping, all of these were emerging. They have not gone away.

CHAPTER 4

Knowing the Elephant

It was six men of Hindustan
To learning much inclined
Who went to see the elephant
(though all of them were blind)
That each by observation
Might satisfy the mind.

(John Godfrey Saxe, 1930)

Six blind men from Hindustan are attempting to define an elephant from touch alone. I remembered this poem from childhood. It was not the racist or disablist overtones that I recalled but the sheer impossibility of ever finally defining an elephant: so large, so exotic, so unknowable, so subject to individual interpretation – and yet so familiar. The poem surfaced out of memory as I began to write this chapter. For inclusive research is like the elephant. We use it and yet it remains elusive, difficult to define. It means what we want it to mean: a projection of values and ideologies that may have little to do with research processes. Its meanings change depending upon the position from which we view it – researcher, person with learning disabilities, critic. We think we know its nature then suddenly we realize that we have only touched one small part of it and are constantly forced to doubt even the adequacy of this partial knowledge.

This chapter is concerned with exploring the contested meanings of inclusive research by analysing the themes emerging from the chapters in the first part of the book. The chapter also reviews the questions which have been the focus of Part 1:

- To what extent does inclusive research owe its origins to particular research perspectives and the broader social context?

- To what extent does it arise from the concerns of people with intellectual disabilities?

The chapter broadens the discussion by using examples from indigenous research in Australia to explore some of the ways in which people who were formerly subject to 'western' style research have taken up the challenge of answering back by increasing ownership of research about them. In our view there is much to be learned from this debate which may be of use in inclusive research. Finally, the chapter provides a preface for the practice questions which are the focus of Part 2.

Contested meanings of inclusive research

In this section we look at some of the reasons why it is so problematic generally to label research as emancipatory, participatory and inclusive. In particular we draw on the previous chapters to look at the power of language in defining and constituting both research and those involved in it, the constantly shifting nature of the research process and the distinction between means and ends in research.

The power of language

As discussed in Chapter 1, within research communities there are many disputes and contested views about the meanings and the value given to particular forms of research: quantitative versus qualitative, empirical versus interpretative, interpretative versus postmodern (Bogdan and Biklen 1992; Brechin and Sidell 2000; Denzin and Lincoln 1998; Ferguson, Ferguson and Taylor 1992; Greenwood and Levin 1998). The dichotomies seem endless. So in introducing yet another label for research which seeks specifically to include people with learning disabilities we are conscious of adding again to the confusion and the disputes. We have done this because we believe that the issues which confront researchers and people with learning disabilities in undertaking research together pose unique problems for both parties. We also believe that the term inclusive research focuses our attention on the exclusion of people with learning disabilities from decision making in the rest of their lives and the continuing struggle they have to be included within their communities.

However we are conscious that there are real problems with the use of the term inclusive research. While inclusion has been a rallying cry for people with learning disabilities in particular for some years (Department of Human Services 2001a; Ramcharan *et al.* 1997; Taylor, Bogdan and Lutfiyya 1995), it also continues the stereotyping of this group of people and reinforces their exclusion from many areas of community life. After all we do not need a phrase like this if we are researching with bank managers, politicians or the wealthy. Indeed one of the underlying features of much qualitative, feminist and participatory action research is that they focus on those who are perceived by the researchers (and others in society) to be marginalized and in need of empowerment. We are not being cynical in noting this but rather raising it as an issue for reflection. The use of specific labels for research with such groups can be positive, but it can also be inherently discriminatory. It can continue by its very nature the 'othering' that the research process seeks to undermine for it provides a variation to traditional research discourse which aims to accommodate and continuously reconstitute a dissident or different group. For example, Edward Said (1978), writing of western discourse which creates the Orient as Other, comments that it is supported by 'institutions, vocabulary, scholarship, imagery, doctrines, even colonial bureaucracies and colonial styles' (p.2). Research has a strong role in this as it is part of the western institution which 'makes statements about [the Orient], authorising views about it, describing it, by teaching about it, settling it, ruling over it' (p.3).

The parallels between this form of othering research applied to cross-cultural research and that which involves people with learning disabilities are clear. Consequently as researchers we are both ambivalent and uneasy about the labels which we apply to our research. Nor is this ambivalence restricted to the term we have coined. How would we feel about being 'subject' to emancipatory research or participatory research? While it can be argued that these terms involve breaking down barriers between researchers and others involved in the research, they can also serve to camouflage or hide real power inequalities which continue to exist in spite of the egalitarian label. Further if we accept the label of inclusive research seriously then (as in emancipatory research) we must look at how the researcher is included. In our zeal to define the research in terms of those we perceive to be marginalized, we sometimes ignore the importance of the role of the researcher as part of the research. Failure to define this clearly can lead either to the continuation of traditional research roles in which the researcher continues, sometimes silently, to wield the real power, or to a silencing of the researcher. Reflection on the researcher's role, however, may lead to new and creative ways of working.

The process of research

The application of a descriptive label to research suggests a static quality. Inclusive research is then imagined to be inclusive from beginning to end. Emancipatory research must reveal itself as emancipatory from its commencement. Yet all our experience suggests that research is an on-going process in which relationships, contents and method may shift and change. Collaboration in research has been described as 'a complex and unpredictable swirl of power relations, and of constantly changing selves' (Hollingsworth, Dadds and Miller 1997, p.56). A similar description can be applied to inclusive research. While those involved in a project may come to recognize the learning which they have gained from it and the way in which they have been changed, this may be an important and gradual part of the process. It may not occur till some time after the research has begun, or even after it has ended. We believe it is important to recognize that while the goals of inclusive research should be involvement, participation, empowerment of all those taking part in it, these will not always be present for all parties at all times during the research. Rather they may emerge slowly. We have found that the researcher is often the last to learn and the most astonished by the learning. For example, a report on participatory research with Koori (Aboriginal) communities in Australia included this comment:

> I remember one of those workers [researchers] actually saying to me one day that one of the benefits of the project was that it really changed her mind about what happens. She had started to realise that she had certain assumptions from the Community about bed wetting – and the research challenged these views. (Anderson 2000, p.10)

Although we have coined the term inclusive to describe a particular set of approaches, we recognize that creating a new category also creates new problems. The application of the label inclusive may lead all those involved in it to assume that the learning has occurred at the beginning of the process and that all participants start at the same point in relation to their involvement in the research. This may not be the case.

Means and ends

We believe that one of the issues which complicates attempts to conceptualize and practise inclusive research is a confusion which exists in the minds of participants about the means and ends of research. Inclusive research is like a rope which is woven from the following strands:

- expectations about the outcome of research
- the need for participants to be involved in its process
- the desirability of people with learning disabilities becoming researchers themselves
- the need for involvement in order to challenge and assert the rights of a marginalized group against dominant 'othering' discourses which seek to colonize it.

In most inclusive research these strands exist to varying extents. However, rarely do those involved in the research seek to separate them and to explore their implications for a particular project. In our experience this leads to a great deal of confusion and misunderstanding among researchers and those with whom they work:

> And I think that in the past that [who the research benefits] has been a little bit of a grey area for people doing the research, which was benefiting them and losing the real focus which should be that when you research a group of people in an area it really needs to benefit the

people which it is designed to help, where the research is taking place. (Mohammed 2000, p.9)

For Mohammed, writing about research with Koori people in Victoria, the end results are of primary importance in the research process. This statement reflects a complaint of research by marginalized groups that it has not really focused on the benefits which its results may have for those involved in it. Rather it was seen as: 'having someone come into the Community, pinch all this information and run away and people never hearing again about it. A lot of people were feeling really quite exploited' (Anderson 2000, p.10). As shown in Chapter 2, this too has been one of the issues about which people with learning disabilities have also complained in relation to research done 'on' or 'about them'.

To achieve an end in research which is acceptable to the groups involved in it would seem to require research which is designed to improve their quality of life, change the society so that it is more just and equitable, and research which can be used by the communities involved in it, that is, research which is accessible and culturally sensitive.

It is possible to conceive of research which might achieve these ends without the direct involvement of people subject to it in the research process. The study of institutional closure (Johnson 1998) discussed in Chapter 1 did not involve people with learning disabilities in its design or implementation, although it met the end goals at least partially. However, there is certainly a risk that the results of such research may end up gathering dust on library shelves, unread by those for whom it is most relevant. My study of institutional closure may have had much more impact on policies and practices of deinstitutionalization had people with learning disabilities and policy makers been involved in it.

For many activists, women, people from culturally and linguistically diverse backgrounds and people with disabilities, making the ends of research relevant and useful is not enough. They believe that direct involvement by their community in the research process is essential. For example, as revealed in Chapter 1, feminist researchers have documented the negative effects of research which does not include considerations of gender or indeed women themselves in research about their issues. Arguments are made by Koori people in Victoria that research should involve members of the community from its beginnings

(Vichealth Koori Research and Community Development Unit 2001). These arguments have been translated into guidelines established by one of the main funding bodies for research in Australia, including the following statement:

> Members of the Aboriginal and Torres Strait Islander community being studied will be offered the opportunity to assist in the research and will be paid for the assistance and the funds to support that assistance are in the research budget. Specifically Aboriginal and Torres Strait Islander women, as advised by the community, will be involved when research deals with women's or children's health issues; and the specific cultural and social needs of Aboriginal and Torres Strait Islander men will be similarly recognised. (National Health and Medical Research Council, cited in Vichealth Koori Research and Community Development Unit 2001, p.35)

One of the key arguments for such involvement relates specifically to the research itself. Without the expertise, the lived experience and the knowledge of people coming from the group involved in the research, results will be likely to be invalid; for example, key issues may be ignored or missed through poor research design and processes. This perspective to involvement in the research positions marginalized community members as experts or consultants who are able to contribute to the process of the research.

Paradoxically, people from a 'marginalized' community may be simultaneously viewed by those undertaking the research as powerless and 'unskilled'. Here the arguments for involvement become those relating to the empowerment of the group or individuals involved in the research. The expectations of the 'researcher' (and perhaps the community) in this situation seem to be twofold. First, through its involvement, the community will become better able to understand its own situation and to act to change it (Freire 1970a, 1970b, 1970c). This argument is predicated on an assumption that the results of the research will be able to be used in this way and that through the research process itself participants will learn how to use them. Second, participants in the research will acquire the skills of social research and in future will be better able to undertake control of their own research. This expectation places responsibility on the part of the researcher to 'teach' research skills to those with whom they are working.

Finally people may be involved in the research to counter and challenge dominant discourses and the way that they are constituted. Through this process they are taking back authority and control, resisting the 'colonization' of their communities and making the research a site for wider political struggle. Tuhiwai Smith describes it in this way:

> The past, our stories, local and global, the present, our communities, cultures, languages and social practices – all may be spaces of marginalisation, but they have also become spaces of resistance and hope. It is from within these spaces that increasing numbers of indigenous academics and researchers have begun to address social issues within the wider framework of self-determination, decoloni-sation and social justice. (Tuhiwai Smith 1999, p.4)

All of these strands in the research rope are worthwhile in our view. However, when they are not made explicit and there is no discussion of the different roles people are playing in the research there can be both confusion and misunderstanding. Are people involved primarily because of their lived experience or their particular skills? Are they there to learn about how to do and use research or is their presence a statement about challenging existing discourses? In any piece of research all or some of these questions may be answered affirmatively. In our view it is important to be clear on the roles and positions of the people involved in the research. If we are not then our relationships become confused and the research itself suffers.

An example of this came my way (JW) as a reviewer for funding bids to a major UK research sponsoring body. The researchers proposed to set up groups of marginalized people so that they, the researchers, could study those groups and the ways in which they could construct their own research. The process had come to dominate the minds of the researchers to the extent that the outcomes of the groups' research were all but irrelevant. The bid was not successful – but it illustrates the potential that the drive to what we have called inclusive research has for confusion and even ethically dubious practice.

To what extent does inclusive research owe its origins to particular research perspectives and the broader social context?

The chapters in this part of the book have explored the way in which inclusive research has developed from a number of different ideological and methodological positions which are outside the disability field. They have also shown how it has been shaped by disability theories, models and the political activity of disabled people. There are implications from both these findings for the practice of inclusive research. First, we argue that inclusive research is a convenient site for political action and challenge. Second, we argue that many of the political issues which become entangled with inclusive research are echoed across other movements, though there are some important differences apparent in the field of learning disability.

Inclusive research: a site for political struggle

Deinstitutionalization and associated rights measures have radically changed the lives of people with learning disabilities over the past 30 years (Booth, Simons and Booth 1990; Chenoweth 2000; Commonwealth Government 1992; Taylor *et al.* 1995). However it is also true that much remains to be done. Research has revealed that many people with learning disabilities experience great difficulties in being included within their communities. Many lead lonely and isolated lives (Booth and Booth 1998; Johnson *et al.* 2001; Ramcharan *et al.* 1997). They are more likely than other members of the population to experience sexual abuse (McCarthy 1999, 2000), find it difficult to access services or to find employment and are likely to be on low incomes or in receipt of pensions or benefits (Department of Human Services 2001a, 2001b, 2002). Many people with learning disabilities continue to experience injustice and discrimination.

Previous chapters have canvassed some of the ways in which research can be used to struggle against societal discrimination and injustice. It can provide evidence to enable groups to fight against such injustices. It can provide a basis for people to become empowered both inside the research and outside it. However it can also become a safe site wherein the external struggles for justice are played out. We argue that inclusive research carries the burden of societal injustice. This affects both the way researchers see themselves and their role and the way people with learning disabilities view the research situation.

There is a profound ambivalence in the position of inclusive researchers. We are committed to promoting justice and equality and at the same time we are part of the oppressing group: well educated, usually with a job and reasonable income, status and access to societal privileges. Inclusive research brings us face to face with colleagues with a learning disability who do not have many of these things. We are apologetic not only for the societal goods which we possess but our apologetic stance extends also to our skills and our lack of learning disability. For example, inclusive researchers seek to identify links which legitimize their research focus. This may involve identification with disability through a connection with a 'disabled relative', an assertion of the amount of time working in this field as an establishment of credibility or a statement of other roles in which they have been involved with people with learning disabilities, for example, as an advocate. It is as if the role of inclusive researcher is not enough to establish a working trust.

Further, in our efforts to create a more just society we take on the burden of trying to make our research achieve the goals we would like to see in the broader context. Our research must be democratic, equal, participatory, emancipatory. However hard we try, it never feels as if we have succeeded. How can we? We cannot create a utopia from within our research projects. We remain comparatively well paid for our work, usually in secure employment and with access to a family life and social resources which are not attainable by some of the people with whom we work. Until we have managed to change the society into a more just place for people with learning disabilities we will continue to feel the guilt and sense of failure of never reaching a desired goal in terms of our research processes. In this respect inclusive researchers join other human service workers for whom what they do is never and can never be enough.

For people with learning disabilities the issues involved in the research process seem to be different. The research presents an opportunity to further goals and to get much needed change. However it continues to present in microcosm many of the injustices experienced outside the research situation. Researchers are paid for their work (albeit often poorly), but even when people with learning disabilities are paid for their involvement it is rarely on equal terms with those undertaking the research. Researchers have access to needed services and bureaucracies and to resources. In essence they have access to power. Further the rhetoric of inclusive research casts these inequalities into sharper relief.

The research can become a site where power struggles are played out. Sometimes these result in compromises and sometimes they result in defeat for people with learning disabilities on issues which they regard as important. For example, timelines established by the funding body may prohibit the use of long-term consultation and restrict the level of involvement of people with learning disabilities in the research process. At other times the researcher becomes silenced, allowing the group to develop the research and unable to find a position from which to use the skills and resources which they bring to the group.

The movement towards an equitable relationship between non-disabled researchers and people with learning disabilities is difficult to establish. It needs to be acknowledged that we as researchers cannot totally change society. What we can do is address our relationships with those with whom we work. We believe that it is only by admitting this and making the underlying conflicts and issues explicit that we can move to more collaborative ways of working.

Inclusive research: the research conscience

If well done, inclusive research offers a space in which people with learning disabilities can exercise power and work towards changing social injustice. However, it is only one stream of research undertaken with people with learning disabilities. A survey of the journals indicates that much research with this group of people remains firmly in an empirical, positivist mode. They are subject to the research, not part of it. Nor is this the only division. Medically based research remains an important part of the research discourse in learning disability. The division between these forms of research is very clear at international conferences on learning disabilities where there are frequently two completely separate streams. Rarely do social scientists attend the medical papers (except as critics) and rarely are the medical scientists active participants in the social research stream.

Many people with learning disabilities, like many indigenous people, women and gay and lesbian people, have experienced both positivist and medical research as oppressive and disempowering. It has after all framed the way they have been constituted as 'sick', as 'stupid' and as powerless over many years. The anger at these forms of research cannot find a space to be heard within them because of their very exclusiveness.

Our seeming inability to work creatively with the anger of people with learning disabilities, anger we may ourselves share about injustice and discrimination, effectively continues the divisions. The very essence of inclusive research is that it posits a dichotomy – us and them. If there were not such a dichotomy, if we were really all 'people first', then inclusive research would be quite unnecessary.

We also contend that inclusive research is the conscience of the research community. If we are doing it, then the rest can get on and do the 'real' research elsewhere. This can become a binary divide based on gender, for we will demonstrate that most inclusive research in learning disability is, surprise, surprise, done by women. There have been moves in the academic community to hive off 'real' work, quantitative studies, which effectively marginalizes not just people with learning disabilities, but also those who work alongside them.

To what extent did inclusive research arise from the concerns of people with learning disabilities?

We have shown in this first part of the book that the concerns of people with learning disabilities actually played a rather small part in getting inclusive research approaches off the ground. Inevitably, given their low levels of power, influence and education, very few people with learning disabilities in the 1960s, 1970s and 1980s even knew what research was, let alone its complexities and internal divisions. So to expect change to have come spontaneously from the bottom up would be entirely unrealistic. This remains the case with the overwhelming majority of people with learning disabilities. A few are able to engage in constructive debate about research – but this is a tiny minority, albeit the group with which we personally have most contact.

This issue is not exclusive to people with learning disabilities. Ramazanaglou (1993) discusses in some detail how important questions can emerge from silences, those things that are *not* talked about. Writing from a feminist perspective, she shows how domestic violence emerged as a concern out of a resounding silence. A combination of researcher-initiated research, heightened consciousness of women's rights and policy developments were involved in the emergence of domestic violence as a significant issue. Now it was just conceivable that women who experience domestic violence will band together to demand research to address the issue. Then, it was unimaginable that they would do so. If we restrict ourselves narrowly to only examining questions which a particular group are able to articulate, we will not necessarily be doing those people a service.

Rather than seeing this as a simplistic either/or question, we need to view the development of inclusive research as a process, which iteratively, if we researchers and others are ready to listen, learn and teach, will lead to people with learning disabilities (or at least some of them) beginning to articulate their own questions and exert influence on us and others to help them find answers. How this has been done to date and the extent to which it has been successful are addressed in Part 2.

Conclusion

Coming to know an elephant is exciting, tantalizing and risky! Writing this book has helped us to come to a deeper understanding of why this is so in relation to inclusive research. In Part 2 we consider how the discourses have been translated into practice – and how the very real dilemmas we have begun to air have been addressed.

PART 2

Exploring the
Research Process

Part 1 of this book revealed that many of the issues confronting researchers in working with people with learning disabilities are common to other forms of research and to working with different communities and groups. The responses of people with learning disabilities to research processes and goals were also seen to be similar to other groups who have traditionally been subject to social research. However we also found particular developments in learning disability which have led to a focus on inclusive research. Part 1 also suggested that there are unique issues that confront researchers working with people with learning disabilities which are often ignored or camouflaged by researchers for ideological reasons.

In Part 2 of the book, we look at the practice issues arising from the emphasis on inclusive research. It consists of two case studies (Chapters 5 and 6) describing research projects which strove for inclusiveness and in which we were closely involved. We have chosen these case studies not because we see them as ideal examples of inclusive research, but because we believe that they illustrate some of the strengths and problems of researching in this way. While we believe each of the case studies illustrates aspects of inclusive research, the emphasis in each is quite different. The first focuses on a project in which inclusion of people with learning disabilities was an integral part of the project development. The second is more concerned with social change resulting from research which included people with learning disabilities.

Following the case studies, in Chapters 7, 8 and 9 we analyse practice issues in inclusive research. In particular we are concerned with exploring the following questions which were raised in the Introduction:

- To what extent did inclusive research arise from the concerns of people with learning disabilities?

- Can and should we manipulate the environment to the extent that people with learning disabilities can be meaningfully included in all stages and aspects of research?

- How can the interests of all parties in the research process be safeguarded?

- Should the researcher have a distinctive voice?

- Do existing research methods stereotype people with learning disabilities?

- Should the researcher be cast in the role of advocate?

Part 2 is not a manual on how to do inclusive research. After all, it is probably clear that we are still struggling with this problem ourselves. Rather it seeks to explore, through an extensive review of the literature, some of the issues which arise in practice and which researchers committed to undertaking inclusive research need to take into account.

CHAPTER 5

Nothing About Us Without Us

Good Times Bad Times

This is the first of two major case studies of inclusive research in which the authors (in this case Jan Walmsley) have been closely involved. It focuses on the processes of inclusive research and fleshes out for the reader some of the challenges of developing projects which have the characteristics of inclusive research listed in Chapter 2:

- a research question owned by disabled people
- furthers the interests of disabled people
- it is collaborative – disabled people involved in the doing of the work
- some control exercised by disabled people over process and outcomes
- question, reports and outcomes must be accessible to people with learning disabilities.

Good Times Bad Times (Atkinson *et al.* 2000) is primarily a collection of accounts by women with learning disabilities. The writing of this book gives an example of the process of inclusive research. In this project I and some colleagues consciously set out to develop an inclusive process, one which had the characteristics listed above. Our purpose was to write a book in which the agenda was set by women with learning disabilities, in order to highlight some distinctive issues which face them and, by implication, to further their interests. A collaborative group was set up to carry forward the work. The intention was to move beyond publications in which non-disabled authors simply recount the stories told by women (see Walmsley 2000b for an example) to enabling women with learning disabilities to interpret as well as tell their stories. We intended to put our expertise as writers and editors at the disposal of women with learning disabilities and to be directed by them. We intended that the final product should be accessible to people with learning disabilities and took steps to further this.

Examining the process will illustrate some of the challenges and costs of working in this inclusive mode.

The origins

The book had its origins in the early 1990s. Two non-disabled women, Michelle McCarthy and Jan Walmsley (who's writing this), had been involved in planning a conference for women staff involved in learning disability services. As we tried to construct an equal opportunities policy for this event, to ensure representation of black and lesbian women, we realized that we were sitting on a massive contradiction. There was no equal opportunity for the women most centrally concerned, women with learning disabilities. We switched tack and became part of a group planning what was billed as the first ever conference for women with learning disabilities in the UK in 1992, Women First. A full account of this event and its significance is to be found in Walmsley (1993). Some important themes were illustrated at Women First. The first was that women with learning disabilities had had very little opportunity to share experiences as women – this was paralleled by the neglect of their situation by the women's movement more broadly. The second was that there were distinct issues for women that had been too little aired. Body Strong, the workshop on abuse, drew 40 women, some of whom spoke of their experiences for the first time – a moving and distressing situation. The third was that the original motivation for holding the conference, addressing issues for women staff, had dropped off the agenda.

Women First was a success, but exemplified some of the challenges in empowering women with learning disabilities. It was a participation event. In keeping with the principles of emancipatory work, every attempt was made to allow women with learning disabilities to lead the agenda, and, although mistakes were made (Walmsley 1993), the principles were firmly adhered to. The consequence was that the conference focus was on recounting experiences. There was no analysis of the links with women's issues or with the politics of the wider disability movement. No specific linkages were made with the social model of disability and important issues for women staff remained unexplored. In the event, the conference was a one-off as far as the women with learning disabilities were concerned. Although many women expressed the desire to get together again, there was no structure and no resources to enable this to happen, except in specific instances where non-disabled women were prepared to set up local and isolated women's groups.

This left some of us troubled. We had our own agendas as feminists which made us want to understand the issues for women with learning disabilities in the context of feminist analysis. Michelle, in particular, was still keen to bring staff issues onto the agenda. I can also own to feeling uneasy that I had let the women down by promising more than I could deliver. These concerns led Michelle and I to meet to consider how we could accomplish the first and second of these two concerns – furthering understanding of the situation of women with learning disabilities and addressing the position of women staff. Without doubt, the idea for a book arose from the concerns of non-disabled women.

The first book

Being academics our thoughts turned to writing a book. We constructed in our minds and on paper a collection of papers on women, most of which were to be written by non-disabled women, although some were visualized as co-written papers. It would, we told ourselves, contribute to improving practice if we addressed it to staff and services. This first book proposal went through several drafts, but I remained troubled. I regarded myself as someone who had supported the inclusion of people with learning disabilities. I had played my part in promoting valued social roles for people with learning disabilities, particularly through Women First and as a member of a team writing the Open University's Equal People course (Open University 1996). I had also been influenced by the disability movement's arguments over emancipatory research and had attempted in my PhD thesis (Walmsley 1995) to incorporate some of its ideals.

How could I justify setting out to write a book about women with learning disabilities without their knowledge or involvement? I concluded that I could not and persuaded Michelle that we needed to change the dynamics, to switch to a more inclusive mode of operation where women with learning disabilities were also editors. Thus was the second book born – the first remains unwritten. This is a good instance of inclusive style research being driven by the values of people who have been constituted (or constitute themselves) as allies; and of a concern over process as well as outcomes, also characteristic of inclusive research.

The editors

In order to put the decision to include women with learning disabilities into effect it was necessary to find some women to join us. The task was accomplished in time-honoured fashion by networking amongst people we knew. My colleague, Dorothy Atkinson, had been editor of *Know Me As I Am* and was working with Mabel Cooper, then chair of People First London and Thames, to write Mabel's life story. It made sense to invite them to join us, and Mabel brought friends, initially Gloria Ferris, later Mary Coventry. I invited some women with whom I had worked to come too – prominent London-based self advocates Jackie Downer and Simone Aspis, and women from Powerhouse, an East London organization which campaigns against sexual abuse. By some means Open Doors, an employment project based in Harlow, Essex, found out about the book and asked to join us, as did Sheena Rolph, then undertaking her PhD (2000) which sought to include people with learning disabilities in constructing a history of community care.

This group formed the core of the editorial team, though it was occasionally supplemented by others. Some also left or attended sporadically. Simone Aspis attended only a few early meetings as she is self-employed so time means money to her. However, her influence was profound. She challenged us not to do what others had done – appropriate people's stories and weave academic arguments around them – in other words, to avoid the academic gaze. This challenge dominated the process. The question of representativeness was raised, particularly over ethnicity. There were two black women in the original group, but no Asian women. Jackie made contact with an Asian women's group in Birmingham, and I was nominated by her to go and talk to them. It was a miserable failure. The group had only just formed, their coordinator (with whom I had made contact) had just left to have a baby, and the new coordinator had no idea why I was there; nor had she had much opportunity to form a relationship with the women. I left a one-hour session with the women feeling that I had in some way assaulted them. We were not on the same wavelength. I realized how much our editorial group knew of the wider world through involvement in self advocacy. Though the new coordinator promised to try to pick up the threads, after about six months she wrote saying they had decided not to take part as she was leaving and handing the fragile baton on to her successor.

This process of finding people to work alongside us illustrates the difficulties of reaching beyond our own personal networks. We tend to go to the same people again and again. There is no recognized group to speak for or network with people with learning disabilities in England, so reaching out is an individualized process. The women who worked on the book were by no means representative of all women with learning disabilities. Even if we had engaged the Asian group, there would still be groups without a voice.

Time, funding and practical considerations

There is no doubt that inclusive research takes more time, energy and resources than comparably sized projects which do not aspire to be inclusive. Writing the book took longer (five years) than assembling most edited books. The costs were higher, largely because most business had to be conducted at face-to-face meetings and because the book is highly illustrated.

The need for money and resources threw the ball firmly back into the non-disabled women's court. Ideally, in an inclusive project, funding is controlled by disabled people. However, initially we had no funds at all. Finding places to meet and money to support travel expenses so that people could attend was no easy task. Initially we borrowed premises we could get for nothing, but this did not resolve the expenses issue. The group would be an empty gesture if only the academics could afford to come. After many abortive attempts to find money from charitable foundations, Dorothy and I obtained funding from the Research Committee at School of Health and Social Welfare at the Open University, where we both work. To obtain this the project had to be cast as action research, with the purpose of ascertaining how women with learning disabilities could edit a book. Thus the women were ascribed their traditional role, as research subjects. Such a compromise was necessary, but undesirable from the point of view of our purpose of working as equals. On the other hand, it was the aspirations to be inclusive that attracted those organizations which did fund us – the Open University, the UK Department of Health (which gave a small grant to pay for illustrations), our generous publisher BILD who agreed to price the book lower than their norm, and very welcome donations from a woman working in services, in lieu of joining us.

In the event, the vexed question of resources meant that we always met in London, a decision which made sense as most of the editors lived in or near London, but which had the effect of skewing membership. It was just too expensive and too tiring for contributors from further afield to attend regularly.

Administrative support for the meetings – mailing out agendas and minutes, circulating drafts, booking rooms – was also a gift from the Open University in the person of Christine Finch, who has worked as a secretary with Dorothy and myself for 15 years and is always prepared to do that little bit extra to support our work with people with learning disabilities. Without that we would have been hard put to continue.

Without doubt, the process was facilitated by the traditions of academic life which allow people to invest time in projects which further knowledge; though none of us had any formal time allocated to us to do this work, which represented another commitment, albeit one we really enjoyed and wanted to do. Inclusive research relies on these informal allocations of time by people who see it as worthwhile. Few projects to date have been generously funded (though there are signs that this may change), so they have often been run on a shoestring.

Power and control

Who's in charge is a critical question in inclusive research. Certainly the idea for a book focusing on women with learning disabilities started with the non-disabled women. However, it is possible to discern a migration of power during the course of the book's gestation. Chairing the meetings, negotiation of contents and format were all areas which witnessed a significant shift.

Chairing the meetings was initially shared between Michelle and myself. I recall feeling that this was inappropriate if the women with learning disabilities were to be in charge, but unavoidable if business was to progress. However, about halfway through the three years during which the editorial group met, once our working practices were established Mabel Cooper agreed to be chair, an arrangement which endured. I think we all felt more comfortable when that happened.

The starting point for our discussions was the book proposal that Michelle and I had drawn up. It did not withstand the critical scrutiny of our disabled colleagues. We were challenged on grounds that such a book would be inaccessible to women with learning disabilities, in academic language, that it perpetuated 'the gaze'. The disabled women were adamant that this was to be a book by and about them and that benefits for staff, one of the original aims, would come if they learnt directly from women with learning disabilities. Only two exceptions were allowed. It was reluctantly agreed to include a chapter by a mother, in order to ensure that children were included. The non-disabled editors were invited to describe the process, a chapter which emerged as 'The Helpers' Story' (Atkinson *et al.* 2000). However, the line was drawn when it came to staff or academics – even the editors – writing chapters on subjects of their own choosing.

Discussions about themes and chapters were lengthy, but largely determined by who could be found to contribute and what they wanted to say. The editorial group knew that it wanted to cover certain topics – relationships, work, family life, health, sexuality, but there was no commissioning; partly because there was no money, and partly because it's a very underdeveloped field, with few acknowledged experts. Because few women with learning disabilities were able to write unaided (Simone Aspis being the exception), we relied on locating people to work together. The upshot was that the 'normal' process of deciding in advance on themes and sections was turned on its head. The chapters came first – thematizing came a lot later.

Other challenges were made to the format. Early on there was a lobby which said a video would be preferable, because women with learning disabilities do not read books. This was resisted, not only by the non-disabled women, partly on resource grounds, partly because the non-disabled women were keen to retain the development of thought processes which they believe writing promotes, and partly because Mabel Cooper had had the experience of being published (1997), something she valued highly. In order to go some way towards meeting the demands for accessibility, it was agreed that there should be a short version of each chapter with illustrations, so that women could read it with support. Line drawings were commissioned to illustrate the short versions. These then had to be sent to authors for approval or otherwise and the illustrator rebriefed, a task I undertook to coordinate.

One of the strengths of the process was the vigour of the debates around key issues. This was no tame tokenistic inclusion – women with learning disabilities genuinely did make many key decisions. One of the ironies is that for a number of pretty obvious reasons such as lack of resources, lack of transport, and sometimes lack of confidence on the part of the disabled women, the 'helpers' as we were termed had to execute the decisions – something that made the process as close to an emancipatory one as I have experienced.

The collaborative process

Having decided that the book was to be by women with learning disabilities, it was necessary to develop a process to deliver it. How this was done is a good illustration of 'experts' putting skills at the disposal of disabled people; one respect in which the project did meet the standards set by the disabled people's movement.

All but one of the chapters was written in partnership between a woman or women with learning disabilities and a non-disabled woman (the exception being Simone's chapter which she wrote herself). Co-publishing with people with learning disabilities has a number of precedents which we were able to draw on (see Atkinson *et al.* 1997;

Souza with Ramcharan 1997; Walmsley with Downer 1997). In this book project, the majority of chapter writing relationships were already established prior to the work beginning. There was one exception, in which I sought out a young woman who had mental health problems as well as learning disabilities. The editorial group was keen to include a chapter by someone with this 'dual diagnosis'. However, the contact was facilitated by and the interview jointly conducted with Jackie Downer, thus ensuring that the author had a familiar person present.

Most of the chapters used the 'writing hand' technique. The idea of a supporter playing the role of 'the writing hand' had been pioneered at the Pecket Well Centre, a college run by people with a variety of disabilities. The process had been recorded on video (Open University 1996) to be used as teaching material, and we were able to draw on this in the editorial group. The process involves listening to and recording the words of the person, at the same time encouraging them with comments or questions. Dorothy Atkinson likens this to the role of the ghost writer employed by prominent people to assist them in writing their autobiographies:

> The recounting of life stories...is a social process. It is important that a relationship of trust exists between the people involved, and that the person who listens does so attentively and sensitively and with respect. (Atkinson 1997, p.7)

The process requires a considerable amount of work by the ghost writer. Atkinson describes this:

> The interviewer's task after each interview is to transcribe the words from the tape into written words on paper. Somehow that untidy and unorganised 'raw' account then needs to be tidied up and put into some sort of coherent narrative. That process needs to be a shared one. The sharing can be at the transcription stage, where the full account is read back and the story teller has a full say in the editing and re-organising process. More usually, the researcher or historian does some preliminary work on the raw material first, organising it in a chronological sequence and/or into themes... This revised version is then read back for additions or alterations. (Atkinson 1997, p.10)

Although these words were written prior to most of the book being compiled, they describe the process well. Drawing on my own experience, I worked with Pam and 'Alice in Wonderland' on their original stories, asking questions, prompting and taping. I then transcribed the tapes, back in the summer of 1997, and reorganized them to make a narrative. I then read these accounts onto tape myself and returned them to the authors by post to listen to. At a later date, I made my way into the depths of East London to play the tapes to the authors. I stopped the tape frequently and noted down any comments or asides. These were then incorporated into the stories. At the end, I asked the authors to draw out messages they wanted people to take away with them, thus offering an opportunity to add a reflective gloss to the chapter. After a final approval stage, in this case taped versions sent by post, these were the chapters.

Finally, just prior to handing the document to the publisher, I compiled a short accessible version myself for each of the chapters. These were submitted to the editorial group, rather than the authors, for approval:

> There also needs to be an understanding and agreement about confidentiality and ownership... The important thing is not to assume what people want but to find out from them what degree of confidentiality and anonymity is thought necessary. (Atkinson 1997, p.8)

In *Good Times Bad Times*, negotiation of anonymity and confidentiality was complex. It was necessary to explain the consequences of owning your story. On the one hand, it was important to be recognized as an author; on the other, publication could bring reprisals of various kinds. One contributor, recounting her experience of resigning from a disabled people's organization because she felt unsupported and undermined, initially wanted to be anonymous. The experience was, at the time it was initially told, raw and recent. She was fearful of reprisals. However, over the time the book was being put together she changed her mind. Some of the wounds healed. At the same time, she felt that she wanted it to be known that she had suffered in this way – to encourage others. It was a brave decision.

In some cases, negotiation of ownership went beyond the author. One contributor asked her mother to look at her chapter. Her mother sought a meeting with me to establish what would happen to the chapter. Once I had explained, she asked me to use only her daughter's first name and to alter some of the contents. As her daughter was present at that meeting in a south London pizza restaurant, I agreed. Similar conditions were imposed by an agency which was overseeing the work being described. Women with learning disabilities are not always in a position to make such decisions autonomously.

However, they were in a position to choose their pseudonyms. 'Alice in Wonderland' was the name chosen by one of 'my' authors. I rather like it. One chapter was written in a different way. Michelle McCarthy took the opportunity to share her research-based findings on sexual abuse with a group of three women who work as volunteers in an agency which runs a women's refuge. They had some claims to expertise in the topic. She summarized her findings in plain English, using charts and illustrations, and asked the group to comment. As the chapter shows, in many respects their views and experiences corresponded with Michelle's findings, though they went further than her in demanding legal and social sanctions for sexual offenders.

There was also a notable instance of the disabled women insisting that our role as helpers was recorded – hence 'The Helpers' Story' which opens the book, co-written by five academics who had been involved throughout most of the process.

Sharing our skills in recording, transcribing and ordering material, as well as being ready to accept and incorporate comments and amendments, was one of the most significant achievements in terms of inclusive practice. However, when it came to developing an editorial voice the task became more complex.

Compromises

The editorial group was committed to do more than collect and publish people's stories. We set out to allow women with learning disabilities to control the agenda by commenting upon their stories as well. It took some careful consideration to establish how this might be done.

At the level of the individual chapters, it was decided that people should be asked to draw out key messages in response to the questions:

- Who do you want to read this?

- What do you want them to remember?

Authors were able to consider and record their key messages, which in each case form the concluding section of their chapter.

At the whole book level this was far less achievable. Our ideal was for the editorial group to read the whole book, with assistance if needed, and work jointly on editorials which drew together themes. This proved beyond our capacity. With one exception, which will be discussed below, reading the whole book or even a section proved to be too onerous. The non-disabled women were left with a dilemma. We wanted to make some general statements which would help readers make sense of and contextualize what they were reading, even to make links with the experiences of other women or other disabled people. However, if we did that we would be perpetuating the researcher/ researched dichotomy we were trying to escape. Eventually, we sought the agreement of the entire editorial group to do this and obtained consent.

However, when the minutes came out, Simone Aspis, who had not been present, telephoned me to remonstrate at the betrayal of principles this represented. After much debate with other members of the editorial group, I agreed that she should write the section introducing her chapter and two others, a task that had originally been assigned to me. I think readers will agree that her comments are more incisive than those of the experienced writers who introduced the other sections, largely because she was, unlike them, unconstrained by a sense of principle that what they were doing was in some sense a betrayal.

As we tried to move from the individual to the general, we encountered real difficulties. All the editors could enjoy and appreciate the stories and learn from them. But summarizing some shorthand themes and making connections to the wider world of ideas was something we failed to achieve in this project. I would not conclude that we could not have done better – undoubtedly we could – but a whole new process of learning and negotiation when we thought we had finished the book (after five years!) was something we collectively felt unable to face.

Conclusion

This co-writing project represents an experiment in adopting the principles of inclusive practice to the writing of a book. I have worked through some of the key stages, as I see them, and attempted as I did so to evaluate the projects against those principles.

In many respects, although the original idea came from non-disabled women, the agenda was taken over and shaped by a mixed group of disabled and non-disabled women. It represents a partnership in the sense that both parties needed one another. It sustains a commitment to political action, in the sense that the disabled women argued for the importance of having their voices heard, as far as possible unmediated by others. The non-disabled women did put aside their own agenda in favour of a book which reflected what the disabled women wanted. Compromises were made over the format. Expertise and skills, whether in terms of finding funds and a publisher, or constructing flowing chapters out of taped conversations, were put at the disposal of women who otherwise could not hope to write a full-length book.

There remains a significant area where power was not shared fully – power over ideas. We found no way to share our expertise, developed over long careers in academic life, in making connections, drawing out themes and writing an authoritative commentary upon the contents. To a great extent, that task remains undone. So great was our discomfort at taking over in the final stages, we pulled our punches and wrote rather bland introductions to the sections in the book.

This was one of the most significant of my personal attempts to put inclusive principles into practice with people with learning disabilities. Each time, I feel, I've crept a little closer to meeting the ideals. Each time, equally, I have felt the tug of regret that the opportunity to develop my own ideas has been subordinated to the ideal. There is no parity because we did not share ourselves, our stories, except insofar as describing the role we played as helpers. Like social workers, we facilitated, but our voices are muted. Does this matter? In some ways it does not – I have other publishing outlets – but in career terms there is a personal price to pay. Within existing academic conventions, projects of this kind do not make a lot of sense. As a publication shared between eight co-authors *Good Times Bad Times* cannot rate very highly on the CVs of any of the non-disabled women. Furthermore, the ambition Michelle and I started out with, to theorize about the situation of women with learning disabilities and in so doing to influence practice, remains unfulfilled. It was possibly an unworthy aim for privileged women to have. Equally possibly, *Good Times Bad Times* may be the foundation for further work in this direction, undertaken by women with learning disabilities, or it may forever be a 'lost book' whose value we will never know. As I wrote this chapter, I felt impelled to put on record that giving up power, if that's what this represents, has its personal costs for the researcher and may not be effective in helping women understand their situation, as opposed to recording their experience.

CHAPTER 6

Living Safer Sexual Lives
Making Research Work

I found out about sex by meself. In me mind. I went to a home when I was fourteen, I lifted up me dress in Nixon St. Just playing on me mind. It was something to do. Wanted sex. The police came along and took me to a home in Thomas Town, a Girls home. I don't remember what happened there.

(Vicki Mulholland, *You're in My World*. In Frawley, Johnson, Hillier and Harrison 2003)

I was thinking of going to a massage parlour but it's over a hundred dollars, and I reckon sex, it depends on the human being, but I reckon sex is free instead of buying it. I've always wanted to try and experience sexual relationships but it hasn't been the time or I haven't found someone.

(David, *I've Got Small Dreams*. In Frawley *et al.* 2003)

These are extracts from 25 autobiographical accounts about the lives of people with learning disabilities. They were told to us as part of a three-year action research project in which I (KJ) was involved in Australia (Johnson *et al.* 2000a). The project focused on the sexual and relationship experiences of people with learning disabilities. One of its primary aims was to change societal barriers so that people with learning disabilities could lead safer sexual lives. However the project was also concerned with issues of inclusion by people with learning disabilities in the research process itself as well as in its outcomes. This chapter reveals the strengths of such an approach but also some of its limitations. It is not concerned with the results of the research or its implementation, but with the degree to which we were able to include people with learning disabilities in a large project which extended over a long period of time. We give the last word to Janice Slattery, one of the members of the reference group.

The origins of the research

The research began with discussions among a small group of academic researchers, of whom I was one. We were concerned at the lack of voice that people with learning disabilities experienced about their sexuality and relationships. While some research had been undertaken on these issues in Australia, there was nothing which was qualitative in nature (Johnson *et al.* 2001). Our concerns were exacerbated by findings that people with learning disabilities were more vulnerable than other people to sexual abuse and also to sexually transmissible diseases (Brown and Turk 1992; Carson 1994; Johnson *et al.* 1987; McCarthy 1999; Millard 1994; Senn 1988; Turk and Brown 1993). We thought that a study which explored with people with learning disabilities how they saw these issues was important. However we were also keenly aware that discussing sexuality and relationships was intrusive and difficult for people. Therefore we began the research with a commitment to ensuring that there would be practical outcomes from it. We also believed that we needed to include people with learning disabilities within the research, both to ensure that it was conducted ethically and because we thought that their contribution to the research would be valuable in shaping its design. Issues around empowerment for those who took part were not really high on our agenda in the beginning.

We started the research process with a consultation which included key self advocacy organizations and service provider groups in Melbourne. The response was unambiguous and strong. About 20 people (many with learning disabilities) came to the meeting and were clear in saying that they thought the research was a good idea. One self advocate commented, 'People will be queuing at the door to talk with you.'

However at this point the involvement of people with learning disabilities was put on hold as we (non-disabled academics) put together a submission for funding. It included a research phase where researchers would work with people with learning disabilities to develop life stories which would include themes of sexuality and relationships. In the second phase of the project we intended to use the findings from the stories to develop actions and interventions designed to increase the possibility of people with learning disabilities leading safer sexual lives.

Although we did not call this research inclusive, it did share some characteristics with this kind of research right from the beginning. Important inclusive features of the submission were:

- a focus on the importance of people with learning disabilities having power and a voice in discussions about sexuality and relationships

- the importance given to the development of a reference group on which people with learning disabilities were represented

- payment to be given to all unwaged workers involved in the research, including reference group members and story tellers

- emphasis on the development of practical outcomes from the research which were to be developed, implemented and evaluated as part of the project.

Obtaining funding

Originally we designed the research as a two-year funded project but the timetable was later extended by another 12 months and some extra funding was given.

We confronted initial difficulties in obtaining funding. Staff at the funding organization expressed grave doubts about the viability of the project. In particular they questioned whether we were really 'doing research' because it was qualitative and action oriented. They queried whether it was possible for people with learning disabilities to contribute life stories because of the perceived effects of their disabilities. They were also concerned that we ensure that the project have strong support, given its sensitive nature.

However the funding organization did believe that the submission had merit and gave us an initial grant of $10,000 to prove through a pilot that we had support from key organizations and that we could actually carry out the methodology outlined in the submission. Using this grant we brought together the reference group and demonstrated that it was possible to work with people with learning disabilities to develop life stories. The original submission was then funded, but not as research; rather it was categorized as community development. I think this raises one of the key obstacles in undertaking research of this kind. Some funding bodies simply do not recognize it as research.

Living Safer Sexual Lives: the project

We believed Living Safer Sexual Lives would fill some of the gaps in our knowledge of how people with learning disabilities see their own sexual lives. We also wanted to work with them to find strategies which would assist them in having more fulfilling and safer sexual expression and relationships. More particularly we were concerned to:

- identify key issues around sexuality and relationships for people with learning disabilities

- place sexuality and relationships in the broader context of the lives of people with learning disabilities

- develop, trial and evaluate workshops and other resources based on stories contributed by people with learning disabilities to assist them to live safer sexual lives.

We were not sure how the project would develop when we began to work on it – after all it was action research. It actually occurred in two stages. The first stage was research in which 25 people contributed their life histories to the project and the second phase was action, which used the research findings to develop specific interventions.

The reference group

We established a reference group at the beginning of the project which had representatives from self advocacy, advocacy and service provider organizations. This remained throughout the entire three years of the project. It was critically important in shaping the design and implementation of both stages of the project.

Originally six people with learning disabilities were representatives on the reference group and there were four representatives from other advocacy and service provider organizations. All unwaged members were paid for their involvement. The three researchers were also members of the reference group. The numbers of participants changed over time for all of these groups as some people dropped out and others came into the group.

In the first six months of the project we worked very hard with the reference group to develop ethical procedures and to explore how best to find people who might want to participate in the project. There were some heated arguments in the group about process which nicely illustrate some of the power issues, for example:

Q: Should people with learning disabilities on the reference group also provide their stories?

A: No, because of problems of confidentiality. (We immediately lost one of the reference group members as a result.)

Q: Should we develop a video as part of the project?

A: We were unsure and lost another member of the reference group (in the end we did make a video).

Q: Should we talk with people in their own homes or restrict ourselves to formal interview situations?

A: We should talk wherever people wanted to providing it was private. This response came from people with learning disabilities and was at odds with the views of service providers.

We took responsibility for making sure that minutes and agendas were in plain English and were heavily criticized whenever 'jargon' was used. People with learning disabilities who were on the reference group were quiet to begin with, but became very vocal as the project developed. We learned later that some people really struggled with embarrassment about sexuality. Two women with learning disabilities joked together about how they went to the 'sex meetings'. We worked with the reference group to design advertising and to go on community radio to talk about the project. Two people with learning disabilities were very involved in both of these enterprises. However, we found it very difficult to find people with learning disabilities who were willing or able to talk with us. Finally, informal networks, access to self advocacy meetings and

---

Box 6.1 Living Safer Sexual Lives: recognizing skills

People with disabilities are often exploited both as research subjects and as members of committees and advisory groups. We're expected to share our expertise – but we're not properly paid for our time and effort. The LSSL project didn't make that mistake. They built consumer (and unpaid worker) participation into their budget from the beginning. The LSSL researchers genuinely attempted to involve people with an intellectual disability in the project. This is, unfortunately, still quite rare. I strongly believe that there should be 'nothing about us, without us'. People with disabilities have a real expertise to share – an expertise that is often under-utilized, even when we do get a seat at the table. Too much jargon, difficult to understand meeting procedures, inaccessible minutes and power imbalances – they make it hard for people with disabilities to contribute. In the LSSL project these barriers were kept to a minimum.

(Harrison *et al.* 2002)

---

college classes enabled us to find 25 people. The view of one of the reference group members about the project is summed up in Box 6.1. As the project developed and reference group members became more comfortable with each other and with the issues, participation by people with learning disabilities increased. The main ways in which people with learning disabilities were involved in the reference group are shown in Box 6.2.

Box 6.2 Changing roles on the reference group

- Attending meetings as members of the reference group. This included giving advice about design and conduct of the research, providing ethical guidance and developing key principles for the research.

- Providing assistance in seeking people who would like to participate in the project. Reference group members advertised the project through their organizations, designed accessible advertising and provided access to a radio programme for people with disabilities so that the project could be advertised.

- Stories were read to people with learning disabilities on the reference group and they worked in small groups with advocates and service providers to contribute editorial comment.

- One member of the reference group was paid to undertake more detailed editing of the stories.

- Two members of the reference group read the stories on video and were paid to do so.

- People with learning disabilities were represented on all working parties established to undertake action arising from the research.

- One woman's insistence on the importance of people knowing their legal rights, which she reiterated throughout the project, led to the inclusion of a pamphlet on legal rights (which she found) into the workshops.

We discovered that making the reference group work entailed a lot of work for us as researchers. We were responsible for calling the meetings (every six weeks), for making sure that accessible large-print minutes and agendas were prepared and for organizing cash payments to unwaged workers on the day. We found ourselves constantly revising minutes at the insistence of self advocates in order to make the language and format accessible to people with learning disabilities.

We organized a lot of small group work in the meetings with structured activities so that everyone had a chance to participate. This too took time. For example, in one early meeting we had a long discussion in pairs about sexual language. At the end of the discussion, people with learning disabilities decided that everyone used different sexual words and we should ask the participants in the project what they preferred. We did this.

Keeping to the agenda was often difficult. We needed a lot of time to talk through issues with people with learning disabilities who had not previously been involved in research. We found to our cost that many research texts were *not* written in plain English and so we had to translate terms into plain English.

The researchers

Four academics were employed as researchers on the project. Three of us were women and one man was included after men with learning disabilities said that they would not talk with a woman about sex. All of us had worked with people with learning disabilities before. However we were aware that this project would challenge us. We were not then aware how much. We had all worked on sensitive research before. We decided that we needed to support each other through the process of the research. We formed peer pairs to check transcripts and to provide support for each other after interviews. We also ran two training days to talk through our anxieties and concerns about the research process. We each kept a journal of our experiences which we shared with our peer pair. The excerpt in Box 6.3 gives an idea of the intensity of some of the interviews.

Box 6.3 Journal entry: interview with Vicki Mulholland

The stories she told in a flat voice of the loss of her children and of sexual abuse left me upset, drained and tired. I don't know how she has survived. And I guess in some ways she has not. Her experiences seem such a long way from my own and yet we were brought up in similar towns and I could relate very closely to the prejudice, the teasing and the stereotyping because I had heard it before at home. I think this was also what upset me... I was very anxious about not causing her any further pain.

After some discussion about sex she suddenly said she felt like having it now and began stroking my hair and shoulder. Asked if I would give her a shower. I backed off, waited a while and asked if she had ever had a relationship with women. She said not. I realized later that assistance in showering and hugs from staff are probably the only physical touching she has had in some years. (Kelley Johnson, journal note, 2000 unpublished)

We did not employ people with learning disabilities as co-researchers during the first phase of the project for a number of different reasons. In spite of our training, we often found the discussions with life story tellers difficult and sensitive. We were concerned that to use co-researchers in this situation would be unfair to all parties. Further the learning disability world in Australia is very small. It was inevitable that some of the co-researchers would have known the life story tellers. This may have created problems for both parties. Although it is true that some of the researchers also knew some of the participants, they were not perceived as being part of the person's world. (This is a telling statement about the relationships between people with and without disabilities.) We were concerned not only about confidentiality, but also about ensuring that privacy was seen to be protected. Even had we decided to employ co-researchers, it is most likely that the university ethics committee and the funding body would have refused permission for the project due to the sensitivity of the topic and the perceived vulnerability of the participants. In writing this paragraph I am conscious even now of some guilt and defensiveness about this. Yet looking back on the research and the emotional and intellectual exhaustion we all experienced during the interview phase, I realize that the guilt is not really related to an intellectual belief that untrained researchers should have been involved because they had a learning disability. It is a much more generalized guilt that the research was not fully inclusive.

The story tellers

Twelve men and thirteen women contributed their autobiographical accounts to the project. We used some starting questions but the discussions with each person were free ranging. We met each interviewee at least three times. We taped each story with the permission of the author and then used the author's own words to condense what were often very long transcripts. Each story was reviewed by the reference group and re-read in detail by a member of the group who had a disability. We then took the stories back to the author and read them through. Any changes which the author wanted to make were made to the story. A title for each story was taken from a quote in the text and pseudonyms (sometimes chosen by the author) were used. Each author was paid for the interviews in which they participated. No one withdrew from the project once they had begun the process, although two people did withdraw early in the discussions. The accounts which were contributed to the project were extremely strong, as the quotations at the beginning of the chapter and in Box 6.4 show.

Box 6.4 She changed my life around

Darren Walters

Won't get married for a while now I think. Because of the fight. I do miss her. Oh I really miss her, oh I know I can cook, but I really miss her cookin'. Oh I miss being with her and watching TV and stuff like that. Oh I miss going shopping with her. Going for a drive with her mum stuff like that. Oh we cuddle, yeah I miss that stuff too, cuddlin' and kissin'. I miss that stuff too... I miss, miss, miss having sex, sex with Simone. Havin' sex and havin' fun with her.

In retrospect I think we could have involved the authors more in the editing and development of their stories. When we talked with them about the finished story they were generally both excited and happy with the results, but we could have been more careful in giving them time to reflect on the stories and ensuring that all of them had the chance to choose a pseudonym and a title for their own story. These views are endorsed by those expressed by a Ria Strong, a self advocate on the reference group in Box 6.5.

Box 6.5 Whose story is it?

The researchers, and those of us who helped edit the stories, made lots of decisions – what would be included in the written stories? What would be left out? How much would we fix people's grammar? Would we add words to make the stories clearer? How would we change the stories to make sure people couldn't be identified? What name would people be given? Where would we say they lived and worked? And so on. The people who told us their stories could have been more involved in shaping the written versions. Some people may not have wanted that – but people should have been given the choice I think. (Ria Strong, cited in Harrison *et al.* 2001, p.65)

Ria's comment raises questions about the representativeness of the reference group in trying to ensure that the rights of people with learning disabilities were asserted strongly in the project. To some extent the reference group itself became part of the research process over time and its members had an increasingly strong commitment to the project. This was good but it may have prevented them from thinking of alternative and inclusive ways of undertaking the research.

Analysing the stories

Each story was workshopped over a period of time with members of the reference group. People with learning disabilities worked in partnership with members of the group who were not so labelled. Each story was read aloud and discussed. Gradually the group came to an understanding of both the individual richness of each story while at the same time identifying key themes arising from them (see Johnson *et al.* 2002a, 2002b for a more detailed account of this process). The key themes were:

- barriers imposed on people with learning disabilities in relation to sexuality and relationships which were due to the attitudes and values of service providers and families

- lack of accessible and accurate information for people with learning disabilities about sexuality and relationships

- confusing and restrictive government policies about sexuality and relationships

- loneliness and isolation experienced by many of the people with learning disabilities who contributed their stories.

Implementing research

At this stage of the research we did not go back to the authors to discuss the findings. Rather we went on to look at ways in which we might move the research into an implementation phase. We set up four planning committees which were developed from the reference group. Each worked on one of the major themes and explored how it might be developed into interventions or resources. It became clear that the people with learning disabilities on the committees were really stretched and we needed their skills and experience. Ria summed up the dilemma (see Box 6.6).

As I reflect on the intervention stage of the research, the balance between inclusion and exclusion of people with learning disabilities becomes clearer, and so do the reasons for it. I feel somewhat uncomfortable at the results of this reflection. The workshops which developed from Living Safer Sexual Lives were innovative and exciting. They involved working with people with learning disabilities, families and service providers to examine attitudes to sexuality and relationships. We used the stories as the main focus of the workshops. They were extensively trialled in Australia and overseas and a manual was developed (Frawley *et al.* 2002; Johnson *et al.* 2001), but people with

---

Box 6.6 Implementing Living Safer Sexual Lives

More self advocates definitely needed to be involved in the Resource and Workshop working groups. Those working groups were a chance for people with an intellectual disability to do something concrete – more so than the Advisory Group meetings. There were only three of us involved, though – and we were all trying to contribute to both working groups. Impossible, when they met simultaneously during Advisory Group meetings. And difficult anyway, it was just too much work. In the end the workshops were mostly developed without us. (Ria Strong, e-mail communication 2000) (Ria Strong, cited in Harrison *et al.* 2001, p.66)

---

learning disabilities were not very involved either in their development or implementation. Why? We found the stories complex and difficult. They raised sensitive and often difficult to manage issues in the workshops. As researchers we decided that the facilitators needed to be skilled in working with groups, able to be flexible and to use the group responses to the material quickly and creatively. We made judgements that the people with learning disabilities would not be able to facilitate the workshops. In retrospect, I believe we could have included them as co-facilitators and explored how we might have adapted the workshops to include them. In our defence, what we were trying was very new and we were learning all the time.

We also developed plain English booklets for people with learning disabilities and for use in the workshops. People with learning disabilities were employed to assist in the editing of the stories and to work with us in ensuring that they were clear and accessible. We also used their discussions about the stories as a commentary on each one. We did not want the stories to become used as 'teaching tools' with questions at the end. It seemed more respectful and more inclusive to put in comments from people with learning disabilities who had read the stories. People who worked with us on this project were paid for their work. We also made a video of three of stories, employing three people with learning disabilities as readers and actors. If people with learning disabilities were included in the making of resources, they were certainly excluded from the policy developments which arose from the research. Forums to discuss the research were held with the state government department and other organizations in the state. Two of the researchers sat on a government working party to develop a new sexuality and relationship policy for people with disabilities in the state. One woman with learning disabilities who was on our reference group was also included but she never attended.

Finally, a working group established to look at ways of increasing social networks for people with learning disabilities did not really achieve its objectives. Few of the non-disabled members of the reference group were interested in this working group. It held one meeting with outside organizations, but without funding and ongoing support the initiatives which it discussed never happened.

On reflection I can see how people with learning disabilities were excluded from those parts of the implementation which we thought were difficult, sensitive or complex. Now if I were doing the research again I would think more carefully about how to extend involvement. But as I write this I am conscious of where the power still lies. *I* will think about how to include people. *They* are not demanding inclusion. As long as this is the case, then it remains the responsibility of the non-disabled researcher to think of ways in which inclusion can happen.

Compromises

This was a project filled with compromises, which included the following:

- Meeting the requirements of the funding organization: we had to prove the research could be done. This took time and resources. Finally the project was undertaken but not as 'research'. As the researchers we were accountable for the funding and for the completion of the project.

- Limits to the extent to which researchers could work with individual life story tellers: we met at least three times (sometimes more) for varying lengths of time. It was clear that for some people with learning disabilities these meetings were important. As researchers we had to be very clear that the contact had an end.

- Little time to assist people other than providing accurate information and support.

- Unable to get funding to use video more creatively and extensively.

- Failure to involve participants as deeply as in retrospect we could have in the development of the stories.

- Too few people with learning disabilities on the reference group.

- Ideally it would have been good to have linked the action phase into the project from the beginning rather than having two quite distinct parts. Resources and time prevented this from happening.

- The networking which might have embedded the outcomes with an organization, thus ensuring their continuity, was done by the reference group and the researchers but only in a limited way.

However in spite of the compromises and difficulties, Ria Strong, as a member of the reference group, provides a vindication for the steps we took towards inclusive research (Box 6.7).

Box 6.7 An assessment

I believe the Living Safer Sexual Lives project was absolutely groundbreaking. Often, people with an intellectual disability are seen as asexual. Either that, or our sexuality is seen as a problem; one that workers and families need to deal with. Our own experiences, good and bad, our own voices – they're just not heard. Living Safer Sexual Lives changed that. People were given a chance to tell their own stories – and those stories are now being used to change people's attitudes towards relationships, sex and people with intellectual disabilities. I'm glad I was part of the process. (Ria Strong, cited in Harrison *et al*. 2001, p.61)

Conclusion

Living Safer Sexual Lives illustrates the excitement and the problems of attempting to work inclusively. When compared with *Good Times Bad Times* it also shows the diversity of work which can occur under this heading. If we were to do the project again I think we would do it quite differently and in ways which might involve people with learning disabilities earlier and in a more organized fashion, but we have all learned from this experience. We include below a commentary from one of the self advocate members of the reference group on what she got out of her involvement (Box 6.8).

Box 6.8 Commentary on Living Safer Sexual Lives

Janice Slattery

What we did

We came together with other people and helped people with intellectual disabilities to tell their life stories. I helped organize the interviews, made a video, went through the stories and picked out the ones we thought should be in the booklets for people with intellectual disabilities.

We got paid for our time.

What I got out of the project

I've learned a lot since I've been involved on the project. I've learned a lot about sex I didn't know. I learned about people. I've made new friends: some old friends and some new ones.

I found one story was like me when I was young and it was like what I went through.

I learned it takes a long time to do research.

We had fun too. One day we walked into the meeting and we saw this Christmas tree. And I said this has a lot of balloons, more than I've seen in a long time. Amanda walked in and said, 'They're not balloons, they're condoms.'

What the project means for people with learning disabilities

For one thing people with intellectual disabilities get the correct information about AIDS, about safe sex. They'll have the information in their hands with the booklets. Then they can go away thinking this is right.

It gives people with disabilities a voice to be heard. It's also good for people with disabilities standing up for what they believe.

It's important for families and service providers to know how to educate their sons and daughters or the people they work with. And to stop treating us like children. And if there are any more projects like this I'd like to be on them. And there should be more funding for it.

Endnote

1.   This chapter uses quotations from Harrison *et al.* 2001.

CHAPTER 7

What Matters to People with Learning Disabilities?

What matters to people with learning disabilities? This is a critical question for both researchers and funders of research. In an applied research field concerned with services and supports, the answer to this question ought to be a major factor in shaping the research agenda. By implication, at least, it follows that people with learning disabilities themselves should have some say in what is seen as a priority for research.

(Ward and Simons 1998, p.128)

One central precept of inclusive research is that it should be on topics that matter to people with learning disabilities, and with good reason. History shows how medical and positivist research has objectified them, pursued goals which set them apart from the rest of humanity and has often led to oppressive policies directed towards them. Work around IQ testing in the early twentieth century falls into this category, as do many current studies of 'challenging behaviour' (see, for example, Danziger 1990; Nind and Johnson 2002; Rose 1979). We believe that as researchers we have a responsibility to people with learning disabilities not to add to this history.

The view that what matters to people with learning disabilities should be what dictates the research agenda is one that has been forcefully expressed in the slogan 'Nothing about us without us'. We have much sympathy with that view, though would argue that there are limitations in people with learning disabilities being the only people shaping priorities for research. People with high support needs who literally do not have a voice are excluded, unless other people with learning disabilities take up their cause. There is little evidence to date that this is happening. But also there are questions which people with learning disabilities are unable to articulate, at least at present. It became clear during the Living Safer Sexual Lives study (see Chapter 6) that issues around sexuality and relationships were of great concern to people with learning disabilities, but strong taboos were held about them and enforced by service providers and families. These effectively silenced people with learning disabilities.

There is also a case for initiating research in areas which might matter to people with learning disabilities if they knew about them. Recent research into, for example, the menopause shows that few women with learning disabilities understand what it means. To expect them to initiate research in such instances is unrealistic and probably not in the best interests of people with learning disabilities.

In this chapter we explore the ways in which people with learning disabilities have been involved in the initiation of research, and the extent to which research should be confined within the parameters of 'Nothing about us without us'. In particular we are concerned with the following three questions which were raised in the Introduction to this book:

- What is the place of people with learning disabilities in initiating research?

- How do we as researchers avoid the continuation of the 'othering' experienced by many people with learning disabilities in research?

- What are the barriers to people with learning disabilities in initiating research?

The chapter begins with a review of work to date which might warrant the description inclusive, and then proceeds to consider the barriers to such research, before turning to ponder the question whether to be inclusive the research must be initiated by people with learning disabilities.

What is the place of people with learning disabilities in initiating research?

As noted earlier, particularly in Chapter 4, many groups, communities and individuals have become angry at the 'othering' process that can be part of even well-intentioned research. A researcher with a 'good idea' and the funds and status to put it into practice enters the community, engages in information gathering and disappears to achieve the results that they intended. However they may leave the researched group feeling disempowered and frustrated. This is not a satisfactory way to do research *with* people. What are the alternatives?

We believe there is not one way in which research questions and ideas arise inclusively. The process can occur in a number of different ways: from an organization or group representing people with learning disabilities, from consultation between researchers and people with learning disabilities, from researchers who then seek support for their idea.

In this section of the chapter we outline some of the main ways in which research has been initiated by people with learning disabilities.

Research generated by advocacy organizations

Research can arise from the concerns and issues of people with learning disabilities directly. Box 7.1 provides summaries of some of the research studies which have been developed by self advocacy organizations in Australia and the UK. With more support and the possibility of being heard, there is little doubt that further research issues and questions would arise from these groups and others. In these situations the researcher's role will be to hear the nature of the proposal, to assist in developing research submissions if asked and to act as a consultant to the group.

Box 7.1 Self advocate initiated research

Reinforce, a self advocacy organization in Australia, receives little government funding, but has over the past ten years generated a number of different research projects.

1. Plain English Less Jargon: an action research project developed in the early 1990s which resulted in the development of videos and a campaign to make language accessible to people with learning disabilities.

2. A history of the self advocacy movement: an idea which remains unfunded at the moment.

3. Spreading the word: an investigation of how people with learning disabilities view their supported accommodation.

4. Self advocacy and deinstitutionalization: working with people in institutions on self advocacy issues.

Central England People First in the UK has undertaken the following studies:

1. A review of people's opinions of day services.

2. Video diaries of people's daily lives.

3. The potential of the internet to empower people with learning disabilities.

4. Consultations with people with learning disabilities to inform research generated by the *Valuing People* White Paper.

They aspire to:

- compile a history of their own organization
- investigate the mental health needs of young people with learning disabilities.

Latterly there have been moves by self advocates to initiate research of this type into matters relevant to people with learning disabilities and to carry it out personally. Perhaps the best known of these is the Bristol Self Advocacy Group's project which involved seven group interviews with other self advocacy groups, each member of the research team taking their themes into the work. One was particularly interested in transport, another in the meaning of disability. Val Williams, their supporter or co-researcher, describes how the group learnt about research and decided it wanted to do some 'finding out of their own' (Williams 1999). She is adamant that this is an example which shows that people with learning disabilities can appreciate what research is, can see its value and plan and carry it out. Her own role is described as a 'supporter'. The support she supplied 'included the practical tasks such as driving the group members to the interviews, making recordings and simply being there' (1999, p.50). She also played a role in helping people understand what the literature said and in helping them raise money because they decided early on that they wanted to be paid for working as researchers.

Self advocacy itself, and other self advocacy groups, are frequently what self advocates want to explore through research. The Bristol Self Advocacy Group, Cardiff and the Vale People First's work (Whittell *et al.* 1998) and the work of the Cumbria People First members (Chapman in progress) are all examples. Swindon People First Research Team (2002) obtained funding to look into the barriers to the setting up of direct payment schemes. Again, this primarily involved work with articulate people with learning disabilities.

Such examples are still rare, though becoming more possible as people with learning disabilities are exposed to research as an activity, and as funders show more sympathy to researchers' aspirations to be truly inclusive. Much has changed in the past decade and it would be hard to visualize a project like the investigation by Simons (1992) into self advocacy being funded now if it did not, at least tokenistically, include a partnership with a user-controlled organization.

Self advocate initiated research rarely includes people with high support needs. Self advocates tend to gravitate towards other self advocacy groups when attempting research (Chapman in progress; Whittell *et al.* 1998; Williams 1999, 2002). This almost always excludes people who cannot speak up.

Whole life approaches

Probably the area where people with learning disabilities have done most to initiate research projects is where they enlist the assistance of people to help them record their own life stories. Such whole life approaches include autobiography and full life stories. They continue to retain a dominant position in inclusive research. They may be initiated by the individual alone who seeks to find a person to assist them to write their autobiography or they may be the result of a researcher seeking information and a life story account. They may be the result of a fortuitous coming together of researcher and person with a learning disability. More rarely, the account is written totally by the person with a learning disability. For example, in a collection of stories written with and by women with learning disabilities around the world, Tamara Kainova already had her stories written:

> On the table beside her, Tamara had two enormous plastic bags filled with stories. Some were in Russian and some were in Czech. Some seemed to have been written a long time ago and others very recently. She was extremely excited at the idea of her stories being in a book and spent a long time going through her collection to find the ones she wanted to include. At the day centre she spent her time embroidering doilies and making woven mats. She wanted a job with money more than anything else. (Johnson and Traustadottir 2000, p.18)

Atkinson and Walmsley (1999) contrast 'true' autobiographies and 'autobiographical accounts'. The true autobiography is written or initiated by the person. It will usually dwell on the ordinariness of life, the aspects that people with learning disabilities have in common with others, however extraordinary the circumstances and settings. By contrast, autobiographical accounts are initiated by others and frequently dwell on difference:

> Two sorts of stories have emerged, and whilst people may see themselves primarily as self determining adults yet they continue to be seen as oppressed and disempowered 'victims'. (Atkinson and Walmsley 1999, p.210)

AUTOBIOGRAPHIES

As mentioned in Chapter 2, the earliest exemplars of publications by people recognizable as having learning disabilities are autobiographies by Nigel Hunt (1967) and Joey Deacon (1974). Ghost writing is common when people have the fame to be in demand for autobiographies, but not the time or writing skills to carry out the work. The need for support is equally true of people with learning disabilities. Joey Deacon enlisted the assistance of fellow patients to record his story; David Barron secured help from his friend Edwin Banks (Barron 2000). Mabel Cooper was equally fortunate in locating an expert writer/ researcher when she felt ready to commit her story to paper. Mabel, an ex- chair of London People First, describes how she came to write her life story with Dorothy Atkinson's assistance:

> Hazel had asked me to do it because she wanted me to do it for college or something she was taking on, and I said 'OK, but will you put it on a tape recorder for me, and I will try and make a little book out of it, because there's a lot more to it than that on it.' And because I'd already done that tape with Hazel I thought well if I find somebody else, I'll ask somebody to help me a bit more… It was an idea, but it's only an idea unless you get somebody to help you. It was just luck I met you. (Cooper 1997, p.7)

Other examples of this genre have been initiated by people with learning disabilities: Traustadottir and Johnson's (2000) collection, *Women with Intellectual Disabilities: Finding a Place in the World*; 'Family, Marriage, Friends and Work: This is My Life', written by Janice Slattery (2000) with Kelley Johnson's support; *Good Times Bad Times* (Atkinson *et al.* 2000) described in Chapter 5. People who are known to be prepared to work with people with learning disabilities to record life stories are in demand. Both of us have been approached by people who would like their stories recorded, once it is known that this is what we do. The autobiography, when carried out with care and respect, is one medium through which inclusive research can be promoted with few of the doubts which attend other approaches. For the author is indeed and without doubt the expert, the ultimate insider who with help can represent him or herself as he or she wishes.

Not all whole life stories are initiated by people with learning disabilities. Bogdan and Taylor's *Inside Out* (1982) was, as far as we know, initiated by the researchers. Collections such as *Know Me As I Am* and *Good Times Bad Times* were, as we have noted, prompted by academics, though adopted with enthusiasm by their contributors/ co-editors. In the Living Safer Sexual Lives project documented in Chapter 6, life stories were sought by researchers. Most autobiographers with learning disabilities are articulate (Andrews with Rolph 2000; Barron 2000; Cooper 1997; Coventry 2000; Ferris 2000; Slattery with Johnson 2000; Tuttleby with Johnson 2000). In the Living Safer Sexual Lives project, one of the criteria for being included as a life story contributor was orally being able to tell the story. Efforts have been made to initiate autobiographies of people who are unable verbally to communicate by some researchers. Di Terlizzi (1994) used biographical reconstruction to tell the story of a woman without speech, drawing on testimony from people who knew her well and on written sources. Rolph (1999) tells the story of Alice, who died in 1989, from documentary fragments, photos taken by Alice and the memories of her employer. Booth and Booth valiantly but unconvincingly attempted to fill in the silences left by Danny Avebury in their interview with him (1996). Kristjana Kristiansen (2000) uses observation and interviews with family and employers to write the work stories of women with learning disabilities.

One might plausibly argue that these cannot be autobiographies, which are essentially told by the person. Certainly they were not initiated by the people themselves in any recognizable sense. Using this approach does provide a way of giving a voice to those who would otherwise be silent. This issue, however, does raise questions about whether all people with learning disabilities can be initiators of research, or whether the initiation criterion can only apply to the articulate.

Finally, it is worth mentioning that few autobiographies/life stories have been the products of funded research. Almost all the examples cited here have come about because someone was interested enough to spend time with the person and assist them in recording and publishing. This certainly appears to simplify the relationship, which is not being used to produce evidence or data for the benefit of funders and their

imagined audience. On the other hand it raises yet again the power dif-
ferential between the person with a learning disability and the supporter
who provides the means for their voice to be heard. Academics working
with people with learning disabilities gain not only the excitement of a
publication but also monetary and professional prizes. It is extremely
difficult to obtain money for this kind of work. Johnson *et al.* (2000a)
managed to obtain some philanthropic trust funding to provide a salary
for Janice Slattery and Amanda Tuttleby as they wrote their chapters.
But this was the exception in a book where women with learning disabilities and feminist researchers gave hundreds of hours to the development of autobiographies.

(AUTO)BIOGRAPHICAL ACCOUNTS

Auto/biographical accounts are those where people with learning
disabilities discuss their own experiences of life to shed light on a
particular topic. These are usually collected for a wider research purpose
than simply recording a person's autobiography. They are often topic
based, designed to get inside an aspect of the lives of people with
learning disabilities as a distinct category rather than as 'people first'.
Not all are truly 'inclusive' in that they draw on people's life accounts,
but are very often initiated by researchers or funders, who then seek
informants.

They commonly portray victimhood and oppression and how people manage to deal with the negative aspects of life as a person who is
socially excluded – institutional life, community life, caring, poverty,
poor services and discrimination. Whereas in autobiographies the
breadth of someone's life is the focus, autobiographical accounts tend to
highlight certain aspects related to having a learning disability. Well-
known exemplars include Tim and Wendy Booth's work on parents
with learning disabilities (1994) and on the children of people with
learning disabilities (1998); Potts and Fido's oral history of 'the colony'
(1991); Rolph's history of two hostels (2000) and the authors' own
work – Johnson's on deinstitutionalizing women (1998) and
Walmsley's on caring (1993, 1995).

Some work of this kind has been initiated by people with learning
disabilities. For example, Potts and Fido's *A Fit Person to be Removed*

(1991) came from a wish by residents of a hospital which was due for closure to record what had happened to them. More recently, less stigmatized subjects have been tackled using autobiographical accounts. Goodley's study (1998) is based on the life stories of five leading self advocates and he used their stories as the data for his thesis and subsequent publications about self advocacy.

In some projects where the life stories of groups of people with learning disabilities are the data, ownership passes from the researcher to the researched in the process. Atkinson's reminiscence-based group work falls into this category. Initially it was her project but, she argues, as the project took shape and became a book it became 'our book'; one which the group members were proud to own and which they played a major role in developing (Atkinson 1997). One of the ironies, however, is that the best known because most readily accessible and to researchers most interesting account of the work is in books and articles published by Atkinson about the project (Atkinson 1997) rather than the book itself which was never published (although it was reprographed and copies were given to the authors). In public at least, unlike Cooper's autobiography, the work is known as that of Atkinson (see, for example, the citation by Chappell 2000). Ownership also shifted during the course of the project in Rolph's study of two hostels in Norfolk (2000). Her Memories Group, comprised of people who had lived in the hostels under scrutiny, worked alongside her through all stages of the research and played a central role both in supplying and analysing the data and advising on interpretations, though it was Rolph's project initially.

As with autobiographies, efforts have been made to ensure that this approach includes people with less well-developed communication skills. Grant, Ramcharan and McGrath (1993) pioneered methods which could include people with little speech and used 'observational techniques', 'interviews, discussions and prompt cards and accompanying people in their daily lives' (1993, p.3). They also interviewed others in the network such as family and key workers. The authors aggregated this information about three people, published it as a third (not first) person account illustrated with discussions and used it to structure a discussion around themes such as 'life at home' and 'participating in the community' (Grant, Ramcharan and McGrath 1993).

Qualitative research

The extent to which qualitative research is inclusive depends greatly on how the research is initiated, designed and implemented. Usually such research uses semi-structured interviews as a means of gathering information. Semi-structured interviews with people with learning disabilities on subjects such as women's health (Johnson *et al.* 2002c), the menopause (McCarthy in press), self advocacy (Simons 1992), advocacy (Simons 1993), adult education (Sutcliffe 1993) and identity (Aull Davies and Jenkins 1997) have been very popular means of accessing views and experiences. Arguably, all are in areas which matter to people with learning disabilities, whether or not they asked for them. In many respects there are overlaps with the autobiographical accounts explored above. One reason for separating them is purely practical – the sheer number of such studies requires some subcategorization. The other reason is that they do not raise the acute issues around self-representation of biographical accounts because the purpose is more focused. Finding out views about a particular set of issues is more straightforward than using people's life stories to make an academic point.

The number of studies of this nature is enormous. Rarely are they fully inclusive, though some examples initiated by self advocates are (Palmer *et al.* 1999; Williams 1999, 2002). Most frequently they are initiated by researchers or funders and have the purpose of illustrating what the world is like for people with learning disabilities and of influencing others (usually services, sometimes parents and family members) to improve things. The subject matter is almost invariably aspects of the lives of people with learning disabilities which are practical and often service related. Rarely, more abstract subjects like identity are the overt focus.

The overwhelming majority of these semi-structured interview projects were initiated by researchers, funding bodies or government agencies; even those which at first sight appeared to be in areas exclusively owned by people with learning disabilities like Ken Simon's

(1992) study of self advocacy *Sticking Up for Yourself.* The rationale for such research is linked in many cases to the increasing emphasis in policy on involving users and carers in service development and evaluation. Research projects which set out to ascertain users' views are a relatively painless way to achieve this. For example, Townsley and Macadam's action research into user involvement in choosing the staff who work with them was inspired by 'an upsurge in the rhetoric surrounding user involvement in community care services' (1996, p.7). Some projects like Holman and Collins' (1998) work on direct payments have also been attempting to push along policy, in this case to address the slow spread of direct payments schemes to people with learning disabilities, by gathering evidence from those who use direct payments and showing how they work for those people and the advantages as they see them. Both of these examples were researcher or funder initiated, though they undoubtedly promoted the interests of people with learning disabilities, including those who became involved in carrying them out.

Service evaluations by people with learning disabilities

This is an area which has been developed in response to the user involvement policies of government, though it would be fair to add that keen researchers have demonstrated what can be achieved, which in its turn has nudged forward the policy agenda.

Involvement in service evaluations began very early in the biography of inclusive research, the earliest we know of being mentioned in Williams and Schoultz (1982). Most such evaluations are initiated by agencies or funders. The first well-known example from the UK was in 1990 when People First London boroughs were invited to evaluate community-based residential services in Hillingdon (Whittaker 1997). Later People First London successfully bid for money to evaluate services in two other London boroughs, Haringey and Sutton. In Australia, the Department of Human Services has trained people with learning disabilities to undertake consultations around service standards and to examine as evaluators the issues of consumer participation. Although not always initiated by people with learning disabilities, sometimes this work is their initiative. At other times, they join in as tenderers for a project that someone else has specified.

Summary

This brief review of work in areas of what matters to people with learning disabilities shows that, whilst few projects are fully inclusive in the sense that they are not initiated by people with learning disabilities, there are an increasing number of examples of self advocate initiated research and life histories/autobiographies, which clearly address what people want done. Much more work has been undertaken that, whilst it arguably benefits people with learning disabilities in a number of ways by getting their voices and opinions aired, developing skills and abilities, pushing forward progressive policy and practice like direct payments, cannot be truly said to have been conceptualized and initiated by those people themselves.

We proceed in this chapter to consider the barriers to people initiating research and to ponder arguments for a broader definition of what matters.

What are the barriers to people with learning disabilities initiating and developing research?

There are barriers which confront both people with learning disabilities and researchers committed to the practice of inclusive research. In this section we canvass some of these, in particular the difficulties associated with funding research and with finding publications willing to accept research initiated by people with learning disabilities.

Obtaining funding

While some philanthropic foundations and trusts are now privileging research which is participatory and inclusive in nature, they remain the minority. Much of the inclusive research we have undertaken or read about has been undertaken without outside funding or with a minimal budget. There are many factors involved in this. For self advocacy groups which have little in the way of resources or paid staff, putting together complex submissions may be beyond them. Some funding bodies remain suspicious about the usefulness or viability of research which includes people with learning disabilities as anything other than subjects. For example, the Living Safer Sexual Lives project had to prove through a pilot study that its methodology of gathering life histories was viable.

Truly inclusive research is almost invariably more expensive and more time consuming than research managed directly by researchers. The timescales for bidding for research tenders are often short, precluding the detailed face-to-face work necessary to ensure that people with learning disabilities can make an input. The costings are often higher than research which does not necessitate the employment of supporters for people with learning disabilities, and the outputs may appear slighter and less sophisticated for the same sum of money. Williams observes of the Norton self advocacy group's investigation of labelling:

> The idea for the project belonged to group members, who could pursue their thinking and action in any way they wished. This was because the working relationship between myself and the group members pre-dated the project and because of our relative lack of funding... I did not have my own agenda for the research, nor was I constrained by any research proposal, employers' expectations or funders' timetable. (Williams 2002, p.236)

Few researchers are as free as she was to invest the time, and few funders would have been content with an open-ended participatory action research project which simply followed the self advocates' evolving agenda.

Investigating the unknown

As noted earlier in this chapter, some research topics may not be best developed by the group involved with them. There are arguments for researchers taking the lead in areas where people with learning disabilities are not well placed to recognize the significance of particular topics. McCarthy's work on the menopause exemplifies this well. It was her idea to investigate women with learning disabilities' experiences of the menopause and she approached the task through semi-structured interviews. She found that the women she interviewed did not know about the menopause because no one had explained it to them. One of her most taxing challenges was to convey to the respondents what it is (McCarthy in press). In such circumstances it is hard to argue that we should restrain researchers from pursuing investigations which might be of ultimate benefit to women with learning disabilities just because those women do not know enough to ask questions. However, it has to be recognized that taking this stance risks work being done which does not benefit people with learning disabilities, as so much past (and some current) research has done. It is indeed a fine line between acknowledging that people with learning disabilities do not know enough to ask the right questions and giving researchers the sense that they have the right to do whatever research they choose.

Balancing interests

There are some instances where the interests of people with learning disabilities may be sacrificed in order to protect others in the group. This kind of situation makes it very difficult for the research to be initiated by members of the group. For example, Brown and Thomson (1997) raise questions about the extent to which people with highly stigmatized identities can or should be empowered to control what is researched, in the context of men who commit sexual offences. Whilst recognizing the value of an ethical position which gives people with learning disabilities the right to be consulted about the value of research, to consent, or not, to take part, they note that where criminal offences are concerned it may not be in the best interests of others to apply these ethical standards. They propose:

> Primary consideration might instead be given to people with learning disabilities, staff or other members of the community who are at risk of victimization by the men. (Brown and Thomson 1997, p.701)

Application of the principles of inclusive research to people whose behaviour is beyond the pale by current moral standards brings into stark relief the limitations of reliance on just one set of criteria to judge whether research should proceed. Inclusive research is not the only answer.

THEORIZING BY PEOPLE WITH LEARNING DISABILITIES

This category is in many respects the least explored and the most challenging. Stalker comments:

> If we are to take seriously the participation of people with learning disabilities in the research process, rather than simply accepting it uncritically, it is important to acknowledge that very little is known about the potential implications of intellectual impairment for involvement in the research process. (Stalker 1998, p.15)

In making this point, Stalker draws attention to the generation of theory as one especially problematic area. There is very little to cite which can be called standard theorizing by people with learning disabilities other than work by Aspis (1997). Indeed, if and when people with learning disabilities manage to theorize in this way, doubt is often cast upon their status as people with learning disabilities. This is not to argue that some people with learning disabilities may not be able to develop theoretical approaches to research. After all theorizing can range from being informed about one's own situation and generalizing to others to highly conceptual arguments based on wide reading and research. As with the rest of the population, some people with learning disabilities will be able to engage with theory at different levels and with varying degrees of sophistication. In our view it is the researcher's responsibility to find ways to engage people in theorizing which are accessible to them and to recognize theorizing when it occurs.

If inclusive research is about anything, it is about changing the way research, including theorizing, is conceptualized. Williams argues forcefully that research is 'finding out' (1999). The work she undertook with the Norton self advocacy researchers, described in detail in her PhD thesis (2002), illustrates some of the subtleties of self advocacy researchers' theorizing. The researchers, working with their respondents in a common cause of exploring self-identification, examined a significant feature of being labelled (a very salient issue). It was not about awareness of being labelled, something about which all were highly ambivalent, but about the impact of being labelled on their lives. This is where they could find common cause between the researchers and the researched. Given that a fair amount of research time and effort has been devoted to discovering whether people are aware of their 'toxic indentity' (Todd and Shearn 1997), the Norton researchers would appear to have made an important contribution to theorizing the impact of labels on people with learning disabilities. The contribution made by Williams, their chronicler, was to recognize what they were doing as theorizing and to give it a name – something the researchers alone may have been unable to do.

One slightly different instance of theorizing is worth examining, namely the chapter I (JW) wrote with Jackie Downer, black self advocate, called 'Shouting the Loudest' (Walmsley with Downer 1997). This was initiated by my being invited to write a chapter on self advocacy in a book by Paul Ramcharan. I asked Jackie to work with me. The chapter examines difference within self advocacy and how, in Jackie's view, men dominate the movement, and the needs of women, black and Asian people and people with higher support needs get neglected. The chapter was based on three meetings I had with Jackie in a Pizza Hut in South London, when we talked about the chapter we had been commissioned to write. I supplied the knowledge of the literature, for example on normalization, to give a context to Jackie's words. In writing it, I made it clear which were Jackie's words and how we had constructed the chapter and, looking back, it did make a contribution to the literature on self advocacy beyond the limits of personal experience. That was very much a product of my sharing my academic knowledge with Jackie's personal and practice-derived knowledge.

However, the belief that people with learning disabilities cannot theorize is one which will remain a barrier to truly inclusive research, unless and until ways are found to accept that some people so labelled can theorize in the conventional sense of the term (Aspis 1997, 2000), work with academics to develop theory (as the Walmsley and Downer chapter illustrates) or recognize it when it occurs (as the work of the Norton self advocacy group shows).

ACCESS TO PUBLISHING

Without the association with people without the label of disability, it remains difficult for people with learning disabilities to be heard publicly through academic or popular publications. The non-disabled ally has a crucial role here. Whilst once more there are exceptions (Aspis and

Strong), few people with learning disabilities have got into print in academic terms without the support of others. Many of the examples already cited in this chapter (Atkinson *et al.* 2000; Cooper 1997; Walmsley with Downer 1997) and others like Spedding *et al.* (2002) illustrate that inclusive research needs the goodwill and support of academics committed to ensuring that the voice of people with learning disabilities is heard. Yet the benefits are two-way, as the description of my (JW's) work with Jackie Downer shows. Without this collaboration, there would be so much less to write! Attribution of authorship remains a problematic area. Should the researcher deny their role (as Atkinson did, keeping her name out of Cooper's 1997 life story), or should their role be fully attributed (as in the Walmsley and Downer example). This was examined above in relation to Cooper's life story and will be reconsidered at various stages in the book.

Should what matters to people with learning disabilities only be defined by people with learning disabilities?

We began this chapter by citing 'Nothing about us without us' and promised to explore its implications for research. Whether or not it is initiated by them, the research which does include people with learning disabilities presents one picture of reality, often one which has been ignored in the past. However it may also exclude groups from contributing to a richer and more extensive view of the issues affecting the lives of people with learning disabilities.

The move to privilege the accounts of people with learning disabilities and the claims being made for their ownership of what is written may preclude the full involvement of parents, carers, staff, policy makers and others who also have experiences which deserve to be explored, and need to be incorporated if a broad picture is to be painted.

Although history as told by people with learning disabilities is beginning to enjoy much deserved popularity (Cooper 1997; Potts and Fido 1991; Rolph 2000), we would contend that the contribution of others to this history needs to be included. Mark Jackson elegantly puts the case for the involvement of a very broad range of people in historical research:

> At one level research should involve the process of uncovering, listening to, and learning from the experiences of people with learning disabilities. And yet, if we are to comprehend those experiences fully, we need to cast our net wide. (Jackson 2000, p.xii)

Whether the interests of all can be safeguarded in research terms by a reliance upon the initiative of people with learning disabilities or their subsequent recognition of the importance of a particular research topic is a question posed by Kellett and Nind (2001) who reflect on their quasi-experimental research involving 'individuals who are preverbal and who have profound intellectual impairments' (p.51). Should such work be abandoned in the name of emancipatory goals is a question they pose; or should inclusive principles be used to inform their work, thus drawing the best of inclusive practice into domains where these have enjoyed far too little attention from researchers. They conclude:

> The growing number of groups involved in qualitative, participatory and emancipatory research may lead the way on research ethics into a new era, but they cannot be left to take the responsibility which all researchers in the area of learning disabilities must share. The changing context of demands for inclusion, for evidence-based practice, and for respect for human rights should lead us to reflect on the practical benefits and ethical issues associated with our research. Having reflected on this study, we conclude that, like any research it is not perfect, that all researchers need to seek compromises, and that dialogue is needed on purposeful ways forward. (Kellett and Nind 2001, p.29)

Conclusion

In this chapter we have surveyed the extent to which research projects have been dictated by what matters to people with learning disabilities. Perhaps simplistically, we initially used as the criterion whether people with learning disabilities initiated the research. There is much to celebrate in this respect. Attitudes have changed and, driven by the precepts of funders such as the Joseph Rowntree Foundation and the Stegley Foundation and the UK Department of Health, there has been a growing recognition that people with learning disabilities have the right to know about the research that is being conducted on them, and that they indeed have the right to ask the questions and expect a response.

However, as editor of the *British Journal of Learning Disabilities*, the leading UK journal in the field, I (JW) know that the overwhelming majority of research is not initiated by or in conjunction with people with learning disabilities; nor is it always evident that the authors have asked themselves whether what they are researching is what matters to people with learning disabilities, as opposed to what matters to services, professionals or even their own careers and the reputation of their universities. Should it be? If all learning disability research should be inclusive, then a lot of questions will not be addressed and many studies will not be carried out because they are either not seen by people with learning disabilities to be in their interests or are currently beyond the ability of many of them to conceptualize.

We believe that this kind of debate is based on a false either/or assumption. Inclusive research is much more than the degree to which it is initiated by the people concerned. Where or not the research is initiated or undertaken by people with learning disabilities, there should be a particular commitment by the researcher to consider carefully why it is being undertaken in the way that it is, and how the research may involve and be of use to people with learning disabilities. They need to ask themselves the question whether this does matter to people with learning disabilities.

CHAPTER 8

Managing Inclusive Research

It is one thing to initiate research and it is quite another to do it. A participatory approach to research raises the possibility of people with learning disabilities working alongside academics as advisors or co-researchers, whilst in emancipatory research, disabled people are expected to control all aspects of the process. In this chapter we consider practice in inclusive learning disability research insofar as it relates to actually managing the research.

The chapter is structured in three parts. The first discusses the roles played by people with learning disabilities in research. The second examines ethical issues which attend all forms of inclusive research. The third looks at the parts played by non-disabled allies in the process. The chapter relates to our key question:

- Can and should we manipulate the environment to the extent that people with learning disabilities can be meaningfully included in all stages and aspects of research?

From advisory groups to control

In this section we describe the roles people with learning disabilities have played in research.

Advisory or reference groups

One of the earliest ways in which people with learning disabilities were engaged in major research projects was as advisory or reference groups. In Chapter 3 we discussed the role played by the Know Me As I Am advisory group. The people on that group were not contributors themselves. Their role was quite distinct and we noted that they influenced significant issues such as corrections to spelling and grammar, though their power did not extend to overriding the editors' preference when it came to the title or the way the book was organized into themed chapters. We also noted the highly significant role of the reference group in Chapter 6, the major means through which people with learning disabilities gained and maintained influence over the project.

Advisory or reference groups have continued to be a popular and often successful way of ensuring that people with learning disabilities have ongoing investment in the project. Ward and Simons (1998) cite the practical benefits of having input from advisors on, for example, designing letters to participants and pictorial questionnaires. In some projects the roles of advisors are conflated with those of respondents. Rolph (2000) constituted a Memories Group which met throughout the project and assisted in shaping its direction. Its members were, however, also respondents or 'life historians' as they were called in this project. Although Rolph did not find it a problem, this can give rise to confidentiality issues if sensitive data shared in a one-to-one situation is made known to the group who already know one another; a situation I encountered in my 'adulthood' project (Walmsley 1991), which is also discussed in Chapter 6.

Not all researchers have felt entirely content with the extent to which such groups do empower people with learning disabilities. Jackie Rodgers set up a group of women to advise on her work on the health of people with learning disabilities. In a perhaps unnecessarily self-critical reflexive paper called 'Trying to Get it Right' she describes how she convened it from women including professionals, carers and service users who had contacted her in relation to the research:

> This seemed particularly helpful as a way of allowing ideas and concerns to be raised from the perspective of people within the group rather than 'consultation' about matters that I defined as relevant. The group provided many useful insights as well as mutual support…and raised my awareness of the sometimes similar and sometimes different needs of carers and those they support. (Rodgers 1999, p.423)

In retrospect, she recognized the limitations of this (and other strategies) as a means of giving people with learning disabilities control over the process and remarked:

> The mechanisms mentioned did contribute to the future direction of the research, but it is true that opportunities for disabled people to formally criticize the research process were lacking. This cannot entirely be excused by time constraints, and must reflect the ideas I then held about the capabilities of people with learning disabilities to understand and influence the research process. (Rodgers 1999, p.431)

In engaging in this level of self-criticism, she demonstrates that the expectations of the degree to which people with learning disabilities should be included had moved on from the role of advisors, which was state of the art in the early 1990s when she did the project, to more intimate and powerful roles within the research process itself.

I had my own encounter with the shifting expectations in 1994 when I met with members of London People First to invite them to participate in an advisory group for the teaching pack I was putting together for people with learning disabilities, carers and staff (Equal People). I was told very politely that this was tokenistic. As a result of this two self advocates became part of the operational course team. We also had an advisory group for the project made up of representatives of leading organizations, including self advocates. Looking back, it is clear that the course team members, not the advisory group, made all the major decisions.

However limited advisory groups may be in giving real power, they do have many advantages in a practical sense. Researchers can and do benefit from advice from people with learning disabilities (and others) on understandings, on issues they encounter as people with learning disabilities (or carers and staff), and on putting things in ways that the respondents are likely to understand.

Co-researching

Co-researching implies an equal partnership, where researchers work with people with learning disabilities to pool expertise. Usually it involves the researcher bringing her (almost invariably it is women who do this work) knowledge and skills, and the people with learning disabilities bringing their unique perspective.

Of all the forms of research in which people with learning disabilities have been major participants, the autobiography probably holds the greatest potential for full and equal partnership since the person who tells is unambiguously the 'expert', the ultimate insider. The telling and recording of one's story as autobiography is an important way in which a person may choose how he or she is portrayed, how the identity is presented, claimed by the person rather than constructed by powerful others as case notes or biographical fragments (Atkinson and Walmsley 1999; Gillman, Swain and Heyman 1997).

It is probably true to say that relatively few people have either the skills or the means to get an autobiography published. However, with imagination, people who cannot read and write can maintain control of the process. To illustrate this we turn again to Mabel Cooper's autobiography. The story, subsequently published as 'Mabel Cooper's Life Story' (1997), had Mabel's name as the author, though as Mabel herself acknowledges it was also Atkinson's work:

> I would like you to put your name on it, in a part of it. I think it should be there. After all, you helped me do the work. (Atkinson *et al.* 1997, p.9)

The means by which the story was produced is chronicled in detail. The story was told in a series of informal interviews which were tape recorded and later transcribed by Atkinson. Atkinson then reworked the information into an account to cover the various milestones, events and turning points in someone's life, but not necessarily in the right order from childhood and schooldays to adult life. Memories are not always organized in this way and people may approach some events, particularly those with painful associations, in a more circumspect way than through a straight chronological account (Atkinson 1997, p.10).

The assembled information was then read back to the author to establish that she was content with the polished account. Various other elements needed to be considered. Attribution of authorship was one, as noted above. Decisions needed to be taken about naming names, particularly where ill treatment was alleged, and the author needed to be able to consider the consequences of naming people.

Subsequently, Atkinson and Cooper have worked and reworked the life story, publishing accounts of how more light was shed through gaining access to Mabel's hospital case notes which explained, inter alia, that her mother had unwillingly been forced to give her up at an early age. This offered Mabel insight into the processes which had led her to be incarcerated in institutions for much of her life. This is published in 'Parallel Stories' (Atkinson and Cooper 2000), an imaginatively co-authored paper in which Atkinson tells her story and Mabel tells hers in words transcribed by Atkinson.

However, it is important to add the caveat that the helper may need to do more than just record and write. Atkinson's help to Mabel in discovering more information about herself to which she had no access enriched Mabel's understanding, and is something Mabel could not have achieved without expert help – the researcher putting her skills at the disposal of the disabled person in the way advocated in emancipatory research. In terms of inclusivity, this example appears to rank highly. The idea was both owned and initiated by Mabel and she controlled the process. It appears to further the interests of people with learning disabilities by shedding light on the ways in which individuals experience historical processes, survive them and indeed make sense of them. It was collaborative in that Mabel was able to exert control at all stages. The resulting life story has been made accessible in a number of ways: there is an audio taped version for an Open University course for people with learning disabilities; conference presentations including many for people with learning disabilities; easy-to-read versions (Cooper, Ferris, Coventry with Atkinson 2000). It has also led to an enhancement of Mabel's career. Initially with Atkinson, but increasingly solo, Mabel has been in much demand as an author, conference presenter and workshop leader (see, for example, Mabel's sole authored article in *Community Care* magazine, 2002).

Another area where people with learning disabilities have been engaged to carry out research is in evaluation of services. Again this is an area where there is considerable value in service user involvement, for they have a particular expertise. As Whittaker (1997) puts it, user-evaluators see services from a different angle, which gives a more complete picture. People with learning disabilities may well get more honest answers and may know better what questions to ask because they have experience of being on the receiving end. Inevitably, the whole project adds value to positive imagery, both for the people in the service being evaluated who see people like themselves (perhaps) in valued roles, and for the people who do the work, who learn new skills, get out and about and get paid for their efforts.

The extent to which the user researchers actually determine the criteria used to judge quality is debatable. I have commented elsewhere (Walmsley 2001) that the Hillingdon evaluation carried out by members of London People First appears to have been influenced by O'Brien's five accomplishments which resulted in the People First evaluators assuming that normalization provided the best yardstick for judgement. This resulted in some rather bizarre interpretations of the last accomplishment – 'relationship':

> They felt they could not make the judgment here because during the two weeks at the house there were not enough opportunities to observe people interacting with ordinary members of the public. (Whittaker 1995, p.101)

The assumption that 'relationship' could not be judged within the home indicates the power of some of the less attractive features of normalization, the importance it accords to interaction with 'valued' people, and throws doubt on the extent to which people with learning disabilities actually determined the criteria by which the services were to be judged.

An illustrated accessible report on five such projects by Whittaker (1997), who worked closely with London People First, gives very detailed descriptions of how the evaluators were trained, how the aims were set and how they went about deciding on a research methodology.

In more complex research projects where mastery of a body of knowledge drawing on the literature is a prerequisite, the task of involving people with learning disabilities as partners is more challenging. Paula Mitchell, in a PhD study which explored the impact of self advocacy on families, engaged three members of Hackney People First as Mitchell was aiming to 'involve people with learning disabilities in the whole research process' (Mitchell 1997, p.50). They took the name 'consultants'. Mitchell made it her business to summarize the research on families with sons and daughters with learning disabilities for the benefit of the co-researchers. This yielded valuable insights:

> One discussion was about stress on parents and the question of support. While in the literature these are usually seen as issues for parents, the co-researchers record that 'There is a lot of stress for everybody in the family, not just parents. And we need support too'. (Mitchell 1997, p.50)

The co-researchers also assisted Mitchell in 'drawing up a list of factors which they thought should feature in a home life in which self advocacy was recognized and encouraged' (p.51), drawing on their personal experience of being self advocates and living with their families to contribute to the framework within which the research was carried out. As in Living Safer Sexual Lives, the line was drawn at people with learning disabilities actually carrying out the interviews or analysing the data in any detail. This was largely their own decision because of matters of confidentiality.

Rolph's Memories Group, initially viewed as an advisory group, in effect became involved in far more depth in the study of the history of two Norfolk hostels. As well as being key contributors ('life historians') as people who had experienced life in the hostels, they also contributed group reminiscence and became involved in analysing the data:

> Aspects of data analysis began to take place from the early stages of the group. Members began to prioritise the most important aspects of their lives in the hostels, highlighting themes for further discussion…
> Comments from some members contested the evidence representing the official voice, challenging the 'known' history. (Rolph 2000, pp.125–6)

Rolph's contribution was to produce a summary of relevant data and historical information to inform the Memories Group discussions and, of course, to act as facilitator, recorder and scribe, and ultimately to write up the PhD.

Beyond co-researching – taking charge

Equal partnerships are perhaps the most co-researching projects are aiming for. They remain within the participatory research framework.

Very few projects have gone beyond that to an emancipatory frame-work. One that has already been referred to, the work of Simone Aspis, consists of theoretical papers rather than research per se. Another is the work of the Bristol Self Advocacy Group, supported by Val Williams. Val describes their work as a genuine initiative, growing out of a desire to find out if their experiences were shared by others, and an awareness that research was a tool to 'make things better' (1999, p.49). As well as initiating the research, they identified the self advocacy groups they wanted to interview, drew up questions and chaired the discussions. Williams also argues, on behalf of the group, that they do engage in the-ory generation:

> If a theory is broadly taken to be a model that helps us understand why things are as they are, then self advocates do engage in theory generation incessantly. For instance, the theory that labeling influences people's thinking is a very powerful one. (Williams 1999, p.51)

The initial results of the group's work have been published in a chapter called 'Telling People What You Think', written by Neil Palmer, Chris Peacock, Florence Turner and Brian Vasey, supported by Val Williams (Palmer *et al.* 1999). In describing why they do it, they write:

> We think we've got on quite well. What research does, is that it takes you outside yourself, and you think about other people more than you do about yourself. We do research because it's interesting to get people's opinions. (Palmer *et al.* 1999, p.33)

The chapter covers 'What is disability?', 'Jobs and work', 'Staff', 'Trans-port' and 'Self advocacy – what does it mean?' The topics reflect the interests of the individual group members, each of whom appears to have taken responsibility for finding the data and writing one section, although details of the process are not crystal clear. In particular, Val's role is not fully transparent.

It is important to note that the group recognizes that not all people with learning disabilities are equally able to do research. Williams writes, on behalf of the group:

> We would maintain that simply being a user of learning disability services does not qualify someone to be a researcher. There are

> aptitudes and skills involved, although these can be developed with
> experience…we agreed that the actual ability level did not matter so
> much as finding people who were interested. People also needed to
> have an ability to listen, to be interested in things, to think for
> themselves, and to understand what others think. (Williams 1999,
> p.51)

This point is important, though underlying some of the qualities identified one might discern a need for the ability to speak and to articulate ideas.

In what is perhaps the most detailed exposition of inclusive research in practice so far, her work with the Norton self advocacy researchers, Williams contends that some research can *only* be done by self advocates:

> The analysis adds to the argument about whether it is possible to be
> both a 'person with learning difficulties' and a researcher. In fact, for
> this kind of research it is not only possible it is actually necessary. The
> common experience of being labeled becomes a positive tool for
> change. (Williams 2002, p.232)

Through analysing video evidence she shows how the self advocates crossed the traditional boundaries between themselves as researchers and the people they were interviewing by calling upon examples of shared experience. She identifies 'the frequent blurring of the strict distinction between the interviewer and the interviewee' (p.230) as a benchmark of inclusive research, and the means by which shared meanings were developed during the interviews. Means and ends, process and outcomes are also blurred and interchangeable. It was, she contends, doing the research and being researchers which was significant:

> By doing research, members took on aspects of a researcher identity,
> and so their challenge to the received social order was achieved not
> only by what they talked about, but by the action of doing research.
> (Williams 2002, pp.233–4)

Although she places this piece of work within the participatory paradigm, it emerges as the most developed piece of emancipatory research to date in the field because so much of it was determined by the self advocate researchers.

Ethical issues

Working inclusively brings in its wake certain ethical issues which cross-cut all types of inclusive research – those of payment, finding participants and gaining informed consent. We discuss these here and offer some tentative ideas about dealing with them.

Payment

It is the orthodoxy that if people with learning disabilities are to become researchers then they should be paid for their work at 'normal' rates (Van Hove 1999; Williams 1999). Researchers have gone to great lengths to ensure that people are paid and recognized for their work, as was shown in Chapter 6. Despite this, as noted in Chapter 7, much inclusive research operates outside the normal funding mechanisms, so there is often not enough cash to pay people the going rate for the job, nor can there be any guarantee of continuing employment.

In a world where the odds are stacked against people with learning disabilities in terms of earning, even when money can be obtained, payment is not a straightforward issue. In one project in which I (JW) was involved, I came speaking the words of equal payment. This was a user controlled project, however, and the users declined the opportunity to be paid. Why? Because very junior research assistants can expect less, after deductions, than the benefits/pensions that these would-be researchers obtain as people with learning disabilities. Not only that, when the project ended as it would after three years and there was no more work, having 'research assistant' as the last paid employment might make it very difficult to resume claimant status at the previous rates based on disability premiums. The users here had much more sense of what was in their interests than I with my unacknowledged social role valorization position. Fortunately, as they were in charge, my ideas were not taken up.

Even where it is in the interests of people with learning disabilities to be paid as researchers, further complications arise. University research staff are paid according to qualifications. It would be rare indeed to find someone working on a research contract who did not have at least a first degree. So appointing people with learning disabilities would challenge the whole set of assumptions upon which academic work is remunerated; no bad thing, one might argue, but practically very difficult to execute within the context of personnel/ human resources policies and agreements with trades unions.

The example of payment illustrates the difficulties of introducing the principles of inclusive research without fully changing the material relations of research production. In a world where people with learning disabilities do not enjoy equal rights but may have other financial compensations, fitting equal research relationships into the equation is problematic; something noted by Zarb in his (1992) paper. The best resolution we can offer is to air the issues and allow those taking part to make informed decisions on how they might be rewarded.

Finding participants

Research which is managed and controlled by the researcher alone is usually reported in terms of criteria which meet the needs of the research. Subjects are randomly assigned to groups or studied because they are perceived to possess certain defined characteristics, for example, a certain level of disability. Difficulties are usually expressed in terms of finding people with particular characteristics. For researchers who want their research to be inclusive, the issues are different. Of course, in the type of research initiated by self advocates this may not be a problem. But much inclusive research, as we have noted, is initiated by researchers who then have to find people who want to be included.

Who takes part and how they might be approached has also been explored. Walmsley (1993) speculated on the viability of approaching people with learning disabilities who are relative strangers with an invitation to take part in research and surmised that few might readily appreciate what it was they were being asked to take part in, research being a somewhat esoteric activity. Certainly advertisements in the media are unlikely to yield willing respondents as few people with learning disabilities read. The problem is exacerbated by the stigma associated with learning disabilities. Researchers may avoid telling people this is why they are of interest, as it could lead to insult or refusal to take part.

Until recently, most researchers appear to have relied on insider status (Atkinson was a social worker who had ready access to people who had recently left hospital for her 1986 study), intermediaries (the Booths approached key workers to gain access to parents of people with learning disabilities in 1994), snowballing through the networks of other people with learning disabilities (Johnson *et al.* 2001; Rolph 2000; Walmsley 1995; all report on this), or captive populations (Johnson's 1998 study of a locked ward in an institution is a good instance).

The increasingly high profile of self advocacy groups makes for another avenue to explore because people with learning disabilities have their own networks and are able to make approaches to other individuals or self advocacy groups if they are keen on the research. Although it was initiated by her, Paula Mitchell found her co-researchers by approaching her local People First group and asking for their assistance. Subsequently people to interview were located through the co-researchers' own networks (1997). Similarly, the need to carry self advocacy groups alongside may in time genuinely empower them because they will have the option of denying access to researchers of whom they do not approve. Chapman, attempting to scrutinize the role of the support worker in self advocacy organizations, was denied access to two that she approached, despite the fact that she was working with self advocate researchers (personal communication 2002).

Of course there are problems in inviting participation using these methods. Making contact through advocacy organizations may increase the possibility of accountability but it may also restrict the numbers of people who participate in research. Using snowballing methods may mean that the same people participate time after time and that others remain excluded.

The issue of inviting participation which is inclusive seems to us to be dependent more on the style and commitment of the researcher rather than on the use of any particular method. Making sure that people are clear about their participation, that there are opportunities for accountability and that the participation is meaningful rather than tokenistic are important steps for involving people in inclusive research.

Informed consent

Associated with this is the question of informed consent. For inclusive researchers informed consent must be more than a one-off signing of a piece of paper worded in jargonistic language. But there are dilemmas in attempting new approaches. Researchers have been imaginative in devising information and consent sheets. Rolph, for example, produced one illustrated with photos, to give her Memory Group insight into what she was proposing to do. She tested this out with an adult education class and amended it according to their feedback (2000, p.107). She later piloted it with six of her 'life historians' and notes that the photographs were useful in enabling people with little speech and no understanding of the written word to recognize what she was seeking to do. One recognized the photo of the hostel where she had spent many years. She argues that gaining informed consent is not a one-off, but needs continual revisiting as people begin to appreciate what the research is about.

However, McCarthy argues that gaining informed consent is not something that can be captured by even the most sophisticated of inclusive research methodologies. In the context of her well-known work exploring the sexual experiences of women with learning disabilities (which she initiated) she writes:

> It is one thing to consent to the face to face aspects of the research i.e. consent to talking to an individual researcher, and it is quite another to consent to the hidden or behind-the-scenes aspects of research, i.e. the researcher going away with your answers, analyzing them, coming to conclusions about you and your situation (which you may not even understand, much less agree with) and then informing other people what they have discovered about you and people like you. Obviously, the more significant the learning disability, the less insight people are going to have, or be able to develop, about the hidden aspects of research. (McCarthy 1998, p.143)

The defender of inclusive research might well be tempted to retort that she ought not to keep these aspects 'behind the scenes'. However, her point that only some people with learning disabilities have the intellectual capacity to comprehend what might be the consequences of consent is an important one. Confining research only to those who can give truly informed consent may well exclude large numbers of people with learning disabilities from being involved at all.

As discussed in Chapter 6, the use of reference and advisory groups can be of assistance in exploring ways to make sure that the consultations with participants about informed consent are as open and accessible as possible. The use of advocates or guardians who can give informed consent is one way to ensure that exploitation of people who are unable to give informed consent is avoided. However, once a third person is involved in this way there may be problems related to confidentiality and privacy. A careful balance needs to be struck by the researcher in consultation with a reference group in exploring the ethics of this issue.

Roles played by non-disabled researchers

The unwritten story of inclusive research is in many respects the roles of the allies, the non-disabled researchers – us. In this section we consider these roles using the headings roles, boundaries and power.

Roles

Working to support inclusive research makes demands on the non-disabled researchers who get involved; variously described as 'allies' (Chappell 1999), inquirers (Knox, Mok and Parmenter 2000), supporter (Williams 1999) and, presumably, co-researchers (if people with learning disabilities are co-researchers then the ally must also be). We can infer from the descriptions of projects in this chapter to date that the non-disabled researcher in practice plays a rather sophisticated role. She has to be someone who can explain research questions and issues clearly, who can summarize the literature in a way that people with little formal education can comprehend, network, conduct group work, record, teach, facilitate, negotiate and advocate. She also needs exceptional sensitivity to power relationships and to be prepared to hold back on her ideas in order that people with learning disabilities can express theirs.

One of the confusions about inclusive research (and, we might add, support to self advocacy) is this role that allies play. It is obfuscated by the language used, something we have struggled with in this book.

Inclusive research has prompted efforts to find language which subverts the traditional power differentials inherent in the research relationship. Without going into the subtle nuances of terms like subject, respondent and informant, we can think of many examples where the linguistic enterprise is far more obviously counter-intuitive. Mitchell worked with co-researchers or consultants to explore self advocacy and families (1997). Knox *et al.*'s (2000) informants were 'experts', the researchers were 'inquirers'. Rolph's collaborators were 'life historians', while she remained without a named role (2000). Van Hove has coined the term 'cooperative research' (1999). Williams calls herself a 'supporter'; the self advocates with whom she works are the real researchers (1999). Johnson refers to research partners, a term also used in citizen advocacy to refer to the person advocated for (Simons 1993). The Booths (and others) parallel their role as researchers with the role of advocates (1994). All are intended to indicate that the relationship is one at least of equality, where the people with learning disabilities enjoy the same (or higher) status as the non-disabled ally.

Whilst recognizing that the intentions are worthy, this proliferation of terms resembles what Sinason, writing in another context, has called 'a manic desire to erase difference' (1992, p.43). She argues that euphemisms are brought in to replace the verbal bedlinen when a particular word feels too raw (Sinason 1992, p.2). Here she is discussing the rapidly shifting terminology used to refer to people with learning disabilities. But the proliferation of labels to describe the roles people play in inclusive research projects suggests a similar level of discomfort on the part of those who invent the new terminology.

The proliferation of terms also makes for some confusions because inclusive research embraces research where people with learning disabilities play the roles of respondents and/or the roles of researchers, and sometimes both, and the language used does not always make it clear who is who. This is important because whilst it is quite legitimate as a researcher working with respondents to see the role as uncovering experience and enabling its articulation, without unduly influencing what is said, the person who seeks to engage people with learning disabilities as co-researchers or as leading research has to do more. In an unpublished conference paper Atkinson (2001) has noted similarities between the role she played as a social worker and the role she now plays as someone who facilitates people with learning disabilities telling their stories. It is true that the co-researcher is in many respects a supporter who plays all the roles that supporters of people with learning disabilities play in non-research life – organizing transport, obtaining the cash advances, generally creating the circumstances which enable people with learning disabilities to play their part, whether as researchers or respondents. However, if inclusive research is ever to go beyond the stage where research is seen as just 'getting inside' the experience of being labelled as having a learning disability, the co-researcher has to be much more. We propose that he or she needs to be a teacher and leader, and language which seeks to obscure that is ultimately unhelpful and dishonest. This is a theme we explore further in Part 3 of the book.

Boundaries

In inclusive research the ally needs to get stuck into people's lives in a way that is unusual in research. Providing transport, organizing, obtaining cash advances for one's colleagues are unusual. Should there be boundaries to the researcher's role? As early as 1989 Atkinson noted that her respondents expected, and received, a continuing involvement from her as a friend. Probably the most extensive defence of the obligations of the researcher to his or her subjects is by Tim and Wendy Booth who describe in graphic detail how they worked with and for people whose lives they studied; how they were called upon to accompany people in court when the custody of their children was at risk; how their involvement with some families extended well beyond the ending of the formal research; how difficult it was to break away when people appeared to need their help so much. As may be recalled, the Booths drew on the philosophy of citizen advocacy when describing their philosophy in approaching their work with parents of people with learning disabilities. They were not only researchers, but also people who got drawn into the often grim reality of the lives of the people they studied (1998). In a subsequent article, 'Doing Research with Lonely People' (1998), Wendy Booth explored the potential and the limitations of the stance they took, and the toll on the researcher whose livelihood may depend upon working with large numbers of individuals, and the ever-increasing encroachment on their personal space. Morally, perhaps the researcher has obligations which go beyond the traditional boundaries, but practically there are limits to what can be done if further research work is to be undertaken, and life is to continue to be lived.

Power

The ally has a lot of power. Even in the most emancipated projects, such as Williams's work with the Norton self advocates, we get to know what is going on through her words. It is she who names what is going on as 'research'; it is she who identifies theorizing. Print is possibly the most difficult communication medium for people with learning disabilities to control, yet print is pre-eminently the medium by which ideas are shared in the public arena. Without the accounts written by the allies we would know very little other than what we can access directly. Well-intentioned researchers who hold to an inclusive perspective to research may (and often do) feel uneasy about the extent to which their research is truly inclusive, and how we can responsibly exercise the power we have.

Until self advocates build up the confidence to challenge (and there is evidence that this is happening at a number of levels), perhaps the best guide for researchers concerned about the inclusive nature of their research is in terms of reflection on research practice. Questions asked of oneself can provide a useful touchstone and guide. These questions might include:

- Would I be willing to participate in this study in its current form?

- What are the problems that any participants may encounter in their involvement?

- Have I considered whether this research is going to make a positive contribution to people's lives?

- Do the advantages of this research outweigh any disadvantages?

- Does this work matter to people with learning disabilities?

Such reflection is more grounded and more participatory when it is part of a group process as an advisory group is more likely to be aware of issues confronting participants and perhaps less committed to undertaking the research itself than the researcher. Yet, ultimately, we have to police ourselves for in the private context in which we are writing this book there is no other control.

Conclusion

In this chapter we have reviewed how inclusive research is managed, through examining the roles people with learning disabilities play, through consideration of how to manage ethical dilemmas and through consideration of the roles played by allies, non-disabled researchers. A huge amount has been achieved, more than many would have thought possible even a decade ago. The environment has been successfully manipulated to promote inclusion. We see a continuous process of negotiation and renegotiation as inclusive research develops. Yet, the power of the ally remains considerable and largely unexplored and unacknowledged. For although in the bubble we have created where inclusive research proceeds there is progress, when the process is described and made public it is overwhelmingly the ally who is the messenger.

CHAPTER 9

Who Uses it and How?

Somehow the products of inclusive research need to be recorded and disseminated or it will remain a small-scale and uninfluential hobby of a few committed activists. This raises the question of ownership: who determines the way people with learning disabilities are represented and how the data is used. Some have expressed doubts about the viability of enabling people with learning disabilities really to gain control over the way data is analysed and research is written up. McClimens (1999) maintains:

> In the field of participatory research…the relationship between the originator of the research question and the participants is hopelessly one-sided. For as long as research continues to be dominated by research interests this is likely to remain so. (McClimens 1999, p.226)

Goodley says 'it remains to be seen exactly how researchers can truly involve informants with the conclusions that are made' (1996, p.344). I (JW) asked whether 'this represents a failure of researchers like myself to enable people with learning disabilities to contribute in this way, or whether we must accept this as a result of the impairment itself' (Walmsley 1997, p.71).

The roles played by non-disabled supporters/researchers are obviously a key issue when trying to access and represent the views and experiences of people with learning disabilities in a participatory model. As Kiernan (1999) and Chappell (2000) observed, it is very difficult to detach the supporter's influence on what's produced.

The chapter relates to the following of our questions:

- Should the researcher have a distinctive voice?
- Do existing research methods stereotype people with learning disabilities?
- Should the researcher be cast in the role of advocate?

Representation and ownership

In the *Good Times Bad Times* case study (Atkinson *et al.* 2000), actually agreeing the who and the how were fairly straightforward. This was a true partnership where each of the editors participated in discussions and agreed how to proceed. It was at the stage of whose ideas prevail in the book that consensus was more difficult.

Tricia Webb, a self advocacy supporter with Skills for People Newcastle, offers some useful insights into the role in reflecting upon her initial efforts to gain data from people with learning disabilities for a commissioned chapter, 'Voices of People with Learning Difficulties'. In introducing the chapter she writes:

> This chapter is about the lives of people with learning disabilities and I decided to talk to three of our volunteers whom I felt I knew relatively well. I wanted to use their experiences to explore issues important to disabled people...at the initial interview we talked about their lives and their experiences of services good and bad. Looking at my notes afterwards, there seemed to be something lacking, something rather impersonal and even clinical about what I had written. I realized I had managed to confine all three people to talking about the things I felt confident I already knew about people with learning disabilities. My paper was full of comments like 'people don't listen to what I want', 'professionals never have time for me', 'I had to do what they thought was best for me', 'they try and run my life for me', 'speaking up for yourself is really hard'. I had unconsciously set myself in the role of expert – leading rather than following – and in some ways the person themselves need not have been there. I had created a caricature of people with learning disabilities and learned nothing new.

> My own challenge in writing this chapter was to give these three people I knew so well the opportunity to tell their stories, yes, but also to help me understand some of the things I might usually miss because of who I am – a professional working in advocacy and committed to the cause! (Webb 1999, pp.48–9)

How familiar those quoted phrases sound. How many reports of research where people with learning disabilities' words are quoted fall into this stereotypical victim category? It is as if people with learning disabilities have learnt the script and know what to say when people ask questions. Many, perhaps all, inclusive researchers are like Webb and 'committed to the cause'. Webb's exceptionally honest reflections open the way for a critical look at the often hidden role of the researcher in determining how people are represented, which words are chosen to help people 'speak for themselves'. The rest of her chapter reveals what she did find out when she really listened. Some of it made for uncomfortable listening for her, particularly hearing about the hurt that 'professional distance' inflicted on people, and the relative insignificance of people like her in the totality of people's lives.

Much research which can be broadly termed inclusive emerges with a strong 'victim' message. Autobiographical accounts are particularly problematic in terms of representation. As we noted in Chapter 7, they are more frequently initiated by researchers or funders than people with learning disabilities themselves. They raise delicate methodological and ethical issues, described by some feminists as 'a tension between giving voice to women's experiences and analyzing those voices' (Ristock and Pennell 1996, p.79). Some feminists take the position that analysis of autobiographical accounts is a violation. Chamberlain refused to analyse her interviewees' stories, wanting them to remain intact: 'I did not want those memories to be plundered, treated as inanimate documents, for evidence in support of a singular point' (Chamberlain 1983, p.1). This is by and large the position that the editors of *Good Times Bad Times* adopted – using the stories people contributed for academic argument was judged as unethical. Goodley, however, sees this resistance as being in danger of 'reducing individual stories into nothing more than sound-bites' (1996, p.343). In this, he shares some of the reservations expressed by Finkelstein who views the elevation of personal experience as 'just a return to the old case file approach to oppression, dressed up in social model jargon' (Finkelstein 1996, p.11). Often the temptation to theorize from people's life stories has not been resisted, though there has been a heightened awareness of the ethical dilemmas and consciences have been assuaged in reflective accounts by the researcher (see, for example, McCarthy 1998; Rodgers 1999; Stalker 1998).

An example of the way auto/biographical accounts have been used to engender sympathy for and empathy with people who bear very negative labels is in the accounts by 'mentally disordered offenders with learning disabilities': 'I am Stuck Here with my Poxy Star Chart' (Flynn *et al.* 1997). This was a publication stemming from a UK Department of Health funded project which aimed to:

> Ascertain from 20 self-selected people with learning disabilities who have committed offences their experiences and their versions of events without recourse to anyone else. To host workshops for the purchasers and providers of services for adults with learning disabilities who offend. (Flynn *et al.* 1997, p.144)

Whether this research can genuinely claim to be inclusive is debatable. Certainly there was a commitment to enabling people to tell their own stories, but there is no evidence that they had any control of the context in which their words were used. The chapter contains two fairly extensive verbatim accounts by people who participated in the study, and uses them to make the point that people had experienced 'inept, inadequate and sometimes abusive service responses' (Flynn *et al.* 1997, p.151). The authors comment that 'they have both been subject to brute force and there is little that is enviable about their lives' (p.151). As part of the project aim was to influence services directly through holding workshops for purchasers and providers, this is a particularly apt illustration of the way funded projects have used autobiographical accounts to change perspectives, with the hope of improving people's lives, but in so doing use a portrayal of people as victims. Whether this victim status is how the contributors would choose to be portrayed if given a free hand is a moot point.

Research which takes a more open-ended approach to recording people's lives, like the autobiographies or Know Me As I Am, has as we have noted tended to portray 'ordinary' aspects of people's lives and to represent them as people first, rather than people with learning disabilities. However they would be unlikely to have been published if they were not people with extraordinary stories to tell because of their distinctive labels and experiences.

Some researchers who work in a self-consciously inclusive framework have made efforts to redress the balance by devoting some space to whole rather than fragmented life stories. Rolph's work on community care in Norfolk has spawned at least one autobiography (Andrews with Rolph 2000). In this Jean Andrews emerges as a person who, despite negative life experiences, has triumphed over adversity with a sense of humour intact. The Booths (1998) devoted one chapter, 'Still Family', to two stories which 'were so compelling that as researchers we are best letting them speak for themselves' (p.122). They use arguments around ownership to justify this: 'Ownership of the story rests where it lies instead of being countermanded by the researcher's claim to interpret its significance' (p.12).

This narrative chapter is juxtaposed with a more traditional 'top-down' approach to analysing what enables some offspring of parents with learning disabilities to flourish in a chapter called 'Risk, Resilience and Competence' where people's autobiographical accounts are used to demonstrate an academic argument. The tightrope that the Booths walk here is one that any inclusive researchers who do not have the luxury of pursuing unfunded research must negotiate. Many funders of applied social research, in this case the Joseph Rowntree Foundation, expect more than open-ended methodological explorations. They (probably rightly) expect some practical benefit to come from their investment in terms of lessons learnt. Thus the researcher, however committed to representing people with learning disabilities as whole people and in their own words, is pushed to offer analyses which are of more obvious practical application. The result is sometimes a compromise. This particular book is a good example of researchers trying to remain true to their ethical commitment to narrative research which allows people space for self-representation while at the same time meeting the expectations of funders and others who expect the researcher to offer more than just people's unvarnished words.

Ownership is probably key to genuinely inclusive research and it is in this area that judgements are most difficult. Researchers have certainly been very aware of ownership issues and we would suggest that this explains why more concrete and practical subjects have been favoured. As I (JW) discovered in 1988, choosing an abstract academic question like the meaning of adulthood does not make it easy for the researcher to share the research with respondents (Walmsley 1991). As a rule of thumb, one can suggest that the more abstract the topic, the less likely it is that people with learning disabilities will have shared fully in producing the analysis and findings.

Chappell, Goodley and Lawthorn (2001) set out to explore issues around the understandings people have of the social model of disability. Using analysis of interviews with self advocates, they propose that although people do not know about the social model as a concept, they do have insights into the barriers people with learning disabilities experience. Ownership by people with learning disabilities was quite limited. The paper is far from accessible and, although valuable insights are offered, the accompanying analysis appears to be very much the work of the named authors. By contrast, finding out about people's experiences of work is something more concrete for people with learning disabilities to tackle and to understand. There can be added value in their being the interviewers and playing a major role in data analysis (see Palmer *et al.* 1999).

We would, however, argue that more sophisticated analysis is possible using the data generated in more concrete applied research, but that many inclusive researchers, including ourselves, have held back in relation to data analysis because of the perceived need to work in ways that enable people with learning disabilities to come alongside. A certain dishonesty is attached to this self-denial because, as we have pointed out, quite sophisticated analyses on the methodology have been published, usually in non-accessible publications. Why is methodological sophistication permissible, but data analysis is not? Where projects address issues relating to the lives of people with high support needs and limited means of communication, ownership is even more problematic. Such projects tend to address ways in which such people can be known, and ways in which they can communicate. They cover issues like talking to people who know the person well, how to record someone's life history, listen with the heart, dream, etc. (Sanderson 1998). Actually eliciting the views of people without speech on particular aspects of life has made far less progress than it has with people who do speak, sign or otherwise communicate fairly complex ideas. The 'quotes', if such they can be called, tend to be in the third rather than first person. There is no way of knowing for certain whether the subjects of these studies have wanted to be included, have known what they were engaged in, or are aware of how they are being represented. It is another example of inclusion in research tending to be the preserve of people who have greater facility with speech, who can, literally, 'find a voice' and 'speak up'.

In surveying the body of work where the words and experiences of people with learning disabilities are the focus, we can see three contrasting trends. The first is for the words to be allowed to 'speak for themselves'. Thus *Know Me As I Am* and *Good Times Bad Times* were conceived. People emerge in these stories in quite rounded ways, but the readers have to do the interpretation for themselves. The second is for the researcher to use people's accounts to portray victims; people who need sympathy, understanding and better services (Booth and Booth 1994). The third is to depict heroes; people who triumph over adversity, demonstrating resilience in the face of negative experiences, such as Rolph's life historians (2000). In all these trends they appear as competent, defying traditional assumptions about their presumed intellectual incapacity. Most frequently what they ask for is straightforward and reasonable – an ordinary life. Although most researchers working in inclusive modes would not admit it, we can see in all three trends the influence of normalization. The whole people are just that – normal human beings with the hopes and fears the rest of us have. The victims need the help of ordinary citizens and services. As far as heroes are concerned, here the task is to reverse the cycle of devaluation and portray positive images. What has been done in the name of inclusive research to date furthers the normalization philosophy well.

We do not say this is wrong. People should be treated with respect and dignity and have every right to expect that their lives are fulfilled. What we do ask is whether that is the whole story or if, as Trish Webb found, there is more to it than that.

Co-writing

The writing up stage is another where efforts have been made to develop partnership working between researchers/authors and people with learning disabilities. *Good Times Bad Times*, 'Mabel Cooper's Life Story' and the work I did with Jackie Downer to write 'Shouting the Loudest' (1997) are instances already referred to in this book. It is interesting to note a gradual shift over time from non-disabled authors writing solo as experts and quoting people with learning disabilities verbatim in soundbites to co-written accounts. This is exemplified by collections edited by the same person, Linda Ward. *Values and Visions* (Philpot and Ward 1994) is almost entirely authored by experts (there's one exception where Margaret Flynn co-authored with her brother), though most of the chapters cite the views or experiences of people with learning disabilities verbatim. *Advocacy and Empowerment* (Ward 1998) has six chapters co-authored by people with learning disabilities. To date, relatively few publications are authored solely by people with learning disabilities.

Some authors are at pains to explain exactly how they approached the co-writing task (Atkinson and Cooper 2000; Walmsley with Downer 1997), though others gloss over this aspect. 'Woman to Woman', a co-written chapter by Doris Clark, Tracey Fry (self advocates) and Jackie Rodgers (researcher) (1998) is one where the process is not described. Although some of the ideas of the self advocate authors appear in italicized quotes, exactly what input they made to the commentary is unclear. Another chapter in the same volume by Whittell, Ramcharan and members of People First Cardiff and the Vale called 'Self Advocacy: Speaking Up for Ourselves and Each Other' is much more explicit:

> This chapter has been written in cooperation... A visit was made to meet and talk with the members and the discussion was taped. After this was transcribed, a draft of the chapter was sent to the group – together with a version on audio tape – so they could check it to make sure they were happy with how it sounded. (Whittell *et al.* 1998, p.39)

Although one might have a few more questions to ask about the process, we would argue that when non-disabled researchers co-author with people with learning disabilities they should always address how it was done. Not only does it assist others who may want to undertake such work, but it is also, we would argue, more honest to clarify exactly how the ideas of people with learning disabilities have been transferred from oral to written accounts, and how far the ideas are owned by people with learning disabilities.

Yet another approach has been adopted by Val Williams. She has published work in her own name about the research undertaken by the groups she worked with, the Bristol, Swindon and Norton self advocacy researchers (1999, 2002). These researchers have also published their own accounts (Palmer *et al.* 1999; Swindon People First 2002). What of the interests of the researcher who co-authors? This is an interesting area. On the one hand, ghost writing does not win many plaudits. We noted in relation to Cooper's autobiography (1997) that she offered Atkinson the opportunity to have her name on the chapter, and that Atkinson refused. As a professional academic, Atkinson needs to have her name on publications. Part of the contract academics have with employers is that they should publish. In this case, and most others we are aware of, any injustice is remedied by the researcher writing about the process; thus gaining the professional recognition denied by a scrupulous adherence to the ethical precepts of inclusive research. One might counter this with the proposition that people with learning disabilities have gained no recognition for their part in infinite numbers of research projects, far more than bend the other way. However, if inclusive research depends upon the support of non-disabled allies, there is potentially at least some injustice if the name(s) of those who have made it possible are deliberately omitted from the authorship in publications, or the role they played is unclear. There is also potential for dishonesty about how the work was carried out. Two wrongs do not make a right.

Accessibility

Accessibility is key to inclusive research in learning disability. It is an absolutely fundamental principle. If, as is the case, most people with learning disabilities cannot read, then imagination is needed to ensure that research findings are open to them. The publications emanating from inclusive research have come to be seen as a means to inform people with learning disabilities; to stimulate their interest in discussion in groups and offering their own insights. For example, the Norah Fry Research Centre's Plain Facts initiative has published a number of very short, plain language illustrated briefings, backed up by audio tapes, covering subjects of likely interest including:

Housing and support options

Living with another family (adult placements)

Making complaints

Closing the last hospitals

College and adult education

Choosing staff

Relationships

Fair shares for all. (Simons 1999, p.48)

There is evidence that this initiative has been widely taken up by self advocacy groups, performing an important educational as well as research dissemination function (Townsley 1998).

In an evaluation of Plain Facts, Townsley (1998) found that the most popular subjects amongst users with learning disabilities were Plain Facts 6 on College and Adult Education, Plain Facts 5 on Supported Employment, and Plain Facts 3 on Making Complaints. She comments that this may be because of their subject matter and style: 'They are based on projects which had very clear outcomes for people with learning disabilities themselves. They also used plenty of quotes and real life examples to illustrate the main points' (Townsley 1998, p.88).

Another method which has been used frequently is the 'short accessible version' of a longer more theoretical discussion. I (JW) wrote one of these for my chapter in Traustadottir and Johnson's (2000) book 'Caring: A Place in the World' (Walmsley 2000a). This was an exploration of the contradictory role that caring plays in people's lives – on the one hand as 'cared for', on the other as carers, sometimes unrecognized and exploited. Yet some women do seem to want to be carers. It was based in part on my PhD. As I look at the short version, I realize that I had dramatically simplified the rather complex argument to three questions:

> Is it true that women with intellectual disabilities need to be cared for?
>
> Do some women with intellectual disabilities care for others?
>
> Does caring give women with intellectual disabilities a place in the world? (Walmsley 2000a, p.191)

The rest of the short version is devoted to a thumbnail sketch of three women whose life stories I used in the chapter to illustrate the argument. At one level, I feel rather proud of this as it manages to concretize an abstract argument. At another, I know that this fails to convey the nuances of debate that the chapter represents; issues important to women with learning disabilities potentially.

Perhaps a more commonly encountered approach is the use of symbols, drawings and plain text to 'translate' for people with learning disabilities. CHANGE, 'the council of organizations representing people with learning disabilities who have a sensory impairment', produced such a document for the Mental Health Foundation's *Building Expectations Inquiry into Community Services and Opportunities for People with Learning Disabilities* (no date). They use 'short words and pictures' (p.1). To us, the short words represent a reasonably coherent summary of the recommendations. The pictures do not add a great deal of value, except as a way of breaking up the page. In the Equal People course, addressed to a mixed audience of people with learning disabilities, family members and staff, we used variants of these approaches. Each topic is introduced with a short, highly illustrated four pages based upon video or audio material. The rest of each topic is more detailed and less illustrated. Story So Far and Key Points boxes summarize the information and ideas, intended for people working as supporters to use to explain the less accessible text. Thus in a topic called 'Working Together for Welcoming Communities' the text was summarized as shown in Box 9.1.

Symbols such as Makaton have also been used as means of making information accessible, though lack of consensus on one set of symbols to use for people with learning disabilities in any context makes symbol use problematic.

Box 9.1 Story so far

We've been thinking about communities.

Sometimes building communities means helping people join in with their local community through sharing leisure and work opportunities.

Sometimes it means helping people get a sense of themselves as a separate community.

Sometimes it means getting together to decide what a particular community wants for itself. (Open University 1996, p.59)

A discussion in print cannot do justice to the potential of audio, video and ICT as vehicles for imparting information. Although audio is very frequently used, being inexpensive to produce and needing relatively low level technology to use, very little has appeared in print on the best ways to structure and convey research findings. Our own experience suggests that drama may well be the ideal medium, though in itself that raises issues about representation and whether those with learning disabilities are the best people to be the actors if their speech is indistinct.

There is little consensus as to what makes for accessibility in presenting information to people with learning disabilities. As we have mentioned, illustrated plain text versions with audio tapes appear to be most successful as a means of disseminating research findings (Plain Facts, Equal People), though symbols, line drawings, videos and websites all have their supporters, and some drawbacks. At the same time, a supporter in the form of a human being is recognized to be a vital adjunct to enabling people with learning disabilities to understand. Efforts have been made to supply short versions of longer papers to facilitate this (Atkinson et al. 2000; Open University 1996; Traustadottir and Johnson 2000).

This brief survey suggests that, whatever mode is used, it is far easier to convey concrete information than it is to convey abstract or theoretical ideas in accessible modes. Accessibility is more readily accomplished for people with relatively mild learning disabilities. It is really problematic for people with high support needs and/or additional sensory impairments. In this sense, the move to create accessible research findings mirrors some of the fundamental challenges in inclusive learning disability research. There is a tendency to privilege concrete applied research over more theoretical or abstract topics and to privilege more able people with learning disabilities.

As far as methodology is concerned, as opposed to content or how the research was actually carried out, researchers have been less concerned about accessibility. Although Val Williams is careful to explain in 'Researching Together' (1999) that it was written with the (self advocate) researchers' approval, most people have been prepared to discuss the ethics and the principles in academic texts. In *Good Times Bad Times*, 'The Helpers' Story' is the one place where the non-disabled women found a voice. Even researchers fully committed to inclusion like Ward and Simons (1998), Rolph (2000) and Mitchell (1997) have been prepared to commit to paper quite complex arguments about methodology. This book is itself an example of the permission we have granted ourselves to discuss our role, and the dilemmas we have encountered. Why methodology is a permissible area for 'research talk' when content is not is an interesting question. Through the examples shown here, certain limitations of accessibility become obvious. Complex abstract arguments are conveyed using biographies, or are squeezed out altogether where symbols and line drawings are used. The belief that accessibility is vital to inclusion is one that was initially argued in disability studies by, inter alia, Zarb (1992) and Barnes (1996). However, this position has not been tenaciously held and the arguments for departing from making all research ideas accessible to people with average or poor reading abilities appear to have won the day. Shakespeare argues:

> Academic work on disability may not always be accessible. I believe writers should use plain language, but this does not equal a duty to be immediately comprehensible. Theories and concepts and social reality itself will often be complex, nuanced and difficult. If Disability Studies is to capture this richness, it will have to use ideas and develop analyses which may not be transparent and simple. (Shakespeare 1996, p.118)

He quoted Einstein to make his point: 'Make everything as simple as possible, but not simpler'.

'Nothing about us without us' is a powerful message and one which appears at first sight to capture the high moral ground. However, it is oversimplistic to use this as the only criterion for worthwhile research and it risks reducing learning disability research to a restricted number of topics and a basic level of interpretation.

Exploitation

One major criticism of research 'on' people is that it is exploitative. However, it has also been argued, and with plausibility, that research 'with' people can also be exploitative. Certainly qualitative research, which comprises almost all inclusive learning disability research, is open to exploitation by the researcher. The person with learning disabilities may well be in a situation where his or her words or story are recorded and used in ways which he or she would not approve of if they knew about it. The moral climate associated with ownership has changed dramatically as inclusive research ideas have begun to infiltrate the literature. From 1990 to 1998, the Open University's undergraduate course on learning disability (of which JW was chair) offered students an option to record a life story with a person with learning disabilities. Many, around 150 a year over ten years, took this option, and some brilliant and ethical work was done. So was some work which was far from ethical, where students had not taken the trouble to seek informed consent; where they failed to recognize the power relationships involved in the interview; where indeed they appeared to have learnt very little. I would see it as unthinkable to offer such an option today because of the increased awareness of the rights people have over their stories, an awareness fostered by sophisticated work in oral history and feminist studies. See a detailed and comprehensive discussion in Ken Plummer's *Documents of Life* (2001), which has influenced inclusive researchers and self advocates.

It is not possible to assert that high ethical standards around ownership, rights and informed consent are always maintained. Although theorizing has developed, the drive to involve users may actually have led to an increase in violation of people's rights to control ways in which their life stories are used. It is most uncomfortable to see 'users' pulled into training sessions to parade the ways in which they have been victimized, in the interests of enlightening would-be social workers or nurses. The temptation for someone in whom few have taken a real interest to offer all they have, their experiences of oppression, in return for a few minutes of fame or a small payment must be great. But does the end justify the means?

Should researchers have a distinctive voice?

This point has been touched upon in a number of places so far and it is far from trivial. We have noted that some non-disabled researchers hold back when it comes to analysing the experiential accounts collected from people with learning disabilities. Others do proffer analysis, some-times to meet the expectations of funders, while at the same time pre-serving space for the authentic voice. Others still show no compunction about taking people's words and using them to make an academic or practice-related argument.

One way around the dilemma that many inclusive researchers face when it comes to having a voice is to provide a commentary on the pro-cess. Thus a space is preserved for the researcher's own story of the re-search. This is usually a reflexive account (see, for example, Atkinson and Williams 1990) which makes forays into the literature around methodology to show where connections can be made to other related fields. Less often, the researchers permit themselves the luxury of some observations on connections between learning disability issues and those raised in the wider literature. Traustadottir and Johnson (2000), for example, draw some parallels between the lives of women with intel-lectual disabilities explored in their book and the feminist/disability studies literature. Non-disabled allies are also prepared to work as advo-cates, to draw from their work messages for service providers, families, communities, policy makers or other academics, usually pointing out their role in making the lives of people with learning disabilities more impoverished than they need to be (Booth and Booth 1994, 1998; Flynn *et al.* 1997; McCarthy 2000, in press; and many others).

Where people committed to inclusive methodologies hold back is in actually analysing the accounts by people with learning disabilities in anything other than a very basic way. Thus, to date there have been no methodologically sophisticated studies of the practice of self advocacy organizations, or of the work of self advocacy supporters, despite self advocacy being, arguably, the most significant development in learning disability in recent years. What work there is, by Bersani (1998) for example, is often adulatory and uncritical; or is undertaken in a co-researching paradigm where people with learning disabilities are seen as equal partners whose role is beyond scrutiny (Mitchell 1997; Williams 1999); or is used to draw up experience-based accounts of the work of self advocates from their own perspective (Goodley 1996) where others are responsible for any failures that develop. This is a risky position for researchers to adopt. We would not want to undermine self advocacy, but we would suggest that the assumption that self advocates are always the best (and only) people to examine the phenomenon that is self advocacy is misguided.

What is the impact?

The impact of inclusive research has been considerable, mainly in practice settings, but also in prompting researchers from other traditions in learning disability to consider where they and their work stands (Kellett and Nind 2001). There is an impact on people's sense of themselves as competent contributors rather than always subject to other people's interpretations and constructs, and this should not be underestimated.

There is very little sign, however, that other areas of academia and social action where empowerment, inclusion and participation are seen as important have been attending to debates in learning disability. Other than people like Ann Chappell writing on behalf of people with learning disabilities in the disability literature, there is little discussion in disability studies on the matters we have been discussing here, and none at all in feminism. Unless allies take the arguments into these areas (as Chappell has done) it seems unlikely that they will be incorporated.

As far as practice is concerned, there is a more optimistic story to tell. We have already noted that the imperative to involve users and carers is a continuing encouragement to inclusive research, for this is where ways of effectively involving users can be tried out. The prestigious UK Community Care Award in 2001 went to a Mencap project in Manchester which aimed to help people tell their life stories using drama. This was inspired by *Know Me As I Am*, which was quite a tribute 11 years after publication. The White Paper *Valuing People* (Department of Health 2000) was produced in part by using consultations with people with learning disabilities. An accessible version was produced which owes much to the work done on making research accessible described in this chapter involving plain English, illustrations and an accompanying audio tape. Subsequent research is including the perspectives of self advocacy organizations.

At a more detailed level, we have noted that Townsley and Macadam's work (1996) on involving users in staff recruitment has been adopted in some English local authorities and there are many examples of services drawing on users to undertake service evaluations. As is often the case with all kinds of research, the impact of these evaluations has been less well described than the process and results. One throwaway remark in Whittaker's account is telling:

> We produced a report and a tape. We said some things that the bosses didn't like. The report was not allowed to be shown to staff... Nothing changed as a result. (Whittaker 1997, p.28)

From some perspectives, however, there appears to be a danger of a service-centred perspective of the world being imposed on self advocacy's agenda, partly through the emphasis on people being involved in research. This is one of Aspis's main criticisms (1997) that self advocacy becomes just another tool in the service provider's toolbox; a position she shares with Finkelstein (1999) who argues that emancipatory research must have as its focus explorations of avenues of political change which will further the interests of disabled people. If they are undertaking service evaluations or even applied research, the energies of people with learning disabilities are channelled away from changing their world for the better to changing or attempting to change services. The outcomes of some inclusive research projects (not all) suggest this may be a point well worth pondering.

Whose career benefits?

One of the most vexed questions in inclusive research is who benefits? Whilst we would agree with those who argue that involvement in research does indeed empower people (Atkinson 2001; Williams 2002), it is above all the allies who stand to gain. Goodley (1996), Mitchell (1997), Rolph (2000), Atkinson (2001) and Williams (2002) all have gained PhDs from their inclusive work. Such accolades are not open to their co-workers – another instance where the idealized world of inclusive research collides with the unequal world beyond. In terms of publications, Williams argues:

> This is one area in which non disabled participatory researchers effectively have their power curtailed. The usual expectation of a string of publications from a project just is not possible, without usurping the rights of the self advocates. (Williams 2002, p.247)

She points out that her colleagues have done better than she has (p.247). However, given her academic career, she stands to gain more. As far as advancement goes, publications matter to academics more than they matter to anyone else!

There are undoubtedly more subtle gains for self advocates who do research. Seeing one's name in print, having one's ideas taken seriously, travel to conferences, invitations to prestigious events, all these opportunities open up to successful co-researchers. Whether they are brief appearances on the world's academic stages or more enduring fame remains to be seen.

Ultimately, it has to be acknowledged that the allies, the non-disabled people who support research, stand to gain most in career terms. It is true that we may have to stand back and let co-researchers take the plaudits or have their names on publications we have midwived, but in the end, as we have shown time after time, the allies gain their rewards.

Conclusion

Debates over representation, ownership, accessibility and personal benefit are alive and well in inclusive research. Whilst there will always be difficulties and challenges, again we need to remember that a great deal has been accomplished in a short time. The challenge now, to ourselves as well as others, is to take these debates back to people with learning disabilities, so that the co-construction of the inclusive research enterprise can continue to challenge boundaries and ultimately change lives.

CHAPTER 10

What Has Been Achieved?

This brief chapter reviews what has been achieved to date in inclusive research and summarizes some of the outstanding unresolved issues which have emerged in the course of the book.

From Edgerton onwards, researchers have found ways of working with people with learning disabilities which were unimaginable when a more pessimistic view of the impairment was prevalent. If, as has been argued (Stainton 2000), the history of learning disability is in part at least a history of swings from optimism to pessimism about the degree to which the impact of the impairment can be remedied, we are living in one of the optimistic eras. Both normalization/social role valorization and the social model of disability are essentially optimistic. Normaliza-tion/social role valorization is premised on the belief that if attitudes and services change, then a better life can be secured for people with learning disabilities. The barriers approach to disability, exemplified in the social model, is also optimistic. If the barriers come down, then the obstacles to equal citizenship will also be lowered. The impact of this belief can be seen in many aspects of policy. For example, the English White Paper *Valuing People* (Department of Health 2000) is essentially about securing for people with learning disabilities rights, independ-ence, choice and inclusion (p.3).

There have been, however, notable limits to inclusion. Probably the most striking of these is the absence of voices of those people who do not speak, sign or otherwise convey their views in a way which others can readily understand. Whilst imaginative and heroic efforts have been made to access the inner worlds of people with profound disabilities (see Goode 1989, for example), there is little evidence that they can be enabled to represent themselves directly, rather than through the eyes of people close to them, or empathetic researchers. This begs the question of who are people with learning disabilities and does it matter that not all of them can be included in research. Oliver (1990) has argued that representativeness is a red herring used by people who want to impede the empowerment of disabled people. While this has some validity, it does not take into account the heterogeneity of disabled people, or within the broad group labelled people with learning disabilities. Most inclusive research reviewed in this book to date has included only those people with mild impairments. Emancipatory and action research models, because they require involvement and control in all aspects of the research enterprise, are inherently more problematic than participatory research which allows more flexibility in defining what inclusion is.

The examples we have quoted in Part 2 suggest that it should not be assumed that those people with learning disabilities who have many of the trappings of social adulthood and citizenship are necessarily better equipped to get inside the worlds of people with more profound impairments than anyone else. Much self advocate initiated research to date has, as we noted above in Chapter 7, been directed at other self advocates, and explicitly in the case of the US-based project described by Ward and Trigler (2001), the Bristol Self Advocacy Group (Palmer *et al.* 1999) and the Norton self advocacy researchers' project (Williams 2002) has been to gain a sense of how others' experiences compared with those of the researchers.

The question of which disabled people should be in charge of research has been addressed by requirements that emancipatory research is accountable to democratic organizations of disabled people (Priestley 1999; Zarb 1992). Debates around solidarity versus diversity have been aired in the disability studies literature, particularly around ethnicity and disability (see Vernon 1996), but also in relation to women's issues (Sheldon 1999). The neglect of issues affecting people with learning disabilities by physically disabled people has also been discussed at some length (Chappell 1997; Traustadottir and Johnson 2000). The evidence so far suggests that self advocate researchers may be as likely to ignore the interests of people who cannot speak for themselves, as

people with spinal cord injuries have been to neglect mental impairments, or older people with acquired impairments.

Arguments for inclusive research, like policies for social inclusion,
may be in danger of recreating subdivisions within the population of
people with learning disabilities – the 'high grades' and 'low grades'.
The high grades can be reabsorbed into 'valued social roles' by imaginative and empowering practices. It remains to be shown that this is
possible for low grades, or that more articulate people can ensure that
the interests of those less well able to voice opinions are protected.

The question whether we can manipulate the environment has been
in part answered by the projects reviewed in this book. If the environent
is changed, people with learning disabilities can contribute experiences
and insights to illuminate research into learning disability. They can also
develop the expertise to undertake tasks associated with carrying out
research.

The evidence is that people with learning disabilities can identify research questions, or come to appreciate and contribute to thinking
about research questions posed by others. They can work out questions
to ask, act as interviewers, assist in evaluations of services, provide valuable information as informants, contribute to written research reports,
act as advisors, help to access other informants with learning disabilities
and play a major part in dissemination. In many of these tasks inclusion
means added value. Most obviously this is when people with learning
disabilities are the experts on their own lives, on the questions to ask
about services. But it is also where they are less trammelled by the ethical
dilemmas that sometimes tie researchers in knots; for example, the
sound advice about corrections to spellings and grammar offered to the
editors of *Know Me As I Am*. It is at the very least highly plausible that
some researchers with learning disabilities obtain information which
others might find more challenging to elicit. For example, Central England People First's project (2000) which investigates the perceptions
that front-line staff have of their training needs has yielded fascinatingly
naive views of what training should be, as well as insights into how service providers respond to people with learning disabilities asking questions! Unfortunately, like so much of what self advocacy organizations

do and know, it has not been written up, so remains a somewhat hidden and marginal activity.

But the 'can' questions are less well answered if we consider the more cognitive tasks associated with research such as awareness of the literature, data analysis and theorizing. Here, although we have cited some isolated instances of people with learning disabilities' contributions, these are rare and many appear suspect. Almost invariably a supporter or co-researcher's hand is present and the degree to which it is their thinking that is represented is often hard to fathom. This may not matter. More often than not research is a collaborative enterprise, where the distinctive contributions of one person rather than another are not explicit, and nor could they be. However, it is worth pondering what this means about the nature of research. If research is only 'finding out', as a number of inclusive research projects have termed it (Palmer *et al.* 1999; Williams 1999), then inclusion is less problematic. We do harbour some lingering doubts, though, about what this means for learning disability research. It does appear to confine it to relatively concrete applied areas like the nature of service provision and it privileges the role of personal experience. Abstract theorizing, such as that which at times seems to dominate disability studies (see, for example, the excellent 'Theory and Experience' special issue of *Disability and Society* 2000) is avoided because it cannot be inclusive. Maybe it should be avoided anyway, because it is remote and often hard to fathom (Corker's *Differences, Conflations and Foundations* 2000, for example). But unless we try it we won't know and learning disability studies may remain the untheorized experience-based poor relation of its intellectually wealthier cousins in disability studies, feminism and black studies. To illuminate this discussion we can look to the road travelled by feminists:

> All too often the slogan 'the personal is political'...became a means of encouraging women to think that the experience of discrimination, exploitation or oppression automatically corresponded with an understanding of the ideological and institutional apparatus shaping one's social status... When women internalized the idea the describing their own woes was synonymous with a political consciousness, the progress of the feminist movement was stalled. (hooks 1984, pp.24–5, quoted in Sheldon 1999, pp.648–9)

One might tentatively suggest that this is where people with learning disabilities are in relation to understanding their oppression through narratives of personal experience. Disability studies and feminism have passed through the stage where narrating pain and oppression is what it is all about. However, just because others have done so does not necessarily mean that learning disability research will follow the pattern. People with learning disabilities can contribute in many ways to research on situations where they possess unique and valuable experience. But to argue that they have the expertise to carry out or control all aspects of research is to go beyond the realms of the rational into a world where the reality of intellectual impairment is wished away and difference is denied. If this is the argument, then there is no reason to confine the involvement of researchers with learning disabilities to learning disability related topics, because they will have the research expertise to do research on any topic.

In the third and final part of the book we look to resolving some of the vexed issues raised in Parts 1 and 2. We cannot promise all the answers, but we believe we have some useful directions to suggest, to take us beyond the stage we have now reached.

PART 3

Beyond Rhetoric to New Realities

So far we have reviewed the origins of inclusive research and celebrated some of its achievements. We have looked in some detail at the ways in which it has been conducted and aired some doubts about its present state. It is clear from the previous chapters that we remain committed to inclusive research. However we believe its development is stalled as researchers and people with learning disabilities look for ever more inventive ways of enabling people with learning disabilities to 'do' research. While we believe that this may be important for some people, it does seem as if it has wrongly become a central issue. We are not necessarily in the business of teaching people with learning disabilities to become researchers, though this is an option for some people. Rather we believe that in addition to exploring ways by which people with learning disabilities may become researchers we also need to be examining with them the kind of research they want; the questions they would like to see answered; how they want to use it and what (if any involvement) they want in the actual doing of it. We also believe that some hard work and some resources have to be invested into making it possible for people with learning disabilities and their organizations to do research. Building research capacity will, we believe, be essential if inclusive research is not to be a marginalized and tokenistic activity.

We are not alone in feeling that there is some clarification and honest reflection needed if inclusive research is not to be discredited and devalued. The following quotation from Braye (2000) on user involvement and participation in social care sums up the broad issues well:

Three things are clear. First, the language of participation is complex: the same thing means different things to different people, and the same concept may be known by a number of different terms. Second, the apparent consensus that participation is a good thing masks major differences of ideology between different interest groups. Third, ends and means are confused; participation is presented both as a means to an end and an end in itself, and at times the purpose and the process appear indivisible. (Braye 2000, p.9)

Suzy Braye goes on to write: 'The fundamental contest is between rhetoric and reality' (p.9). Although the book is on a different though related topic, user involvement in social care, its messages are also relevant to inclusive research:

1.   The language is often confusing, masking as much as it communicates.

2.   Many people agree that what we have termed inclusive research is a 'good thing', but they may well be coming from different ideological standpoints.

3.   At times the ends and means are confused – is it the process or the outcome which is most important?

Part 3 of this book seeks to explore the gap between rhetoric and reality and to propose some new realities for people with learning disabilities and non-disabled researchers working together. Chapter 11 focuses on the role of the researcher in inclusive research. Chapter 12 outlines some possible ways of working together to create truly inclusive research.

CHAPTER 11

Beyond Rhetoric...

In Chapter 8 we discussed the language adopted by inclusive research-ers to describe what they do – supporters, co-researchers, research part-ners, inquirers – and suggested that not only is this confusing, but it can also be misleading and mask some very real skills that researchers have to use if they are effectively to support inclusive research. These labels also conceal the often continuing power imbalances which persist in such research.

In contrast to the prevailing practice, which takes for granted the roles and skills of the researcher, our argument will be that their roles deserve more than just the passing and self-effacing mention they often receive in the literature. Supporting inclusive research is a skilled activ-ity. It needs be recognized as such because if it is not then researchers are silenced and left almost ashamed of their skills. It also makes it very dif-ficult to train people in this way of working if we pretend it is 'just sup-port' as some have claimed (Williams 1999). The power imbalances between people with learning disabilities and the researchers continue to be camouflaged by a rhetoric of participation. This kind of hidden devaluing is often difficult for people with learning disabilities to do anything about. Until there is more debate about the roles played by all participants in inclusive research, we believe it will be trapped in confu-sion which ultimately fails to serve the cause of people with learning disabilities.

One of the keys to progress is to clarify what roles we can play as supporters of inclusive research and how we can develop our skills and help new entrants to develop theirs. This is the focus of Chapter 11.

The final chapter brings together the two voices of inclusive research to explore some of the ways in which they may create new realities together.

What roles do non-disabled researchers play in inclusive research?

In answering this question we have to find our way through a stack of issues which have camouflaged and distorted the roles of people in research. These are the confusing language and confusing roles which are applied to the non-disabled researcher in inclusive research.

Language and terminology

In exploring the researcher's role in inclusive research, the first difficulty is in terms of the language which is used to label the roles of different people in the research.

Inclusive research has spawned a new language. As discussed in Chapter 8, this language struggles to find words to describe the work of the inclusive researchers (whether they have a disability or not) and those who would have been subject to it in non-inclusive research. A whole range of terms has been coined to describe the roles of people engaged in inclusive research:

- Mitchell (1997), who studied the impact of self advocacy on families, called her colleagues (and by implication herself) co-researchers.

- Rolph (2000) described the people she worked with as 'life historians' while she remained without a named role.

- Williams (1999) calls herself a supporter; the self advocates she works with are the 'real' researchers.

- Atkinson *et al.* (2000) refer to themselves as helpers while the women with learning disabilities became known as the 'disabled women'.

- Kelley Johnson refers to research partners (personal communication, 1999). Interestingly this is also the term adopted in citizen advocacy circles for the person who enjoys the benefit of an advocate.

- The informants of Knox *et al.* (2000) were 'experts' while the researchers were 'inquirers'.

- Van Hove (1999) describes research with people with learning disabilities in Belgium as 'cooperative research'.

This is a confusing list. It is difficult to know if the writers are using the terms interchangeably or applying them differently because there is little attempt by anyone actually to explore what these roles mean in practice or where the boundaries between roles lie.

One of the interesting things to note in these definitions is the negation of the researcher role or the blurring of the boundaries between roles of researcher and those involved in the research who are not by training or experience researchers in the formal sense. In at least some cases there is an effort through language to reverse the power roles. The researcher becomes an 'inquirer' and people with learning disabilities become 'experts', for example. We argue that the boundaries of the researchers' roles and their expertise and limits need to be a subject of open reflection and discussion by those taking part in the research.

For this purpose, we need to reclaim the word researcher as it describes our skills and experience. Anything else takes away from the task. There may not be one label for the researcher doing inclusive research. Underlying the researcher's work is a strong commitment to inclusion and empowerment. However, the way this commitment is played out in a particular piece of research may be very different, depending on the people involved and the nature of the project. What does seem to be important to us is that clear language is used which is understood by all those taking part in the research. For example Box 11.1 shows how reflection led to a particular use of language between two researchers, one labelled as having a disability and one not.

Confusing roles

One of the hidden stories about inclusive research is frequently the role played by the researcher. We should comment that these researchers are

Box 11.1 Finding a way through the language maze

I (KJ) was one of the initiators of a project to examine the barriers which women with disabilities experience in accessing cervical screening. The project also employed Ria Strong, a woman with a disability, as 'co-researcher'. Ria and I struggled for some time to come up with labels which felt comfortable to both of us. Co-researcher immediately positions her as a woman with a disability and as someone with a lesser power role in the research. In fact she was employed for her skills (in computers), her networks and her experience as an advocate. Neither of us felt comfortable with co-researcher. Our concern was validated when one organization made it clear they did not want to talk with the co-researcher but with the *researcher*. The university employed Ria as a research assistant. This at least stated formally what she was in management terms but when we developed a list of jobs this too did not seem adequately to describe what she was doing. In the end we decided that in this instance we were both researchers, but that I had the lead role because of my experience and because the responsibility for the research was finally mine. Together we carefully worked out what our separate roles were in the research and we now raise the issue of language in public forums about the project. Ria and I intend to write about the issues that arose for us in this work relationship at the end of the project. (Kelley Johnson, unpublished note)

overwhelmingly women. Sometimes their stories are told (see, for example, Atkinson *et al.*'s chapter 'The Helpers' Story', 2000), but frequently they are not or referred to only in passing. Like supporters who work with self advocates, the roles and qualities are described in deceptively simple terms. Williams, for example, reduces her role to such activities as driving the car (Williams 1999).

Although one cannot overstate the importance of such practical supports, without which few self advocates could aspire to do much research, we would contend that, to be effective, researchers need to do a great deal more than merely provide these practical services.

Furthermore this negation of skills is like a reflection of the devaluing of people with learning disabilities (see Chapter 4).

One of the most common forms of inclusive research has been the autobiography. Here some researchers have been explicit in describing what is involved in assisting people to tell their stories. Atkinson, for example, describes in a series of papers, some co-written, how she worked with Mabel Cooper to create 'Mabel Cooper's Life Story' (Cooper 1997), and subsequent autobiographical accounts (see Atkinson 1997; Atkinson and Cooper 2000); something that was discussed in some depth in Chapter 8. An interesting paradox is that Cooper's original (1997) account, a much quoted chapter, is attributed to Cooper alone. Formally, Atkinson's role is not acknowledged, although in her account of their joint work Atkinson does mention Mabel's suggestion that her name should be included (Atkinson 1997). Another example of a researcher facilitating an autobiographical account is Sheena Rolph's work with Jean Andrews, shown in Box 11.2.

Much is hidden behind Jean's words: the processes of building trust, prompting, skilful editing of an oral account into something which

---

Box 11.2 The story teller's perspective: how I wrote this chapter

Jean writes of her experience in writing her story in the following terms:

> Sheena came here and saw me about it and we got together, didn't we. And I got to write the story, because I told the story. I told the story into a tape. Then Sheena types it out. Then we read it together, and I took bits out and put bits in. (Andrews with Rolph 2000, p.35)

---

flows easily in print; the stuff of qualitative methodological textbooks such as Ken Plummer's (2001) on life histories and Paul Thompson's (1988) on oral history. But in inclusive research it has become the convention to play down the skills of the researcher.

McCarthy (2000) describes a different role. She worked with women from Powerhouse, an East London organization for women who have been abused. McCarthy set herself the task of exploring the published research on abuse of women with learning disabilities with the three women, themselves with some claim to expertise given the function of Powerhouse and, as it transpired, their own experience. The process of this research is described in Box 11.3.

This process is a significantly different one to that employed with Mabel Cooper and Jean Andrews. Michelle was not setting out to tap into and

---

Box 11.3 The researcher's perspective

This chapter is the result of a number of conversations between four women, three of whom have learning disabilities. All conversations were taped, then transcribed by Michelle, who also edited them, adding some structure and contextualising comments and references. A draft of the chapter was put on tape for Anastasia, Pam and Deborah to listen to. They were then able to comment on it and thus also contribute to the editing process. When research findings on sexual abuse were discussed, Michelle presented these in as accessible way as possible, including using pictorial forms to represent percentages. (McCarthy with Anastasia, Pam and Deborah 2000, pp.48–9)

---

record direct personal experience. Rather she was sharing with the Powerhouse volunteers as fellow experts her experience of an area of academic knowledge hitherto unknown to them, and pooling ideas with them on the accuracy of the research vis-à-vis their own practice-derived knowledge. This involved summarizing a complex literature, making it accessible as far as possible and facilitating discussion, before assembling into written form and re-editing with the involvement of the three co-authors. Here is an instance where the researcher is overtly sharing her own knowledge and expertise as an academic in addition to the facilitating skills implied in the previous examples.

This example is relatively rare, or at least its acknowledgment is. Most inclusive researchers claim, at least in public, merely to be aids to recording and writing for publication – the concept of the 'writing hand' (Pecket Well College, quoted in Open University 1996, Work-book One). The process of authorship is often obscured, as with the chapter 'Telling People What You Think' written by four self advocates which is introduced thus:

> This work was researched and transcribed by the Bristol self advocacy Research Group which are people with intellectual talent. (Palmer *et al.* 1999, p.33)

The supporter's contribution is not described.

Similarly, Janice Slattery's chapter in Traustadottir and Johnson's edited book (2000) is entitled 'Family, Marriage, Friends and Work: This is My Life' and attributed to Janice 'with Kelley Johnson'. But my (KJ's) contribution is not explained. A reviewer of this book commented on this significant omission:

> I wonder how the other women worked together to produce the stories I read – not a minor detail considering that this is a rare attempt to publish the first person accounts of individuals who for the most part have difficulty communicating verbally and in writing; and their collaborators, apparently, were professionals. (Wickham 2001, p.215)

It is, one might suggest, typical of women to be prepared to remain in the background while others take the centre stage: behind every suc-cessful man is a...; behind every successful co-researcher is a...skilled researcher. The arguments for hiding the role of skilled women re-searchers behind the broad notion of supporter, co-researcher, partners, etc. are nowhere made explicit, though one is tempted to suggest that it is done with the best of motives, as a way of enhancing the image of the person with a learning disability as a competent adult, in other words social role valorization. Interestingly though, it also serves to undermine the empowerment of people with intellectual disabilities. Few women researchers (especially academics) would willingly give up their author-ship to refereed articles or other products on which they had worked with other researchers. We have argued elsewhere in this book that we researchers in learning disability are more influenced by a crude inter-pretation of normalization than we care to admit, an interpretation which attempts to deny difference. Like the endless changing terminology in the field, the proliferation of terms to describe the researcher may be an example of what Sinason (1992) bravely described as a manic desire to erase difference.

Ways forward

Inclusive research covers many different kinds of research. Perhaps we need to reclaim the labels that were used previously for people who worked in particular ways, for example, oral historian. But perhaps we also need to indicate in the label that we are committed to inclusive research. More importantly it seems that we need to be very clear ourselves about our boundaries. These should be a source of discussion early in the project with everyone who is involved in it. Questions that identify the kind of project we are working on, who is working on what and who wants to be involved in particular parts of the project are important issues which are rarely openly canvassed.

It should be clear from this discussion that we are not in a position to be prescriptive, but we do urge that researchers and those employing them are clear in their roles. It may be that in some projects people with learning disabilities initiate the description of the researcher's role. In other projects the researcher may undertake this task. It is then a subject for negotiation. Similarly we believe that the roles of people with learning disabilities (and others) involved in particular projects should be open for discussion and negotiation, nor should this be restricted to individuals involved. Projects which use a critical reference group as an advisory or management committee shaping the research design should also have clear boundaries which will differ depending on the nature of the project. Box 11.4 shows one example of the role of an advisory group. This was developed through discussion with advisory group members and then drafted by the researcher before going back to them for final approval.

Box 11.4 Learning Partners

The reference group

1. WHAT WE BELIEVE

We think it is very important that we share a set of beliefs about how the reference group might work.

- *Learning Partners* aims to assist people with intellectual disabilities to be included in their communities. It also aims to help change the attitudes of other community members. So the reference group should make sure that people with intellectual disabilities are included fully in its work.

- It is important that reference group members own the project from the beginning and are part of it till the end. This will help us make the project successful. It will also help us to make sure it is used after it is finished.

- It is important that all different views from members of the reference group are heard and that we come to agreements together about decisions for the project.

- All reference group members are seen as having a valued and important role in the project.

2. WHO SHOULD BE PART OF THE REFERENCE GROUP?

- The reference group should include one representative from all organizations and groups included in it.

- People with intellectual disabilities should be key representatives on the reference group.

- The reference group will be chaired by someone from Gawith Villa for the first three months. After that we will make a decision about how the meetings are chaired, for example a new person each meeting.

- The reference group should have a secretary who sends minutes and agendas to members within two weeks of a meeting.

- A financial report should be given to the reference group at least at three-monthly intervals for the information of the members.

- All unwaged workers should be paid $30 for their attendance at reference group meetings.

- All members of the reference group should report back to their organization about the work of the project. They should report any feedback from their organization to the reference group at each meeting.

- Unless otherwise agreed to, the project officer should provide a written progress report in plain English to each reference group meeting. This should clearly state the work done and raise problems and issues for discussion.

- The management group for the project should report to the reference group at each meeting.

3. HOW THE REFERENCE GROUP WILL WORK

- The reference group will meet every six weeks for the first three months of the project and then a new decision will be made about its meeting times.

- Agendas and minutes should be produced in large print and plain English.

- The project officer should be available for one hour before each reference group meeting to discuss issues with reference group members. Meetings should be kept to between one and two hours.

4. WHAT THE REFERENCE GROUP WILL DO

- Advice. The reference group will advise the project officer.

- Shaping the project. The reference group will actively help to design, carry out and evaluate the project.

- Providing skills and services. Some members may be asked from time to time to share their skills and experience.

- Payment. All unwaged workers will be paid for work done in the project. Sometimes members will become co-workers. Except where an organization has said it will give these things for free, people will be paid for work and time.

- Accountability. The reference group will provide accountability for the project. The project officer will make regular reports to the reference group and reports are also expected from partners on a regular basis where these are relevant.

- Gawith Villa and Deakin University are key partners in the project. Gawith Villa will be accountable to ANZ Trustees. A small management group will be appointed at the first reference group meeting.

- Appointment of staff. Staff for the project will be appointed through advertisement and interview.

- Reference group members may become part of subcommittees during the project.

- We expect that at a minimum reference group members will come to reference group meetings. When they are unable to do so it is important that they try to find someone else to come.

Should the researcher have a distinctive voice?

Given the camouflaging of the role of the researcher in many accounts of inclusive research, this is a live question. In our view the researcher should have some form of distinctive voice in the project to protect both them and the people they work with. We believe that this is important for a number of different reasons: because it is important for people with learning disabilities that their voices be heard clearly and unambiguously; because the research itself is richer and more credible when this happens; and because without a clear voice researchers can become devalued and burned out.

Without the researcher being clear about their voice in the research, the research itself becomes blurred and subject to misinterpretation. For example, Taylor *et al.* (1976) reported that some readers of the personal accounts of people with learning disabilities commented that they couldn't have written the words. Rather the reader assumed that the words belonged to the researchers. While Taylor *et al.* sought to disabuse people of these assumptions, the failure to make clear the break between researcher and the person telling the story left the latter without real credibility.

As noted in an earlier part of this book, some feminist researchers have argued strongly that the position from which the researcher is coming, their values and attitudes are an important part of the research. Failure to clarify these makes it difficult for the reader to understand the research. Further self-reflection by the researcher involved in inclusive research would provide a service to other researchers and to people with learning disabilities as it would make clear the contributions each was making to the research.

Johnson (1998) describes why she thought it was important for her to have a voice in a four-year study of institutional closure (which did not aspire to be inclusive):

> There are many voices in this study, but inevitably they are all heard through my voice. For this reason, if for no other, it was important that I become subject to my own research... Further examining my own emotional reactions to situations and exploring some of the unconscious means I used to defend myself against the stress of the women's world enabled me to hypothesize about some of the reactions of others in the situation. This was particularly so in interpreting the reactions of the women during the closure process, for they were very often not able to articulate their concerns verbally... As a woman working primarily with women, it was important to recognize as part of the research the mutuality and the differences in our experience if I were to develop a view of the world in which they lived (Oakley 1981). (Johnson 1998, pp.10–11)

I (KJ) took the reflective nature of my research very seriously, providing a series of personal accounts throughout the book. Of course it is possible that such reflection and the focus on the researcher can become both precious and can screen out the other people in the research or reduce them to subjects. For example, Gelya Frank's *Venus on Wheels*

(2000) focuses on the life of a woman with physical disabilities and leaves this reader with no clear sense of the woman at all, but with a very detailed view of the concerns of the non-disabled researcher.

If researchers have a distinct voice so should those with whom they work. The voices of people with learning disabilities should be the focus of the research and their part in it should be well documented. In our view there need to be more reflective accounts of what being involved in inclusive research actually means to people with learning disabilities beyond a statement of what they did.

We argue strongly that researchers have a duty to have a clearly articulated voice in inclusive research. The right to a distinctive voice is based on their expertise as social researchers and this needs to be acknowledged clearly, just as the lived experience, skills and experience of people with learning disabilities involved in research need to be acknowledged. Not only is the researcher's claim to be voiceless disingenuous because it hides what is really going on and masks the reality with rhetoric, but it also does a disservice to people with learning disabilities who will remain for ever in the dark, their real participation devalued.

Should the researcher be cast in the role of advocate for people with learning disabilities?

Given the widespread view in the learning disability and wider disability field that research cannot be neutral and that the researcher should be 'on the side' of disabled people (Barnes 1996), this is important to air. But we find it difficult. Underpinning much of what inclusive researchers do is a commitment to values which are focused on social justice, equity and fairness. We believe that it is impossible to be involved in inclusive research without at some level also being involved in advocacy for these issues and sometimes for individuals. Both of us have been involved in these different aspects of advocacy. However the situation is neither simple nor straightforward. For example in my (KJ's) study of institutional closure I became advocate for some women during the closure project as the following example shows:

> During these proceedings (of matching women living in the institution to houses in the community) I found that my role as researcher became blurred with that of advocate. In many of the panels I was the person who knew the woman best and at times I was a source of information about her. I was anxious that I might provide incorrect information or that I might jeopardise a person's opportunities by speaking out and thus antagonising those making the decision. There were also issues of fairness to be considered. If I argued for a particular individual then others would be disadvantaged. (Johnson 1998, p.129)

The intermingling of advocate and researcher roles was a difficult and soul-searching one, but also one which could not be denied in this situation. Anxieties about how the research information will be used when applied in a practical situation, questions of the ethics of using such information in a different forum and the possibilities of the advocate's role threatening not only those with whom one works but also the research itself were difficulties.

I (JW) encountered a particularly challenging instance when supervising a postgraduate student who was co-researching with four people with learning disabilities, all of whom she had known for some time. During the course of the work, it emerged that one co-researcher had been suspected (but not convicted) of viewing child pornography on the internet some years before. As the field work involved contact with both disabled children and vulnerable adults, she was torn between her loyalty to her co-researching colleague (and friend) and the need to protect the people who were subject to the research. Fortunately, in this instance, matters were amicably resolved. However, it is a stark example of the tension between advocacy and the role of a professional researcher. The researcher cannot always be unequivocally 'on the side' of people with learning disabilities as a citizen advocate can be.

The position assumes a homogeneity amongst people labelled as having learning disabilities which is in itself a gross misrepresentation. Like all human beings, people with learning disabilities are different from one another and some may behave in ways few researchers would be wise to support (see, for example, Brown and Thomson 1997). McCarthy discusses the problems of making public her findings that men with learning disabilities were among the sexual abusers of women with learning disabilities. This finding ran the risk of perpetuating community stereotypes of men with learning disabilities as dangerous (McCarthy 2000). Similarly I (KJ) in a study of sexuality and people with learning disabilities was confronted not only with similar dilemmas but also with the problem of whether or not to report in my research the alleged rape of a woman with learning disabilities by members of another marginalized group.

This question of homogeneity also relates to people with severe and profound disabilities. For as long as we have been involved, a holy grail of participative research at least for the researchers has been to find ways of including them, although, as we noted in Chapter 7, many researchers with learning disabilities are more interested in the phenomenon of self advocacy. It is probably sensible to conclude that in a conventional sense of what research means, we lack the skill and/or techniques to include people with severe learning disabilities as equal partners. Nevertheless, people with severe impairments can play a valuable role. For example, the very presence of Emma, a young woman without speech and with limited ability to sit upright, caused one researcher with learning disabilities to stop and reflect on his own limitations. 'I don't think I know how to find out what Emma wants,' he commented (JW personal observation). As Kellett and Nind (2001) observe, the inability of researchers with learning disabilities alongside other researchers to work inclusively with people with severe and profound disabilities does not negate the need to work hard to access their perspectives and represent their interests. Of all people with learning disabilities they may well need research most, for they are so easily forgotten, neglected and abused. Work such as that of Goode (1989), whether inclusive or not, does as much as anything to remind us of the essential humanness of people with such limited power.

It is undoubtedly part of the 'messiness' of inclusive research that advocacy and researcher roles will blur. The researcher in our view needs to be reflective about this, willing to discuss the ethical and political dilemmas which are confronted during the process of the research with others and should where possible be open about their values and stance on advocacy prior to commencing the research. An advocacy stance in relation to people with very limited ability to communicate their views and experiences does, on the other hand, seem an important role for researchers. Admitting that this probably will not be inclusive in the way we have defined it is important too!

Conclusion

This chapter has attempted to open up for discussion questions which focus on the role of the researcher in inclusive research. We intend that this chapter will provide a starting point for more open and detailed discussion of these issues. While we hide them from others and from ourselves they will not be resolved.

In the next chapter we look at some ways by which people with learning disabilities and researchers might come together to do inclusive research.

CHAPTER 12

...To New Realities

This chapter is concerned with how trained researchers and people with learning disabilities who are not trained researchers might work together. We suggest some ways that we have tried or have seen used by others which seem to us to break through some of the issues which we have raised in earlier parts of this book. We then go on to flag some other possibilities that we do not think exist at the moment but in our view should do so. It also touches on the major but little explored issue of building the capacity of user-controlled organizations to commission, manage and, in some cases, carry out research.

To expect all people with learning disabilities to be involved in every aspect of the research undertaken about them is in our view both unrealistic and oppressive. The choice to be involved and how that involvement occurs are to us the most important issues. It is possible that people with learning disabilities may be tokenistically included through membership on management or advisory groups for research projects, but in fact be given little say in the way the research happens and often little support to participate. When a research project originates with a researcher we believe that they have a responsibility to reflect on their research project and to consider carefully in what ways people with learning disabilities may be involved and to invite their participation, opening up for debate the best ways this might be achieved. When a research project originates with people with learning disabilities, they may well need support in considering how best the roles are distributed and what expert assistance they may need.

So what are the shared ways in which research can be undertaken? We believe that there are at least three different ways in which researchers and people with learning disabilities can work together: in a teacher/student relationship; in a consultant/employer relationship; in a co-researching relationship and in jointly making use of theory. We would also argue that if inclusive research is to make real inroads, then capacity building investment in self advocacy organizations will be necessary.

Researcher as teacher and coach/person with learning disability as learner or student

The inclusive research mode of working has been particularly effective in enabling the personal experiences of people with learning disabilities to be brought to public knowledge. Mabel Cooper's story appeared in the magazine *Community Care*, incidentally as sole author (Cooper 2002) Most books on learning disability topics, like the recent volume on advocacy edited by Barry Gray and Robin Jackson (2002), include accounts by and draw on evidence from the testimonies of people with learning disabilities. Such stories are of great significance to the teller and have contributed enormously to changing perspectives of people with learning disabilities. However, we would propose that there are limits to what can be achieved politically, or in terms of developing group empowerment through a continuing proliferation of predominantly personal individualized accounts.

In this view we are at one with Simone Aspis (2000) who argues that we need to move beyond a personal sense of oppression into an understanding of the political processes which contribute to the continuing oppression of people with learning disabilities as a group:

> What is clear is that individuals and groups of disabled women with learning difficulties do not have the opportunity to develop ideas which explain their discrimination and their relationships with other people in society. Such a tool would need to be developed at a personal and collective level, which would enable us to understand the barriers which we face and explain how we would fight back. (Aspis 2000, p.71)

However, if this process is to occur, it is argued by Rohhss Chapman (Spedding *et al.* 2002), who calls herself a co-researcher, that it is important for support workers to help people move into a broader understanding:

> Opportunities arise to make open and clear these important shifts from the personal to the political aspects of self advocacy work. This then provides a wider framework for supporters to act within that links directly into the social model of disability... If this link is not made then advocacy work will remain locked into an ever revolving wheel of personal issues so wider challenges to service systems and governments will fail to be made. (Spedding *et al.* 2002, p.150)

Chapman argues here for the supporter to offer their own knowledge and understandings to help people with learning disabilities to put their own experiences into a broader context, and thus to understand it better. The life story is often a good place to start, but it needs to be seen as a potential starting point rather than necessarily an end in itself.

Failure by the researchers to put their existing expertise into the project can lead to poor research which is less effective than it could be. An example of this comes from one of the rare US experiments in participatory research, in an article by Ward and Trigler (2001). They describe how they worked with People First members using a participatory action research approach to conduct a quality of life survey (at the instigation of the steering committee of the 1998 People First international conference). Their reflections on the process are refreshingly honest. Of the construction of the questionnaire they write:

> The sub committee made all the final decisions on how to word questions, which questions to include in the survey, and the rating scale. Because this was their study we had decided that our role as researchers was to identify conceptual issues, highlight problems and state technical concerns about particular questions for discussion purposes only. Unfortunately, in our eagerness to give self advocates control of the questionnaire we created methodological problems which compromised the results. (Ward and Trigler 2001, p.58)

One of their conclusions is that 'role clarification at the beginning of the process, identifying areas of expertise, and establishing guidelines for the team process will mediate power and control issues' (Ward and Trigler 2001, p.58). We would wholeheartedly agree with this view.

Until people like us who seek to support inclusive research offer concrete skills which will make research effective and reputable, we would suggest that inclusive research in learning disability will remain at the point at which women found themselves in the early 1980s:

> When women internalized the idea that describing their own woes was synonymous with a political consciousness, the progress of the feminist movement was stalled. (hooks 1984, pp.24–5)

Describing their woes is something people with learning disabilities have been helped to do through the development of inclusive research and the work of supporters. Sometimes it seems as if that is the only knowledge and expertise they are required to bring to the research. We would argue that there is now a case for those supporters to change roles and to offer not just help in accounting and recording personal experience, but also in sharing their knowledge as teachers and coaches, telling people what they know and guiding people towards effective strategies. The example quoted from McCarthy's (2000) work with the women from Powerhouse illustrates the potential of this approach. Her summary of the research into abuse of women with learning disabilities alongside facilitation offered them both a yardstick by which to judge their own experiences and an opportunity to learn about the wider context.

Nor is this a one-way process. Once we start defining our skills and experience and exploring how we might act as teachers or coaches, we can also begin to focus on the specific experience and skills which people with learning disabilities bring to the research process. This means that the research process becomes an exciting one of uncovering skills and abilities, rather than making assumptions that all people with learning disabilities and researchers are the same. The example in Box 12.1 offers an illustration.

Box 12.1 Soliciting the views of people with learning disabilities

I (JW) was asked to support Karen Spencer, an experienced self advocate, in working with a group of people with learning disabilities with a varied experience of speaking up for themselves to find out what matters to people with learning disabilities. This work was commissioned by the UK government who were planning a major survey of people with learning disabilities, following the *Valuing People* White Paper, and who commissioned Central England People First to assist the market research company employed to ensure the survey asked the right questions in the right way. My role was strictly defined as Karen's supporter and the scribe who wrote down what everyone said. I was not there to have my own opinions. As the ground rules put it: *Support people must not take charge and cannot interfere.*

It was a fascinating experience. Karen is an excellent facilitator who knows how to pace a workshop, and who uses humour to defuse some awkward moments. She can also feed in her own experience on topics like direct payments, about which she has very positive things to say – far more effective as a way of teaching people than an impersonal account. I was privileged to be there, with a defined role, and to learn more about how to work with people with learning disabilities and more about what really matters.

Subsequently I was able to put my skills as a social researcher into the project by helping CEPF write the report, by clustering people's comments under headings, something which I can do speedily, but which might be very time consuming for them.

Researcher as consultant/people with learning disabilities as employers

Working together does not necessarily mean that the project has to be undertaken totally by all parties. After all organizations and businesses do not involve their executives in undertaking research. In many cases they employ consultants to do the work. In this kind of arrangement the consultants are accountable for their work to a management group from the organization which holds the resources for the project. Of course people on the management group may have a role in shaping the research design but their primary role is to ensure that the researcher does the job and does so within the budget. It is a management role. There is potential for the social researcher to be employed as a consultant by organizations or groups of people with learning disabilities.

This is a topic we find particularly challenging to tackle because it is built on our own personal experience and has not, to our knowledge, been written down anywhere. As well-trained academics we find this rather uncomfortable. Nevertheless we are convinced that this is a useful model which, like the teacher/coach/student partnership described above, offers the potential for role clarification and a route forward.

As Zarb (1992) and Oliver (1992) pointed out, the social relations of research production are cast in ways which make it very difficult for non-experts to find a way in. You have to know what opportunities for funding are out there. You need to know how to fill in the forms, what literature to refer to, how to describe methodologies which will convince funders that you know what you are doing and will offer good value for money. Successful social researchers will have this knowledge and probably a track record which funding bodies will recognize and value.

We believe that strong partnerships between researchers and people with learning disabilities can be formed using a consultancy approach (Box 12.2). Some groups may need to develop skills in managing consultants, but these skills may be of more generalized interest and relevance than the development of specific research skills. After all, researchers themselves tend to be narrow in their approach and learning how to do one kind of research may not serve the longer term interests of an organization or group.

Box 12.2 The researcher as consultant

Supporting the development of a major funding bid

In 2000 the UK Department of Health put out a message that it was ready to disburse substantial funds for learning disability research which would, inter alia, increase our understandings of social exclusion. One of five criteria for judging the bids was user and carer involvement. Central England People First decided that it would bid for funds to extend its work on social exclusion, using 'user' researchers who would offer their own perceptions and access the views and experiences of other people in the Central England geographical area. They called on one of us (JW) and two other academics with whom they had worked before to assist them. We held a number of meetings over two months preparing the bid. My contribution was a literature review on participatory and emancipatory research, written in both 'accessible' language and in academic language, and an offer to be part of the research team, for which I would be bought out of my day job.

In the end the bid was unsuccessful. In my view there were two reasons for this. One was that it was too expensive at £400K. Because funding a self advocacy organization to undertake a major piece of government-funded research would have been a first, had we pitched it at half that amount the Department might have been willing to risk it, but not to the tune of one-fifth of the total funds. The other (and this was based on official referees' feedback) is that it was not original enough. Central England People First's major claim to do this work was that they were a user-controlled organization, but beyond that it was not so very different from many other similar pieces of work (some quoted in this book). In fact CEPF have some very valuable insights to offer on being an organization which seeks to engage with policy and practice, and research which would unpick the challenges and dilemmas was something they are in a very good position to do.

As an unpaid advisor I had felt unable to say these things forcefully enough at the right time for fear of being seen as too pushy. Had I been formally a consultant I would have felt in a stronger position – and would have had to be prepared to be overruled by the organization which was employing me.

Subsequent to the failed bid described in Box 12.2, the two colleagues and I who work with CEPF have sought to clarify what we can do to support the organization's ambitions to secure research funding, by acting as consultants to advise them of where they might get funding and for what. We have made three proposals for projects where we have the necessary expertise to support a major funding bid. These have emerged from discussions with CEPF management committee. One of these proposes that the organization itself should be the subject of research by recording its history, including the memories of key players. A successful self advocacy organization which has survived against many odds for over 15 years is something which should be researched, understood and celebrated. The research can be commissioned and controlled by CEPF, but they do not need to do it all.

The other bids are to do with the mental health needs of young people with learning disabilities and bottom-up research on social exclusion as defined by people with learning disabilities. We now await instructions from CEPF as to which, if any, they would like us to pursue with them. This to me makes sense of my involvement, with quite good prospects of a positive outcome. At the same time, the power to make final decisions rests with CEPF. The funding will be in their name, thus preserving the inclusiveness of the process.

One of the difficulties is that consultants generally need to be paid and many organizations representing people with learning disabilities do not have the money to do this. Forming partnerships with other (and wealthier) organizations may assist with this. Alternatively research consultants with a commitment to inclusive research may be willing to work up a project on the understanding that if it is successful they will have a paid role within it. Private consultants are used to working in this manner and academic consultants often put in months of effort alone to develop funding bids. In these instances the holder of the resources and the power is the organization, not the researcher.

Co-researching: trained researchers and people with learning disabilities

Co-researching is a term used in relation to inclusive research which often does mean something like the teaching/student relationship described above. It is frequently applied to a situation where a group of people with learning disabilities work with (often for no money) a trained researcher. However we believe that it may occur on a different basis; one which involves a more equal sharing of responsibility and skills for a particular project. Currently I (KJ) am working on a project which involves co-researching with individuals with disabilities. This is described in Box 12.3.

Box 12.3 Leadership and people with disabilities

This is a small project funded by philanthropic trusts. It aimed to identify the needs of people with disabilities for leadership training and the availability of inclusive courses in the community which dealt with this issue. The aim of the project was to make recommendations that would enable people with disabilities to access leadership training which they saw as relevant and useful. KJ was employed as the researcher for this project but is working with a man with learning disabilities. Colin Hiscoe was employed, not because he had a disability only. He had skills and experience in self advocacy, and was passionate about leadership and the development of skills for people with disabilities. He also had good networks through the advocacy movement, was skilled in running meetings with people with learning disabilities and was able to provide a critique of current courses in terms of their accessibility. Both researchers are learning from each other.

The examples provided here suggest a number of factors which need to be considered by researchers (whether or not they have a disability) in undertaking co-researched work:

1. The skills which both researchers bring to the study: in successful examples the skills of the co-researchers complement each other.

2. While the people with disabilities bring with them a knowledge of disability issues, the focus needs to be on the

skills and experience which they can contribute to the research itself.

3. It is important that the person with a disability is paid an acceptable and legitimate rate for their labour, comparable with non-disabled researchers. It needs to be made clear that the researchers are not volunteers but paid workers. Frequently this presents problems in terms of paid work interfering with disability pensions and entitlements. This reflects wider inequalities, but does need to be resolved if we are to move forward.

4. A clear contract is established between the researchers involved in the study, indicating what their rights and responsibilities are to each other and to the study itself.

Clearly not all people with learning disabilities would want or have the necessary skills to undertake this kind of co-researching, but then neither do people without disabilities!

Working together on outcomes

Discussions with people with learning disabilities in Victoria, Australia, about leadership training have indicated that they have little access to the kind of information which might influence policy developers or politicians. Their attempts to lobby for changes to the way disability services are run or to demonstrate needs for particular policy changes are often limited to 'stating what we know' or anecdotal experience. Yet there is much research available on the needs of people with learning disabilities. As noted earlier in the book, researchers often fail to make this information available to groups which need it in accessible forms. Nor do they often take the time to explain their research findings to such groups, either at conferences or in forums. There is a notable exception to this in the Plain Facts initiative, where projects funded by the UK-based Joseph Rowntree Foundation are made accessible to people with learning disabilities through tapes and booklets (Townsley 1998).

Researchers who are serious about their commitment to inclusive research need to take account of how their findings might be used by a

---

Box 12.4 Making research accessible

As part of its commitment to the European Year of Disabled People (2003), the *British Journal of Learning Disabilities*, a leading UK journal, is piloting a scheme to persuade authors of papers to supply an accessible abstract along with the paper. This will be published in large-print format in the journal.

---

group of people with learning disabilities. This should not be simply restricted to providing information, but should also include discussions about how to use the information effectively, its strengths and limits.

Theorizing

We have noted at several points in the book that theorizing is particularly challenging in inclusive research. The non-disabled researchers are likely to come to the enterprise with knowledge of theoretical models; people with learning disabilities less often have this knowledge. For example, there has been a recent trend to using Foucauldian ideas to understand the situation of people with learning disabilities (Veck 2002). Essentially, Foucauldian analyses are premised on 'the gaze' of the researcher on the lives of the subjects to understand how disciplinary power is exercised. It is not readily adaptable to inclusive approaches, unless other people with learning disabilities are coopted into the gazing at others – which simply pushes the problem down the hierarchy. Does this mean that such theorizing is antithetical to inclusive research and should not be employed by people claiming to work in inclusive ways? We would argue that there is a place for such theorizing, but there needs to be a commitment on the part of the researcher ultimately to make the findings available to people with learning disabilities, to assist them in understanding, in this case, the nature of power to which they are subject, and to using that knowledge.

Undoubtedly there are dangers in this. Many people may not take the trouble to 'translate' their work in this way, thus perpetuating the 'othering' which has been characteristic of learning disability research for so long. However, we would contend that non-disabled researchers do sometimes need the mental space in which to explore ideas before having to consider the challenge to give others access to it. This is the argument we have used to justify writing this book, as described in the Introduction. As we have been writing the book, so we have been able to clarify for ourselves (and others) some of the contradictions we have encountered in our work. We hope that this will benefit people with learning disabilities, by clarifying the choices we are making when we embark on research together.

Training and qualifications

This chapter has sought to open a debate about how people with learning disabilities and researchers might work together. There is no one right way to do this but we all need to be open to exploring different strategies and possibilities depending on the nature of the research and the needs of the group. One issue which has not been canvassed and yet seems central to all the issues is that of acquiring skills. Researchers attend courses in research strategies at university. They learn about specific methodologies and they also learn how to use research in relation to policy. In Chapter 11 we argued that there may be a need for specific training in working inclusively, once there is more of an evidence base on which to establish such training. Here we propose that people with learning disabilities who aspire to be researchers may also want and need to develop their skills. Courses that provide some people with learning disabilities with skills in research and which offer certification are important and may be attractive to some people. Such courses may focus on how to do research themselves or how to work with other researchers. A text used with community groups (Wadsworth 1996) provides an excellent model for developing such a programme with people with learning disabilities. We find it interesting and disturbing that people with learning disabilities are expected by 'inclusive researchers' to participate in research without the kinds of knowledge and skills which people without disabilities accept as a necessary precursor for their professional roles. Is this another example of devaluing?

Building research capacity in user-controlled organizations

As suggested in this chapter and as advocated by Zarb (1992), the optimum conditions for users to gain control of a research agenda is when a user-controlled organization holds the funds and employs the researchers. At present in the UK and Australia the research capacity of even the leading self advocacy groups is very limited, confined to a few star performers and often unable to meet the challenges offered by policy makers and practitioners ever more driven to show they are working alongside 'users'. Such organizations, far from being a solid basis on which to build effective partnerships, are all too often ephemeral, dependent on unreliable external funds and inexperienced in bidding for or managing research. If we are seriously committed to promoting inclusive research, then investment in these organizations will be vital.

Conclusion

In this chapter we have sought to identify models for research relationships if inclusive research is to move forward and develop beyond the rather anecdotal stage it has reached in the early twenty-first century. We hope these begin to point the way to a vigorous next stage in the inclusive research enterprise.

Conclusion

Why Do It?

No need to hear your voice when I can talk about you better than you can speak about yourself. No need to hear your voice. Only tell me about your pain. I want to know your story. And then I will tell it back to you in a new way. Tell it back to you in such a way that it has become mine, my own. Rewriting you, I rewrite myself anew. I am still author, authority. I am still the colonizer, the speaking subject, and you are now the centre of my talk.

(hooks 1990, pp.151–2)

We have explored in this book the past history and present state of inclusive research and have tentatively proposed some directions for future development. Much of what has been done in the name of inclusive research has been inspired, we believe, by a desire to redress wrongs, to show that we are not like the colonizers described by hooks above. We have suggested in Part 3, however, that it is time to move on, to leave the guilt behind and to reinvigorate the enterprise.

What we have termed inclusive research has already made a major contribution to changing the way that people with learning disabilities are viewed and has revolutionized approaches to research in learning disability. Although there is some way to go before everyone working in the learning disability research field puts principles into practice, we believe that the case for asking researchers to consider the interests of people with learning disabilities in the work they do is irrefutable, thanks to the work of the pioneers. At the very least they need to consider:

- demonstrating that what they do matters to people with learning disabilities

- how they can help people with learning disabilities access the outcomes of their work.

Nevertheless, we have also identified some real conundrums and challenges in the way inclusive learning disability research has been heading. The belief that in order to serve the interests of people with learning disabilities all research needs actively to include them is, we believe, responsible for stalling the enterprise as people look for ever more inventive ways to enable people with learning disabilities to 'do' research. What we should be seeking, we argue, is ways of enabling people with learning disabilities to influence, even control, research projects which they have identified as being relevant to them. Indeed, this is the position reached in the disability arena – Zarb (1992) made changing the social relations of research production, not changing the actual doing of research, the focus of his paper. Significant projects like Priestley's work on community care (1999) were not emancipatory because they were carried out by disabled people, but because they were controlled by an organization of disabled people.

Inclusive learning disability research, like normalization/social role valorization and many other developments in learning disability, has been largely driven by values – of social justice, redressing past and present wrongs, promoting valued social roles – rather than an evidence base. We have shown that often the people who have pioneered the work have done so because they want to change things, to show that in the small world of research we can do things differently and better. A lot of what we personally have done has been driven by guilt and we can never get it right because we are operating in a context where, whenever the research meets the real social barriers confronting people with learning disabilities (inability to travel independently, an inadequate education, restrictions on what can be earnt because of welfare benefit rules etc.), the inequality in the world beyond spoils things. Inclusive research has for us and most others operating as researchers in this field been driven not by organizational partnerships and goals, but by one-to-one relationships. Neither researchers nor people with learning disabilities have been selected for the work based on competencies and job descriptions. In most cases, people have been working with those they know on projects they themselves have set up. There is nothing inherently wrong with this. It is a classic way for change to start. But if we are to move the agenda beyond the realm of anecdote and story into research which develops theory, or promotes change on a larger scale, then this needs to change too. At present, 'big' research, the sort policy makers listen to, is still the preserve of the non-inclusive research centres. The inclusive enterprise is marginalized, left to a few (mainly women) to pursue, while the well-funded prestigious centres carry on much as they have always done.

The failure of people like us to explain what we do and how we do it when working inclusively has led to a mystification of the process. The myth is that somehow some people magically get it right, but how the magic works is obscure. The hard work, the finely honed skills, the self-restraint researchers need to exercise, are camouflaged. In the book we have tried to look behind the curtain and to describe some of what is involved. This is important because for inclusive research to penetrate beyond its present narrow confines we argue that there needs to be a focus, not on people with the right values but people with the requisite skills to work on inclusive research. This goes for both sides of the binary divide – training courses for the career researchers and for those people with learning disabilities who have the potential and the inclination to 'do' research, opportunities for organizations controlled by users to learn about research, how it is funded and carried out, and how to manage it. If we genuinely want to support inclusive research, then people with learning disabilities and their organizations will need investment of time and money to develop their capacity to commission and manage research. Precious few such organizations have this sort of capacity at present.

We would also argue for an extensive dialogue between funders and commissioners of research, research centres and organizations representing people with learning disabilities to decide what sort of research needs to be done and how fruitful partnerships can develop. We firmly believe that without this dialogue the present agenda of user groups is too narrow and the skills base too small to be the foundation for all learning disability related research. But given the right sort of conditions, organizations of people with learning disabilities should be able to look beyond the preoccupations of their individual members to consider wider issues, and should expect to harness the capacity of university research centres to work for what they consider important.

We also need another sort of language. We struggle with the language at the end of the book as we did at the beginning. The binary divide, the polarizing of the non-disabled and the disabled, the researcher and the co-researcher, the inquirer and the expert, is perpetuated, not dissolved, through inclusive research. As we commented in Chapter 1, only the excluded need inclusive research. This is not to argue for difference to disappear; it is to argue for some clarity over language. People with learning disabilities have made and will continue to make valuable input to research. They do not need obscurantist language to prove that. Rather they need the contributions they make to be named and described and recognized for what they are, not for what we wish they could be.

Finally we make a plea for people like us, the researchers, to have permission to take some space of our own to consider, reflect and come up with ideas and suggestions. This permission has been lacking to date. 'Nothing about us without us' rings in our ears as we write this. Yet after working for ten or more years in a challenging and ill-charted field as we have, it is essential to have time and space to reflect. Of course, this must be shared. There needs to be a commitment to make these insights available to colleagues with learning disabilities and to accept that they will be challenged and refuted. That is the essence of a vigorous research community. As authors of this book we have needed this space to work through our own ideas and experiences, to make sense of them and to come up with ideas for change. We know we have not come up with all the answers. But we hope at the very least to provoke some useful discussion as we take these ideas back into the field where we have worked for so long, and to be forgiven for airing those questions we dare not ask.

References

Abbott, P. and Sapsford, R. (1987) *Community Care for Mentally Handicapped Children.* Milton Keynes: Open University Press.

Anderson, I. (2000) 'Vichealth Koori Health Research and Community Development Unit, University of Melbourne.' In Vichealth Koori Health and Research and Community Development Unit *We Don't Like Research. But in Koori Hands It Could Make a Difference.* Melbourne: Vichealth Koori Health Research and Community Development Unit.

Andrews, J. (with Rolph, S.) (2000) 'Scrub, scrub, scrub…bad times and good times: some of the jobs I've had in my life.' In D. Atkinson, M. McCarthy, J. Walmsley *et al.* (2000) *Good Times Bad Times: Women with Learning Difficulties Telling their Stories.* Kidderminster: BILD.

Armstrong, D. (1983) *Political Autonomy of the Body: Medical Knowledge of the Twentieth Century.* Cambridge: Cambridge University Press.

Aspis, S. (1997) 'Self advocacy for people with learning difficulties: does it have a future?' *Disability and Society 12*, 4, 647–654.

Aspis, S. (2000) 'Researching our history: who is in charge?' In L. Brigham, D. Atkinson, M. Jackson, S. Rolph and J. Walmsley (eds) *Crossing Boundaries: Change and Continuity in the History of Learning Disabilities.* Kidderminster: BILD.

Atkinson, D. (1986) 'Engaging competent others: a study of the support networks of people with a mental handicap.' *British Journal of Social Work 16*, Supplement, 83–101.

Atkinson, D. (1989) 'Research interviews with people with mental handicaps.' In A. Brechin and J. Walmsley (eds) *Making Connections.* Sevenoaks: Hodder and Stoughton.

Atkinson, D. (1997) *An Auto/biographical Approach to Learning Disability Research.* Aldershot: Ashgate.

Atkinson, D. (2001) 'Researching the history of learning disability using oral and life history methods.' Unpublished PhD thesis. Open University, Milton Keynes.

Atkinson, D. and Cooper, M. (2000) 'Parallel stories.' In L. Brigham *et al.* (eds) *Crossing Boundaries.* Kidderminster: BILD.

Atkinson, D., Jackson, M. and Walmsley, J. (eds) (1997) *Forgotten Lives: Exploring the History of Learning Disability.* Kidderminster: BILD.

Atkinson, D., McCarthy M., Walmsley, J. *et al.* (2000) *Good Times Bad Times: Women with Learning Difficulties Telling their Stories.* Kidderminster: BILD.

Atkinson, D. and Walmsley, J. (1999) 'Using autobiographical approaches with people with learning difficulties.' *Disability and Society 14,* 203–216

Atkinson, D. and Williams, F. (1990) *Know Me As I Am: An Anthology of Prose, Poetry and Art by People with Learning Difficulties.* Sevenoaks: Hodder and Stoughton.

Aull Davies, C. and Jenkins, R. (1997) '" She has different fits to me": how people with learning difficulties see themselves.' *Disability and Society 12,* 1, 95–110.

Ayer, S. and Alazewski, A. (1984) *Community Care and the Mentally Handicapped.* London: Croom Helm.

Baddou, F. (1946) 'Intergroup relations and action programs.' *Journal of Social Issues 11,* 4.

Baldwin, S. and Glendinning, C. (1983) 'Employment, women and their disabled children.' In J. Finch and D. Groves (eds) *A Labour of Love: Women, Work and Caring.* London: Routledge and Kegan Paul.

Bank-Mikkelson, N.E. (1969) 'Modern service models.' In *Changing Patterns in Residential Services for the Mentally Retarded.* Washington, DC: President's Committee on Mental Retardation.

Bank-Mikkelson, N.E. (1980) 'Denmark.' In R.J. Flynn and K.E. Nitsch (eds) *Normalisation, Social Integration and Community Services.* Baltimore: University Park Press.

Barnes, C. (1996) 'Disability and the myth of the independent researcher.' *Disability and Society 11,* 1, 107–111.

Barron, D. (2000) 'From community to institution and back again.' In L. Brigham, D. Atkinson, M. Jackson, S. Rolph and J. Walmsley (eds) *Crossing Boundaries: Change and Continuity in the History of Learning Disabilities.* Kidderminster: BILD.

Bayley, M. (1973) *Mental Handicap and Community Care.* London: Routledge and Kegan Paul.

Benmayor, R. (1991) 'Testimony, action research and empowerment: Puerto Rican women and popular education.' In S. Berger Gluck and D. Patai (eds) *Women's Words. The Feminist Practice of Oral History.* New York: Routledge.

Benn, C. (1981) *Attacking Poverty through Participation. A Community Approach.* Melbourne: PIT Publishing.

Beresford, P. (2000a) 'Service users, social policy and the future of welfare.' *Critical Social Policy 21,* 4, 488–512.

Beresford, P. (2000b) 'What have madness and psychiatric system survivors got to do with disability and disability studies?' *Disability and Society 15,* 1, 167–172.

Bersani, H. (1998) 'From social clubs to social movement: landmarks in the development of the international self advocacy movement.' In L. Ward (ed) *Innovations in Advocacy and Empowerment.* Chorley: Lisieux Hall.

Blunden, R. (1988) 'Quality of life in persons with disabilities: issues in the development of services.' In R. Brown (ed) *Quality of Life for Handicapped People.* London: Croom Helm.

Bogdan, R. and Biklen, S. (1992) *Qualitative Research for Education. An Introduction to Theory and Methods.* Boston: Allyn and Bacon.

Bogdan, R. and Taylor, S. (1976) 'The judged, not the judges: an insider's view of mental retardation.' *American Psychologist 31,* 47–52.

Bogdan, R. and Taylor, S. (1982) *Inside Out.* Toronto: University of Toronto Press.

Bogdan, R. And Taylor, S. (1989) 'What's in a name?' In A. Brechin and J. Walmsley (eds) *Making Connections.* Sevenoaks: Hodder and Stoughton.

Booth, W. (1998) 'Doing research with lonely people.' *British Journal of Learning Disabilities 26,* 4, 132–134.

Booth, T. and Booth, W. (1994) *Parenting under Pressure: Mothers and Fathers with Learning Difficulties.* Buckingham: Open University Press.

Booth, T. and Booth, W. (1996) 'Sounds of silence: narrative research with inarticulate subjects.' *Disability and Society 11,* 1, 55–70.

Booth, T. and Booth, W. (1998) *Growing Up with Parents who have Learning Difficulties.* London: Routledge.

Booth, T., Simons, K. and Booth, W. (1990) *Outward Bound: Relocation and Community Care for People with Learning Difficulties.* Milton Keynes: Open University Press.

Braye, S. (2000) 'The language of participation.' In H. Kemshall and R. Littlechild (eds) *User Involvement and Participation in Social Care.* London: Jessica Kinglsey Publishers.

Brechin, A. and Sidell, M. (2000) 'Ways of knowing.' In R. Gomm and C. Davies (eds) *Using Evidence in Health and Social Care.* London: Sage Books/Open University.

Brown, H. and Thomson, D. (1997) 'The ethics of research with men who have learning disabilities and abusive sexual behaviour: a minefield in a vacuum' *Disability and Society 12*, 5, 69–708.

Brown, H. and Turk, V. (1992) 'Defining sexual abuse as it affects adults with learning disabilities.' *Mental Handicap 20*, 2, 44–45.

Brown, S., Johnson, K., Jackson, A. and Wyn, J. (1998) 'Healthy, wealthy and wise? The health implications of gambling for women.' *Australian Journal of Primary Health – Interchange 4*, 3, 147–157.

Brown, S., Johnson, K. and Wyn, J. (2001) 'Minimising the health impacts of gambling: Horn of Africa community.' *Australian Journal of Primary Health 7*, 1, 124–128.

Brydon-Miller, M. (1993) 'Breaking down barriers: accessibility self advocacy in the disabled community.' In P. Park, M. Brydon-Miller, B. Hall and T. Jackson (eds) *Voices of Change. Participatory Research in the United States and Canada.* Westport, CT: Bergin and Garvey.

Butler, K., Carr, S. and Sullivan, F. (1988) *Citizen Advocacy: A Powerful Partnership.* London: National Citizen Advocacy.

Campbell, J. and Oliver, M. (1996) *Disability Politics: Understanding our Past, Changing our Future.* Leeds: Disability Press.

Caplan, P. (1977) *African Voices, African Lives: Personal Narratives from a Swahili Village.* London: Routledge.

Carr, W. And Kemmis, S. (1983) *Becoming Critical. Education, Knowledge and Action Research.* Geelong: Deakin University.

Carroll, L. ([1872] 1990) 'The walrus and the carpenter.' In M. Roberts (ed) *The Faber Book of Comic Verse.* London: Faber and Faber.

Carson, D. (1994) 'The law's contribution to protecting people with learning disabilities from physical and sexual abuse.' In J. Harris and A. Craft (eds) *BILD Seminar Papers No. 4. People with Learning Disabilities at Risk of Physical or Sexual Abuse.* Kidderminster: BILD.

Cattermole, M., Jahoda, A. and Markova, I. (1988) 'Leaving home: the experience of people with a mental handicap.' *Journal of Mental Deficiency Research 32*, 47–57.

Central England People First (2000) *Submission to the Department of Health Learning Disability Research Initiative.* Northampton: Central England People First.

Chamberlain, M. (1983) 'Review of *Women's Words: The Feminist Practice of Oral History.*' Oral History II, 2, 1–2.

CHANGE (nd) *Building Expectations: Inquiry into Community Services and Opportunities for People with Learning Disabilities.* London: MHF.

Chapman, R. (in progress) *Self Advocacy and the Work of Supporters*. PhD thesis. Milton Keynes: Open University.

Chapman, R. and Carlisle People First Research Group (in progress) *The Role of the Advisor in Self Advocacy Organisations*.

Chappell, A. (1992) 'Towards a sociological critique of the normalisation principle.' *Disability, Handicap and Society 7*, 1, 35–51.

Chappell, A. (1997) 'From normalization to where?' In L. Barton and M. Oliver (eds) *Disability Studies Past Present and Future*. Leeds: Disability Press.

Chappell, A. (1999) 'Research and people with learning difficulties.' In J. Swain and S. French (eds) *Therapy and Learning Difficulties*. London: Butterworth-Heinemann.

Chappell, A. (2000) 'The emergence of participatory methodology in learning disability research: understanding the context.' *British Journal of Learning Disabilities 28*, 1, 38–43.

Chappell, A., Goodley, D. and Lawthorn, R. (2001) 'Making connections: the relevance of the social model of disability for people with learning difficulties.' *British Journal of Learning Disabilities 29*, 45–50.

Chenoweth, L. (2000) 'Closing the doors: insights and reflections on deinstitutionalisation.' In M. Jones and L. Basser Marks (eds) *Explorations on Law and Disability in Australia*. Melbourne: The Federation Press.

Clark, D., Fry, T. and Rodgers, J. (1998) 'Woman to woman: setting up and runnning a health advocacy group for women.' In L. Ward (ed) *Advocacy and Empowerment*. Chorley: Lisieux Hall.

Cocks, E. and Cockram, J. (1995) 'The participatory research paradigm and intellectual disability.' *Mental Handicap Research 8*, 1, 25–37.

Colin, T. and Garrow, A. (1999) *Thinking, Listening, Looking, Understanding and Acting as You Go Along. Steps to Evaluating Indigenous Health Promotion Projects*. Alice Springs: Council of Remote Nurses of Australia.

Commonwealth Government (1992) *Disability Discrimination Act*. Canberra: Australian Government Printing Service.

Cooper, J. and Vernon, S. (1996) *Disability and the Law*. London: Jessica Kingsley Publishers.

Cooper, M. (1997) 'Mabel Cooper's life story.' In D. Atkinson, M. Jackson and J. Walmsley (eds) *Forgotten Lives: Exploring the History of Learning Disability*. Kidderminster: BILD.

Cooper, M. (2002) 'This life.' *Community Care*, 21–27 February, 22.

Cooper, M., Ferris, G., Coventry, M. with Atkinson, D. (2000) 'Croydon lives.' In D. Atkinson *et al.* (eds) *Good Times Bad Times: Women with Learning Difficulties Telling Their Stories*. Kidderminster: BILD.

Corker, M. (2000) 'Disability politics, language planning and inclusive social policy.' *Disability and Society 15*, 3, 445–462.

Cosier, J. and Glennie, S. (1994) 'Supervising the child protection process: a multidisciplinary inquiry.' In P. Reason (ed) *Participation in Human Inquiry.* London: Sage.

Coventry, M. (2000) 'Croydon lives 3.' In D. Atkinson *et al.* (eds) *Good Times Bad Times: Women with Learning Difficulties Telling their Stories.* Kidderminster: BILD.

Daly, J. (1996) 'Social science health research.' In J. Daly (ed) *Ethical Intersections. Health Research, Methods and Researcher Responsibilities.* St Leonards: Allen and Unwin.

Danziger, K. (1990) *Constructing the Subject. Historical Origins of Psychological Research.* Cambridge: Cambridge University Press.

Deacon, J. (1974) *Tongue Tied.* London: National Society for Mentally Handicapped Children.

Denzin, N.K. and Lincoln, Y.S. (1998) 'Introduction: entering the field of qualitative research.' In N.K. Denzin and Y.S. Lincoln (eds) *The Landscape of Qualitative Research. Theories and Issues.* Thousand Oaks: Sage.

Department of Health (DoH) (2000) *Valuing People.* London: DoH.

Department of Human Services (2001a) *The Aspirations of People with a Disability.* Melbourne: Department of Human Services.

Department of Human Services (2001b) *One Community in 2011. Draft State Disability Plan.* Melbourne: Department of Human Services.

Department of Human Services (2002) *Victorian State Disability Plan.* Melbourne: Department of Human Services.

Di Terlizzi, M. (1994) 'Life history: the impact of a changing service provision on an individual with learning disabilities.' *Disability and Society 9*, 4 501–16.

Edgerton, R. (1967) *The Cloak of Competence.* Berkeley: University of California Press.

Edgerton, R. and Bercovici, S. (1976) 'The cloak of competence: years later.' *American Journal of Mental Retardation 80*, 485–497.

Edgerton, R., Bollinger, M. and Herr, B. (1984) 'The cloak of competence: after two decades.' *American Journal of Mental Retardation 88*, 345–351.

Emerson, E. (1992) 'What is normalization?' In H. Brown and H. Smith (eds) *Normalisation: A Reader for the Nineties.* London: Routledge.

Evans, G., Todd, S., Blunden, R., Porterfield, J. and Agar, A. (1987) 'Evaluating the impact of a move to ordinary housing.' *British Journal of Mental Subnormality 33*, 1, 10–18.

Felce, D. and Grant, G. (eds) (1998) *Towards a Full Life: Researching Policy Innovations for People with Learning Disabilities.* London: Butterworth Heinemann.

Ferguson, P.M., Ferguson, D.C. and Taylor, S.J. (1992) *Interpreting Disability: A Qualitative Reader.* New York: Columbia University Teachers College.

Ferris, G. (2000) 'Croydon lives 2.' In D. Atkinson *et al.* (eds) *Good Times Bad Times: Women with Learning Difficulties Telling Their Stories.* Kidderminster: BILD.

Fine, M. (1998) 'Working the hyphens: reinventing self and other in qualitative research.' In N. Denzin and Y. Lincoln (eds) *The Landscape of Qualitative Research.* Thousand Oaks: Sage.

Fine, M. and Gordon, S. (1992) 'Feminist transformations of/despite psychology.' In M. Fine (ed) *Disruptive Voices: The Possibilities of Feminist Research.* Ann Arbor: University of Michigan Press.

Finkelstein, V. (1996) 'The disability movement has run out of steam.' *Disability Now,* February, 11.

Finkelstein, V. (1999) 'Doing disability research.' Extended book review. *Disability and Society 14,* 6, 859–867.

Flynn, M. (1986) 'Adults who are mentally handicapped as consumers: issues and guidelines for interviewing.' *Journal of Mental Deficiency Research 30,* 369–377.

Flynn, M. (1989) *Independent Living for Adults with Mental Handicap: A Place of My Own.* London: Cassell.

Flynn, M., Griffiths, S., Byne, L. and Hynes, K. (1997) 'I am stuck here with my poxy star chart: listening to mentally disordered offenders with learning disabilities.' In P. Ramcharan, G. Roberts, G. Grant and J. Borland (eds) *Empowerment in Everyday Life: Learning Disability.* London: Jessica Kingsley Publishers.

Foster, M. (1972) 'An introduction to the theory and practice of action research in work organizations.' *Human Relations 25,* 6, 529–556.

Frank, G. (2000) *Venus on Wheels.* Berkeley: University of California Press.

Frawley, P., Johnson, K., Hillier, L. and Harrison, L. (2002) *Living Safer Sexual Lives Workshop Manual.* Brighton: Pavilion Publishing.

Freire, P. (1970a) 'Conscientization and cultural freedom. In *Cultural Action for Freedom. Harvard Educational Review.* Monograph Series No. 1.

Freire, P. (1970b) 'Cultural action and conscientization.' *Harvard Educational Review 40,* 452–477.

Freire, P. (1970c) *Pedagogy of the Oppressed.* New York: Seabury Press.

Freire, P. (1972) *Cultural Action for Freedom.* Harmondsworth: Penguin.

French, S. (1999) 'Controversial issues: critical perspectives.' In J. Swain and S. French (eds) *Therapy and Learning Difficulties.* London: Butterworth-Heinemann.

French, S. and Swain, J. (1997) 'Changing disability research: participating and emancipatory research with disabled people.' *Physiotherapy 83,* 1, 26–32.

Gerber, D.A. (1990) 'Listening to disabled people: the problem of "voice" and authority in Robert B. Edgerton's *The Cloak of Competence.' Disability, Handicap and Society 5,* 1, 3–23.

Gillman, M., Swain, J. and Heyman, B. (1997) '"Life" history or "case" history: the objectification of people with learning difficulties through the tyranny of professional discourses.' *Disability and Society 12,* 5, 675–693.

Gluck, S.B. (1991) 'Advocacy oral history: Palestinian women in resistance.' In S. Berger Gluck and D. Patai (eds) *Women's Words. The Feminist Practice of Oral History.* New York: Routledge.

Gluck, S.B. and Patai, D. (1991) 'Introduction.' In S. Berger Gluck and D. Patai (eds) *Women's Words. The Feminist Practice of Oral History.* New York: Routledge.

Goffman, E. (1963) *Stigma.* Harmondsworth: Penguin.

Gomm, R. and Davies, C. (1999) *Using Evidence in Health and Social Care.* London: Sage.

Goode, D. (1989) 'The world of the congenitally deaf blind: towards the grounds for achieving human understanding.' In A. Brechin and J. Walmsley (eds) *Making Connections.* Sevenoaks: Hodder and Stoughton.

Goodley, D. (1996) 'Tales of hidden lives: a critical examination of life history research with people who have learning disabilities.' *Disability and Society II,* 3, 333–348.

Goodley, D. (1998) 'Appraising self advocacy in the lives of people with learning difficulties.' Unpublished PhD thesis, University of Sheffield.

Goodley, D. (2001) 'Learning difficulties, the social model of disability and impairment: challenging epistemologies.' *Disability and Society 16,* 207–231.

Grant, G., Ramcharan, P. And McGrath, M. (1993) *Living in the Community: Views of Three People with a Learning Difficulty.* Bangor: Centre for Social Policy Research and Development.

Gray, B. and Jackson, R. (eds) (2002) *Advocacy and Learning Disability.* London: Jessica Kingsley Publishers.

Greenwood, D. and Levin, M. (1998) *Introduction to Action Research. Social Research for Social Change.* London: Sage.

Gridley, H., Moore, S., Higgins, J. and Johnson, K. (1998) 'Improving women's health care: the experiences of women patients and general practitioners in the western region of Melbourne.' *Australian Journal of Primary Health – Interchange 4*, 3, 119–134.

Harding, S. (1987) *Feminism and Methodology.* Milton Keynes: Open University Press.

Harrison, L., Johnson, K., Hillier, L. and Strong, R. (2001) '"Nothing about us without us": the ideals and realities of participatory action research with people with an intellectual disability.' *Scandinavian Journal of Disability. Research 3*, 2, 56–70.

Hevey, D. (1992) *The Creatures Time Forgot.* London: Routledge.

Hollingsworth, S., Dadds, M. and Miller, J. (1997) 'The examined experience of action research: the person within the process.' In S. Hollingsworth (ed) *International Action Research: A Casebook for Educational Reform.* London: Falmer Press.

Holman, A. and Collins, J. (1998) 'Choice and control: making direct payments work for people with learning difficulties.' In L. Ward (ed) *Advocacy and Empowerment.* Chorley: Lisieux Hall.

hooks, b. (1984) *Feminist Theory: From Margin to Centre.* Boston: South End Press.

hooks, b. (1990) *Yearning: Race, Gender and Politics.* Boston: South End Press.

hooks, b. (1992) 'Revolutionary black women.' In *Black Looks: Race and Representation.* London: Turnaround.

hooks, b. (2000) *Feminist Theory. From Margins to Centre.* 2nd edition. London: Pluto Press.

Horton, B (1993) 'The Appalachian land ownership study: research and citizen action in Appalachia.' In P. Park, M. Brydon-Miller, B. Hall and T. Jackson (eds) *Voices of Change. Participatory Research in the United States and Canada.* Westport, CT: Bergin and Garvey.

Humphreys, S., Evans, G. and Todd, S. (1987) *Lifelines: An Account of the Life Experiences of Seven People with a Mental Handicap who use the NIMROD Service.* London: King's Fund.

Hunt, N. (1967) *The World of Nigel Hunt.* Beaconsfield: Darwen Finlayson.

Jackson, M. (2000) 'Introduction.' In L. Brigham *et al.* (eds) *Crossing Boundaries.* Kidderminster: BILD.

Jackson, T. (1993) 'A way of working: participatory research and the aboriginal movement in Canada.' In P. Park, M. Brydon-Miller, B. Hall and T. Jackson (eds) *Voices of Change. Participatory Research in the United States and Canada.* Westport, CT: Bergin and Garvey.

Jahoda, A., Markova, I. and Cattermole, M. (1989a) 'Day services: a purpose in life?' *Mental Handicap 17*, 4, 136–139.

Jahoda, A., Markova, I. and Cattermole, M. (1989b) 'Stigma and self concept of people with a mild mental handicap.' In A. Brechin and J. Walmsley (eds) *Making Connections*. London: Hodder and Stoughton.

Johnson, K. (1998) *Deinstitutionalising Women. An Ethnographic Study of Institutional Closure*. Cambridge: Cambridge University Press.

Johnson, K., Frawley, P., Hillier, L. and Harrison, L. (2002a) 'Living Safer Sexual Lives: research and action.' *Tizard Learning Disability Review 7*, 3, 4–9.

Johnson, K., Frawley, P., Hillier, L. and Harrison, L. (2002b) 'Living Safer Sexual Lives: Working research.' *Health Sharing Women 12*, 4, 12–16

Johnson, K., Frawley, P., Holopainen, D., Hillier, L. and Harrison, L. (2000a) *Living Safer Sexual Lives. Workshop Evaluation*. Melbourne: Australian Research Centre in Sex Health and Society, La Trobe University.

Johnson, K., Hillier, L., Harrison, L. and Frawley, P. (2000b) *Living Safer Sexual Lives*. Melbourne: Australian Research Centre in Sex Health and Society.

Johnson, K., Hillier, L., Harrison, L. and Frawley, P. (2001) *People with Intellectual Disabilities. Living Safer Sexual Lives*. Melbourne: Australian Research Centre in Sex, Health and Society, La Trobe University.

Johnson, K. and McIntyre, D. (2001) 'The researcher, the psychoanalyst and supervision in the room at the back.' In A. Bartlett and G. Mercer (eds) *Postgraduate Research Supervision. Transforming (R)elations*. New York: Peter Lang.

Johnson, K., Strong, R., Hillier, L. and Pitts, M. (2002c) *Screened Out. The Experiences of Cervical Screening for Women with Disabilities*. Melbourne: Cancer Council of Victoria.

Johnson, K. and Tait, S. (2003, in press) 'Throwing away the key.' In I. Freckleton and K. Diesfeld (eds) *Involuntary Detention and Civil Commitment: International Perspectives*.

Johnson, K., Topp, V. and Andrew, R. (1987) *Silent Victims. People with Intellectual Disabilities as Victims of Crime*. Melbourne: Office of the Public Advocate.

Johnson, K. and Traustadottir, R. (2000) 'Finding a place.' In R. Traustadottir and K. Johnson (eds) *Women with Intellectual Disabilities. Finding a Place in the World*. London: Jessica Kingsley Publishers.

Kaplan, S.J. and Alsup, R. (1995) 'Participatory action research: a creative response to AIDS prevention in diverse communities.' *Convergence 28*, 1, 38–55.

Keith, L. (2001) *Take Up Thy Bed and Walk: Death Disability and Care in Classic Fiction for Girls*. London: Women's Press.

Kellett, M. and Nind, M. (2001) 'Ethics in quasi-experimental research on people with severe learning disabilities: dilemmas and compromises.' *British Journal of Learning Disabilities* 29, 2, 51–55.

Kiernan, C. (1999) 'Participation in research by people with learning disability: origins and issues.' *British Journal of Learning Disabilities* 27, 2, 43–47.

King's Fund (1988) *Ties and Connections.* London: King's Fund.

Knox, M., Mok, M. and Parmenter, T. (2000) 'Working with the experts: collaborative research with people with an intellectual disability.' *Disability and Society* 15, 1, 49–62.

Krech, D. (1946) 'The challenge and the promise.' *Journal of Social Issues 11*, 4, 2–6.

Kristiansen, K. (2000) 'The social meaning of work. Listening to women's own experiences.' In R. Traustadottir and K. Johnson (eds) *Women with Intellectual Disabilities: Finding a Place in the World.* London: Jessica Kingsley Publishers.

Lather, P. (1991) *Getting Smart. Feminist Research and Pedagogy with/in the Postmodern.* New York: Routledge.

Lewin, K. (1946) 'Action research and minority problems.' *Journal of Social Issues 11*, 4, 34–46.

Liffman, M. (1978) *Power to the Poor.* Sydney: George Allen and Unwin.

Lyons, J.F. and Heaton Ward, W.A. (1955) *Notes on Mental Deficiency*, 3rd edn. Bristol: John Wright.

McCarthy, M. (1998) 'Interviewing people with learning disabilities about sensitive topics: a discussion of ethical issues.' *British Journal of Learning Disabilities 26*, 4, 140–145.

McCarthy, M. (1999) *Sexuality and Women with Learning Disabilities.* London: Jessica Kingsley Publishers.

McCarthy, M. (2000) 'Consent, abuse and choices: women with learning disabilities and sexuality.' In R. Traustadottir and K. Johnson (eds) *Women with Intellectual Disabilities: Finding a Place in the World.* London: Jessica Kingsley Publishers.

McCarthy, M. (in press) 'The menopause and women with learning difficulties.' *British Journal of Learning Disabilities.*

McClimens, A. (1999) 'Partcipatory research with people who have a learning difficulty: journeys without a map.' *Journal of Learning Disabilities for Nursing, Health and Social Care 3*, 4, 219–228.

McTaggart, R. (1997) *Participatory Action Research. International Contexts and Consequences.* New York: State University of New York Press.

Maguire, P. (1987) *Doing Participatory Research: A Feminist Approach.* Amherst, MA: Center for International Education.

Maguire, P. (1993) 'Challenges, contradictions and celebrations: attempting participatory research as a doctoral student.' In P. Park, M. Brydon-Miller, B. Hall and T. Jackson (eds) *Voices of Change. Participatory Research in the United States and Canada.* Westport, CT: Bergin and Garvey.

Mairs, N. (1986) 'On being a cripple.' In *Plaintexts: Essays.* Tucson: University of Arizona Press.

Mansell, J., Felce, D., Jenkins, J., de Kock, U. and Toogood, S. (1987) *Developing Staffed Housing for People with Mental Handicap.* Tunbridge Wells: Costello.

March, J., Steingold, B., Justice, S. and Mitchell, P. (1997) 'Follow the yellow brick road. People with learning difficulties as researchers.' *British Journal of Learning Disabilities 23*, 3, 94–97.

Markova, I., Jahoda, A. and Cattermole, M. (1988) 'Towards truly independent living.' *The Psychologist*, October, 397–399.

Marris, P. and Rein, M. (1969) *Dilemmas of Social Reform.* London: Routledge and Kegan Paul.

Mercer, J.R. (1973) *Labelling the Mentally Retarded: Clinical and Social Systems Perspectives on Mental Retardation.* Los Angeles: University of California Press.

Millard, L. (1994) 'Between ourselves. Experiences of a women's group and sexual abuse.' In A. Craft (ed) *Practice Issues in Sexuality and Learning Disabilities.* London: Routledge.

Millear, A. (with Johnson, K.) (2000) '39 months under the Disability Discrimination Act.' In R. Traustadottir and K. Johnson (eds) *Women with Intellectual Disabilities: Finding a Place in the World.* London: Jessica Kingsley Publishers.

Mitchell, P. (1997) 'The impact of self advocacy on families.' *Disability and Society 12*, 1, 43–56.

Mittler, P. (1996) 'Advocates and advocacy.' In P. Mittler and V. Sinason (eds) *Changing Policy and Practice for People with Learning Disabilities.* London: Cassell.

Mohammed, J. (2000) 'Administrator Rumbalara Aboriginal Co-operative, Shepparton.' In Vichealth Koori Health Research and Community Development Unit *We Don't Like Research but in Koori Hands it Could Make a Difference. A Community Report from the Vichealth Research and Community Development Unit.* Melbourne: Vichealth Research and Community Development Unit, University of Melbourne.

Moore, S., Gridley, H. and Johnson, K. (2000) 'Women's views about intimate examinations and sexually inappropriate practices by their general practitioners.' *Psychology and Health 15*, 71–84.

Morris, J. (1993) *Community Care or Independent Living.* York: Joseph Rowntree Foundation in association with Community Care.

Nicholls, R. and Andrew, R. (1990) *A Stands for Advocacy.* Melbourne: The Office of the Public Advocate.

Nind, M. and Johnson, K. (2002) 'Listening not labelling: extending the social model of disability to people with learning difficulties whose behaviour challenges.' Unpublished.

Nirje, B. (1980) 'The normalisation principle.' In R.J. Flynn and K.E. Nitsch (eds) *Normalisation, Integration and Community Services.* Baltimore: University Park Press.

Oakley, A. (1979) *Becoming a Mother.* New York: Schocken.

Oakley, A. (1981) 'Interviewing women: a contradiction in terms.' In H. Roberts (ed) *Doing Feminist Research.* London: Routledge.

Oakley, A. (2000) *Experiments in Knowing. Gender and Method in the Social Sciences.* Cambridge: Polity Press.

O'Brien, S. and Johnson, K. (1987) *Having a Real Say. A Report on Developing Consumer Participation within Organisations for People who are Intellectually Disadvantaged.* Melbourne: AMIDA.

O'Brien, S. and Johnson, K. (1988) 'Improving consumer participation.' *Community Quarterly 13*, 4–14.

Oliver, M. (1990) *The Politics of Disability.* London: Macmillan.

Oliver, M. (1992) 'Changing the social relations of research production.' *Disability, Handicap and Society 7*, 2, 101–114.

Oliver, M. (1994) 'Capitalism, disability and ideology: a materialist critique of the normalisation principle.' Paper presented to the conference *Twenty-five Years of Normalisation, Social Role Valorisation and Social Integration: A Retrospective View.* University of Ottawa, Ontario, 10–13 May.

Open University (1996) *Learning Disability: Working as Equal People.* Milton Keynes: Open University.

Osman, L. (1986) *Finding the Way. People with Intellectual Disabilities and the Criminal Justice System.* Melbourne: Office of the Public Advocate.

Palmer, N., Peacock, C., Turner, F. And Vasey, B. Supported by V. Williams (1999) 'Telling people what you think.' In J. Swain and S. French (eds) *Therapy and Learning Difficulties.* London: Butterworth-Heinemann.

Park, P. (1993) 'What is participatory research?' A theoretical and methodological perspective.' In P. Park, M. Brydon-Miller, B. Hall and T.

Jackson (eds) *Voices of Change. Participatory Research in the United States and Canada*. Westport, CT: Bergin and Garvey.

Patai, D. (1991) 'US academics and third world women: is ethical research possible?' In S. Berger Gluck and D. Patai (eds) *Women's Words. The Feminist Practice of Oral History*. New York: Routledge.

Pecket Well College (1996) In Open University *Learning Disability: Working as Equal People*. Milton Keynes: Open University.

Philpot, T. and Ward, L. (eds) (1994) *Values and Visions*. London: Butterworth Heinemann.

Plummer, K. (1983) *Documents of Life*, 1st edn. London: Routledge.

Plummer, K. (2001) *Documents of Life*, 2nd edn. London: Sage.

Potts, M. and Fido, R. (1991) *A Fit Person to be Removed*. Plymouth: Northcote House.

Priestley, M. (1999) *Disability Politics and Community Care*. London: Jessica Kingsley Publishers.

Race, D. (1999) *Social Role Valorisation and the English Experience*. London: Whiting and Birch.

Ramazanaglou, C. (1993) *Up Against Foucault. Exploration of Some Tensions between Foucault and Feminism*. London: Routledge.

Ramcharan, P., Roberts, G., Grant, G. and Borland, J. (1997) *Empowerment in Everyday Life: Learning Disability*. London: Jessica Kingsley Publishers.

Rapoport, R.N. (1970) 'Three dilemmas in action research.' *Human Relations 23*, 6, 499–513.

Reason, P. (1998) 'Three approaches to participative inquiry.' In N. Denzin and Y. Lincoln *Strategies of Qualitative Inquiry*. London: Sage.

Reinforce (1992) *Plain English Not Jargon*. Melbourne: Reinforce.

Reinforce (2000) personal communication.

Richards, S. (1984) *Community Care of the Handicapped: Consumer Perspectives*. Birmingham: University of Birmingham.

Riddell, S., Wilkinson, H. and Barron, S. (1998) 'From emancipatory research to focus group: people with learning difficulties and the research process.' In P. Clough and L. Barton (eds) *Articulating with Difficulty: Research Voices in Inclusive Education*. London: Paul Chapman.

Ristock, J.L. and Pennell, J. (1996) *Community Research as Empowerment: Feminist Links, Postmodern Interruptions*. Don Mills, ON: Oxford University Press.

Roberts, H. (1981) 'Women and their doctors: power and powerlessness in the research process.' In H. Roberts (ed) *Doing Feminist Research*. London: Routledge.

Rodgers, J. (1999) 'Trying to get it right: undertaking research involving people with learning difficulties.' *Disability and Society 14*, 4, 421–433.

Rolph, S. (1999) 'Enforced migrations by people with learning difficulties: a case study.' *Oral History 27*, 1, 47–56.

Rolph, S. (2000) 'The history of community care for people with learning difficulties in Norfolk 1930–1980.' Unpublished PhD thesis, Open University, Milton Keynes.

Rose, N. (1979) 'The psychological complex: mental measurement and social administration.' *Ideology and Consciousness 5*, 5–68.

Russell, F. (1946) 'Oil for the lamps of democracy.' *Journal of Social Issues 11*, 3, 7–14.

Said, E. (1978) *Orientalism.* London: Vintage Books.

Sanderson, H. (1998) 'A say in my future: involving people with profound and multiple disabilities in person centred planning.' In L. Ward (ed) *Advocacy and Empowerment.* Chorley: Lisieux Hall.

Saxe, J.G. (1930) 'The blind men and the elephant.' In *The Victorian Reader's Third Book.* Melbourne: Government Printer.

Saxton, M. And Howe, F. (1988) *With Wings: An Anthology of Literature by Women with Disabilities.* London: Virago.

Senn, C. (1988) *Vulnerable: Sexual Abuse and People with Intellectual Disability.* Toronto: Allan Roeher Institute.

Shakespeare, P., Atkinson, D. and French, S. (eds) (1993) *Reflecting on Research Practice.* Buckingham: Open University Press.

Shakespeare, T. (1996) 'Rules of engagement: doing disability research.' *Disability and Society 11*, 1, 115–120.

Sheldon, A. (1999) 'Personal and perplexing: feminist disability politics evaluated.' *Disability and Society 14*, 643–658.

Sigelman, C.K., Budd, E.C., Spanhel, C.L. and Schoenrock, C.J. (1981) '"When in doubt say yes": acquiescence in interviews with mentally retarded persons.' *Mental Retardation 19*, 53–58.

Simons, K. (1992) *'Sticking Up for Yourself'. Self Advocacy and People with Learning Difficulties.* York: Joseph Rowntree Foundation.

Simons, K. (1993) *Citizen Advocacy: The Inside View.* Bristol: Norah Fry Research Centre.

Simons, K. (1999) *A Place at the Table.* York: Joseph Rowntree Foundation.

Sinason, V. (1992) *Mental Handicap and the Human Condition.* London: Free Association Books.

Slattery, J. (with Johnson, K.) (2000) 'Family, marriage, friends and work: This is my life.' In R. Traustadottir and K. Johnson (eds) *Women with Intellectual Disabilities: Finding a Place in the World.* London: Jessica Kingsley Publishers.

Souza, A. (with Ramcharan, P.) (1997) 'Everything you ever wanted to know about Down's Syndrome, but never bothered to ask.' In P. Ramcharan, G. Roberts, G. Grant and J. Borland (eds) *Empowerment in Everyday Life: Learning Disability.* London: Jessica Kingsley Publishers.

Spedding, F., Harkness, E., Townson, L., Docherty, A., McNulty, N. and Chapman, R. (2002) 'The role of self advocacy: stories from a self advocacy group told through the experiences of its members.' In B. Gray and R. Jackson (eds) *Advocacy and Learning Disability.* London: Jessica Kingsley Publishers.

Spelman, E. (1988) *Inessential Woman. Problems of Exclusion in Feminist Thought.* London: Women's Press.

Stainton, T. (2000) 'Equal citizens? The discourse of liberty and rights in the history of learning disabilities.' In L. Brigham, D. Atkinson, M. Jackson, S. Rolph and J. Walmsley (eds) *Crossing Boundaries: Change and Continuity in the History of Learning Disability.* Kidderminster: BILD.

Stalker, K. (1998) 'Some ethical and methodological issues in research with people with learning difficulties.' *Disability and Society 13*, 1, 5–19.

Stancliffe, R. and Lakin, K. (1998) 'Analysis of expenditures and outcomes of residential alternatives for persons with developmental disabilities.' *American Journal on Mental Retardation 102*, 6, 552–568.

Steier, F. (1992) *Research and Reflexivity.* London: Sage.

Sutcliffe, J. (1993) *Adult Education and People with Learning Difficulties.* Leicester: NIACE.

Swantz, M.-L. and Vainio-Mattila, A. (1988) 'Participatory inquiry as an instrument of grass-roots development.' In P. Reason (ed) *Human Inquiry in Action.* London: Sage.

Swindon People First Research Team (2002) *Journey to Independence: Direct Payments for People with Learning Difficulties.* Report to BILD. Swindon: Swindon People First.

Taylor, S.J., Bogdan, R. and Lutfiyya, Z. (eds) (1995) *The Variety of Community Experience. Qualitative Studies of Family and Community Life.* Baltimore: Paul H. Brookes.

'Theory and Experience' (1992) in *Disability Handicap and Society 7*, 2 (Special Issue).

Thompson, P. (1988) *The Voice of the Past.* Oxford: Oxford University Press.

Todd, S. and Shearn, J. (1997) 'Family dilemmas and secrets: parents' disclosure of information to their adult offspring with learning disabilities.' *Disability and Society 12*, 3, 341–366.

Townsley, R. (1998) 'Information is power: the impact of accessible information on people with learning difficulties.' In L. Ward (ed) *Innovations in Advocacy and Empowerment for People with Intellectual Disabilities.* Chorley: Lisieux Hall.

Townsley, R. and Macadam, M. (1996) *Choosing Staff: Involving People with Learning Difficulties in Staff Recruitment.* Bristol: Norah Fry Research Centre.

Trausradottir, R. (2001) 'Research with others. Reflections on presentation, difference and othering.' *Scandinavian Journal of Disability Research 3*, 2, 9–28.

Traustadottir, R. and Johnson, K. (eds) (2000) *Women with Intellectual Disabilities: Finding a Place in the World.* London: Jessica Kingsley Publishers.

Traylen, H. (1994) 'Confronting hidden agendas: co-operative inquiry with health visitors.' In P. Reason (ed) *Participation in Human Inquiry.* London: Sage.

Tredgold, A.F. (1947) *A Text Book of Mental Deficiency (Amentia),* 7th edn. London: Baillière, Tindall and Cox.

Treleaven, L. (1994) 'Making a space: a collaborative inquiry with women as staff development.' In P. Reason (ed) *Participation in Human Inquiry.* London: Sage.

Tuhiwai Smith, L. (1999) *Decolonizing Methodologies. Research and Indigenous People.* London: Zed Books.

Turk, V. and Brown, H. (1993) 'The sexual abuse of adults with learning disabilities: results of a two year incidence survey.' *Mental Handicap Research 6*, 193–216.

Tuttleby, A. (with Johnson, K.) (2000) '39 months under the Disability Discrimination Act.' In R. Traustadottir and K. Johnson (eds) *Women with Intellectual Disabilities: Finding a Place in the World.* London: Jessica Kingsley Publishers.

Van Hove, G. (1999) 'Cooperative research with people with learning disabilities in Belgium.' *Tizard Learning Disability Review,* European issue, 40–45.

Veck, W. (2002) 'Completing the story: connecting relational and psychological processes of exclusion.' *Disability and Society 17*, 5, 529–540.

Vernon, A. (1996) 'Fighting two different battles: unity is preferable to enmity.' *Disability and Society 11*, 2, 285–290.

Vichealth Koori Research and Community Development Unit (2001) *Research Understanding Ethics. A Community Report from the Vichealth Koori Health*

Research and Community Development Unit. Melbourne: Vichealth Koori Health Research and Community Development Unit, University of Melbourne.

Victorian Government (1986) *The Intellectually Disabled Persons Services Act.* Melbourne: Victorian Government Printing Service.

Wadsworth, Y. (1994) *Understanding and Involvement. Consumer Evaluation of Acute Psychiatric Hospital Practice. A Project's Beginnings.* Melbourne: Victorian Mental Illness Awareness Council.

Wadsworth, Y. and Epstein, M. (1996a) *Understanding and Involvement. Consumer Evaluation of Acute Psychiatric Hospital Practice. A Project Unfolds.* Melbourne: Victorian Mental Illness Awareness Council.

Wadsworth, Y. and Epstein, M. (1996b) *Understanding and Involvement. Consumer Evaluation of Acute Psychiatric Hospital Practice. A Project Concludes.* Melbourne: Victorian Mental Illness Awareness Council.

Walmsley, J. (1989) 'The meaning of adulthood in the lives of people with learning difficulties.' Unpublished MSc dissertation. Open University, Milton Keynes.

Walmsley, J. (1991) 'Adulthood and people with learning difficulties: report of a research project.' *Mental Handicap Research 4*, 2, 141–154.

Walmsley, J. (1993) 'Women first: lessons in participation.' *Critical Social Policy 38*, 86–99.

Walmsley, J. (1994) 'Learning disability: overcoming the barriers?' In S. French (ed) *On Equal Terms.* London: Butterworth Heinemann.

Walmsley, J. (1995) 'Gender, caring and learning disability.' Unpublished PhD thesis, Open University, Milton Keynes.

Walmsley, J. (1997) 'Including People with Dearning Difficulties: Theory and Practice.' In L. Barton and M. Oliver (eds) *Disability Studies: Past, Present and Future.* Leeds: The Disability Press.

Walmsley, J. (2000a) 'Caring: a place in the world.' In R. Traustadottir and K. Johnson (eds) *Women with Intellectual Disabilities: Finding a Place in the World.* London: Jessica Kingsley Publishers.

Walmsley, J. (2000b) (with Atkinson, D.) 'Oral history and the history of learning disability.' In J. Bornat *et al. Health Welfare and Oral History.* London: Routledge.

Walmsley, J. (2001) 'Normalisation, emancipatory research and learning disability.' *Disability and Society 16*, 2, 187–205.

Walmsley, J. (with Downer, J.) (1997) 'Shouting the loudest: self advocacy, power and diversity.' In P. Ramcharan (ed) *Empowerment in Everyday Life.* London: Jessica Kingsley Publishers.

Ward, L. (1989) 'For better, for worse.' In A. Brechin and J. Walmsley (eds) *Making Connections: Reflecting on the Lives and Experiences of People with Learning Difficulties.* London: Hodder and Stoughton.

Ward, L. (ed) (1998) *Advocacy and Empowerment.* Chorley: Lisieux Hall.

Ward, L. and Simons, K. (1998) 'Practising partnership: involving people with learning difficulties in research.' *British Journal of Learning Disabilities 26*, 4, 128–131.

Ward, K. and Trigler, J.S. (2001) 'Reflections on participatory action research with people who have developmental disabilities.' *Mental Retardation 1*, 57–59.

Webb, P. (1999) 'Voices of people with learning difficulties.' In J. Swain and S. French (eds) *Therapy and Learning Difficulties.* London: Butterworth Heinemann.

Welsh Office (1983) *All Wales Strategy for the Development of Services for Mentally Handicapped People.* Cardiff: Welsh Office.

Whittaker, A. (1995) 'Partnership in practice: user participation in services for people with learning difficulties.' In T. Philpot and L. Ward (eds) *Values and Visions: Changing Ideas in Services for People with Learning Difficulties.* London: Butterworth Heinemann.

Whittaker, A. (1997) *Looking at Our Services: Service Evaluation by People with Learning Difficulties.* London: King's Fund Centre.

Whittell, B., Ramcharan, P. and members of People First Cardiff and the Vale (1998) 'Self advocacy: speaking up for ourselves and each other.' In L. Ward (ed) *Innovations in Advocacy and Empowerment for People with Intellectual Disabilities.* Chorley: Lisieux Hall.

Wickham, P. (2001) 'Review essay: *Women with Intellectual Disabilities: Finding a Place in the World.' Mental Retardation 3*, 237–240.

Wilkinson, J. (1989) 'Being there: evaluating life quality from feelings and daily experience.' In A. Brechin and J. Walmsley (eds) *Making Connections: Reflecting on the Lives and Experiences of People with Learning Difficulties.* London: Hodder and Stoughton.

Williams, P. and Schoultz, B. (1982) *We Can Speak for Ourselves.* London: Souvenir Press.

Williams, V. (1999) 'Researching together.' *British Journal of Learning Disabilities 27*, 2, 48–51.

Williams, V. (2002) 'Being researchers with the label of learning difficulty: an analysis of talk carried out by a self advocacy research group.' Unpublished PhD thesis, Open University, Milton Keynes.

Wolfensberger, W. (1972) *The Principle of Normalisation in Human Services.* Toronto: National Institute on Mental Retardation.

Wolfensberger, W. (1980) 'The definition of normalisation: update, problems, disagreements and misunderstandings.' In R.J. Flynn and K.E. Bitsch (eds) *Normalisation, Social Integration and Community Services*. Baltimore: University Park Press.

Wolfensberger, W. and Thomas, S. (1983) *Passing: Programme Analysis of Service Systems Implementation of Normalisation Goals*. Toronto: National Institute on Mental Retardation.

Wolfensberger, W. and Tullman, S. (1982) 'A brief outline of the principle of normalization.' *Rehabilitation Psychology 27*, 131–145.

Zarb, G. (1992) 'On the road to Damascus: first steps towards changing the relations of disability research production.' *Disability, Handicap and Society 7*, 125–138.

Zuber-Skerritt, O. (1996) 'Emancipatory action research for organisational change and management development.' In O. Zuber-Skerritt (ed) *New Directions in Action Research*. London: Falmer Press.

Subject Index

ability, to undertake research 153–4
academic gaze 98, 217
access
  to publishing 142–3
  to research 53–4
accessibility
  inclusive research 62, 172–7, 217
  Know Me As I Am 77–8
achievements, inclusive research 183–7
action research 10, 24
  see also participatory action research
advisory groups *see* reference groups
advocacy
  researchers 203–6
  see also citizen advocacy; self
    advocacy
Advocacy and Empowerment 171
advocacy organizations, research
  generation 128–30
All Wales Strategy 45–6
allies, sympathetic 66–7, 159
AMIDA, consumer participation 33–4
anonymity, *Good Times Bad Times* 104
association with valued others 48
audio 175
Australia
  qualitative studies 71
  self advocacy movement 70
authorship 143, 149, 197
autobiographical accounts 134–6
  representation and ownership
    166–8
autobiographies 131, 132–4
  equal partnership 149
  feminist research 36
  researchers' roles 195–6
  self advocates 57

barriers approach, to disability 183
biographical accounts 131, 134–6
biographies, feminist research 36
boundaries, non-disabled researchers
  161–2, 193
Bristol Self Advocacy Group 129–30,
  153, 172, 184
*Building Expectations Inquiry into
  Community Services and Opportunities for
  People with Learning Disabilities* 174

Campaign for the Mentally
  Handicapped (CMH) 70
carers, focus of research on 65–6
Caring: A Place in the World 173–4
change
  in learning disability research
    69–73
  see also social change
Changing Perspectives 74
Chicago school, ethnographic research
  68
Chronically Sick and Disabled Persons
  Act (1976) 51
citizen advocacy 49–50, 55, 161
co-publishing 102–3, 214–16
co-researching 148–54
co-writing 171–2
coaches, researchers as 208–10
collaboration 82
  Good Times Bad Times 102–5
  Know Me As I Am 75–6
  see also partnerships
collective identity, inhibition of 48
colonizing the other
  qualitative research 39–40
  resistance to 86
communities, involvement in research
  84–6
Community Care 208
Community Care Award 179–80
community living 49
compliance 70

compromises
    Good Times Bad Times 105–7
    Know Me As I Am 77
    Living Safer Sexual Lives project
        122–3
confidentiality, Good Times Bad Times
    104
confusing roles, researchers 194–8
consent, informed 158–9
consultants, researchers as 211–14
consumer participation, AMIDA 33–4
control, over research 101–2, 148
criticism, opportunities for 148

data analysis, denial of 169
data gathering, qualitative research
    35–6
deinstitutionalization 49, 87
Department of Health Learning
    Disability Research Initiative 13
dichotomy, through inclusive research
    90
difference
    focus on, autobiographical accounts
        131
    pride in 55
    terminology to erase 160
Differences, Conflations and Foundations
    186
differentiation, in disability 51
dilemmas, inclusive research 73–8
disability
    social model 50–4, 169
    see also intellectual disability;
        learning disability; physical
        disability
Disability and Society 52
Disability Discrimination Act 37
Disability, Handicap and Society 52, 186
Disability Politics 52
disability studies 187
    emphasis on embodiment 52
    learning disability 51–2

disabled people's movement
    emancipatory research 50–4
    group consciousness 56
    self advocates in research 58–9
distinctive voice, of researchers 178–9,
    201–3
Documents of Life 36, 177
Doing Research with Lonely People
    161
domestic violence 91

editors, Good Times Bad Times 98–9
emancipatory research 10, 24, 28
    challenge imposed by 59–60
    characteristics 63
    disabled people's movement 50–4
    espousal by disabled people 38
    political change 180
embodiment, disability studies 52
empathy, through auto/biographical
    accounts 167
empiricist model 64–5
employers, learning disabled as 211–14
empowerment
    of marginalized groups 43
    of participants 32–5
    reference groups 147–8
    women with learning disabilities
        96–7
equal partnership 148–54
equal payment 155–6
Equal People course 97, 174
ethical dilemmas, researchers 185
ethical issues 155–9
ethnographic research 68
euphemisms 160
expert advisors, researchers as 50–1
expertise, learning disabled 114
exploitation 177–8

families, focus of research on 65–6
'Family, Marriage, Friends and Work:
    This is My Life' 197

feminism 27, 186, 187
feminist research 24, 25, 26–7
    empowering participants 32, 35
    focusing on the individual 36
    self-reflection 39
    social change 30
feminist researchers, negative effects of
    research 84
Finding a way through the language
    maze 194
A Fit Person to Be Removed 135
Foucauldian analyses 217
funding
    access to 54
    expectation of practical benefit 168
    Good Times Bad Times 99–100
    importance of inclusion 13
    initiating research 138–9
    Living Safer Sexual lives project
        111–12
    researcher as consultant 213, 214

ghost writers 103
ghost writing 132
Good Times Bad Times 95–108
    co-writing 171
    collaborative process 102–5
    compromises 105–7
    the editors 98–9
    first book 97–8
    initiation of 132, 133
    methodology 176
    origins of the book 96–7
    power and control 101–2
    representation and ownership 165,
        166, 170
    time, funding and practical
        considerations 99–100
government policies 58
group consciousness, disability
    movement 56
group level, self advocacy 55

Hackney People First 151–2
Having a Real Say 33–4
'The Helper's Story' 101, 105, 176,
    194
helpful research 9–10
high grades, learning disabilities 185
homogeneity, of learning disabled
    204–5

'I am Stuck here with my Poxy Star
    Chart' 167
ICT (information and communications
    technology) 175
image, disadvantaged people 45
immediacy, participatory action research
    27
impairment, and evil 50
inclusion 13
    limits to 183–4
    stereotyping 81
inclusive research
    accessibility 62, 77–8, 172–7, 217
    achievements 183–7
    building research capacity 219
    co-writing 171–2
    contested meanings 80–6
    defining 10–11
    exploitation 177–8
    impact of 179–81
    key questions 17
    learning disability 61–78
        defining 61–4
        methodologies 64–73
        revealing potential and
            dilemmas 73–8
    managing 146–63
        ethical issues 155–9
        from advisory groups to control
            146–54
        non-disabled researchers, role of
            159–63

with people with learning
  disabilities
    concerns of 90–1
    short history of 12
    working together on outcomes
      216–17
  philosophical influences 44–60
    disabled movement and
      emancipatory research 50–4
    normalization 44–50
    self advocacy 54–9
  political perspectives and broader
    social context 87–90
  principles 16
  process
    Good Times Bad Times 95–108
    Living Safer Sexual Lives
      project 109–25
  representation and ownership
    165–70
  research perspectives
    common principles 28–41
    influence of 23–8
    translating principles into
      practice 41–2
  researchers see researchers
  theorizing 217–18
  training and qualifications 218
  who benefits 181
individual level, self advocacy 55
individuals, focusing on 35–8
inequalities, in research situation 89
informed consent 158–9
Inside Out 68, 133
insider status, finding participants 157
institutional closure, qualitative study
  29–30, 40, 84
integrationist policies 48
intellectual disability
  disability studies 52
  terminology 51
  see also learning disability
Intellectually Disabled Persons Services
  Act (1986) 46, 51

interests, balancing 140–3
intermediaries, finding participants 157
interpretation, empowerment 34–5
interviewer, blurring of boundaries
  between interviewees and 154
interviews, semi-structured 136–7,
  139–40

Joseph Rowntree Foundation 168, 216
justice, research as a fight for 87–8

Kainova, Tamara 131
Know Me As I Am: An Anthology of Prose,
  Poetry and Art by People with Learning
  Disabilities 180
  initiation of 133
  potential and dilemmas of inclusive
    research 73–8
  representation and ownership 12,
    167–8, 170
  valued social role 49
knowledge production 39

labels, for research 81–2
language
  non-disabled researchers 192–5
  and power differentials in research
    160
  power of 80–2
  terminology, intellectual disability
    51
leadership, learning disabled 215
learners, learning disabled as 208–10
learning disability
  disability studies 51–2
  inclusive research 61–78
    defining 61–4
    methodologies 64–73
    revealing potential and
      dilemmas 73–8
  terminology 51
  see also people with learning
    disabilities

Learning Partners 199–201
liberationism, feminist research 27, 30
life historians 147, 152
life stories
    feminist research 36
    initiation of research 131–6
    violation of rights to control 177–8
Living Safer Sexual Lives 109–25
    compromises 122–3
    implementing research 120–2
    inclusion of life stories 133
    obtaining funding 111–12, 139
    origins of the research 110–11
    reference group 112–16
    researchers 116–18
    stories, analysing 119–20
    story tellers 118–19
London People First 132, 137, 148, 151
low grades, learning disabilities 185

'Mabel Cooper's Life Story' 149, 171, 195
Maketon 53, 174
marginalized groups
    empowerment of 43
    importance of inclusion 13
    involvement in research 84–6
    social change through PAR 31
means and ends, of research 83–6
mechanical aids 53
medical model, learning disability 64, 70
medically based research 89–90
Memories Group 135, 147, 152, 158
mental handicap
    normalization 45
    terminology 51
Mental Health Act (1959) (Australia) 51
Mental Health Act (1959) (UK) 51
Mental Health Act (1983) (UK) 51
mental retardation 69
methodology, and accessibility 176

naturalistic approach, to research 25–6, 36
NIMROD 47
non-disabled researchers
    boundaries 161–2
    equitable relationship between learning disabled and 89
    power 162–3
    roles 159–61
        challenge to 58
        confusion 194–8
        language and terminology 192–4
    theorizing 217–18
Norah Fry Research Centre's Plain Facts initiative 173, 216
normalization 44–8, 59
    and inclusive research 48–50
    judgement of service quality 151
normalization-inspired models, of research 52
North American model, normalization 45
Norton self advocacy group 139, 141–2, 154, 172, 184

objectivity, in research 26, 32, 62
Open Doors 98
open-ended approach, to research 167–8
oppression 208
Orient as Other 81
othering 39, 81, 217
ownership
    Good Times Bad Times 105
    inclusive research 169–71
    moral climate 177

PAR *see* participatory action research
'Parallel Stories' 150
participants
    empowering 32–5
    finding 156–7

inclusion in research process 13
participation
  inviting 157
  social care 189–90
  traditional research 65
participatory action research (PAR) 25,
  27–8
  characteristics 62
  empowering participants 32
  focusing on the individual 38
  self-reflection 39
  social change 31
participatory research 10, 24
partnerships
  consultancy approach 212
  in research 148–54
  see also collaboration
PASS 47
PASSING 47
Patterns for Living 78
payment 155–6
People First 55, 209
People First Hackney 151–2
People First International conference
  209
People First Language 56
People First London 132, 137, 148,
  151
people with learning disabilities
  126–45
  association with valued others 48
  challenging assumptions about
    working with 11–12
  co-researching 214–16
  creation of subdivisions 185
  disability studies 52–3
  early voices of 67–9
  as employers 211–14
  empowering participants 33–4
  identification of research questions
    185
  inclusive research
    accessibility 62, 77–8, 172–7,
    217

co-writing 171–2
  due to concerns of 90–1
  ethical issues 155–9
  exploitation 177–8
  Good Times Bad Times 95–108
  Living Safer Sexual Lives
    project 109–25
  representation and ownership
    165–70
  roles 146–54
  short history of 12
initiating research
  barriers to 138–43
  by advocacy organizations
    128–30
  Know Me As I Am 75
  qualitative research 136–7
  service evaluations 137–8
  whole life approaches 131–6
  as learners or students 208–10
  reason for non inclusion in book
    15–16
  research on perception of life 72
  researchers as advocates 203–6
  self advocacy 56–7, 58
  service provision 45–6
  silence of, prior to late twentieth
    century 67
  soliciting views of 211
  terminology 19–20
  training and qualifications 218
  who should define what matters
    143–4
  see also learning disability
philosophical influences, inclusive
  research 44–60
physical disabilities
  access to research 53
  focus on, disability studies 52
Plain English Less Jargon 129
Plain Facts 173, 216
political change, emancipatory research
  180
political focus, action research 27

political struggle, inclusive research as
site for 87–9
positive imagery, disadvantaged people
45, 49
positivist research 25, 26, 35, 90
postcolonialism 24
potential, inclusive research 73–8
power
    Good Times Bad Times 101–2
    non-disabled researchers 162–3
    self advocacy 57
Powerhouse 98, 196, 210
pride, in learning disabled 55
print 162
process of research 82–3
    Good Times Bad Times 95–108
    Living Safer Sexual Lives project
    109–25
pseudonyms 105
publishing, access to 142–3

qualifications 218
qualitative research 25–6
    colonizing the other 39–40
    empowering participants 32
    exploitation 177
    focusing on the individual 35–6
    inclusiveness of 136–7
    learning disability
        glimmerings of change 71–3
        traditional research 65–6
    self-reflection 38–9
    social change 29–30
quality of services, normalization 47,
151

reductionist approach, to research 26
reference groups 146–8
    Learning Partners 199–201
    Living Safer Sexual lives 112–16
    need for clear boundaries 198
reflection, on research 38–41
Reinforce 55, 70, 129

reminiscence-based group work 135
representation
    inclusive research 12, 165–8
    see also self-representation
representativeness 184
reputable research 9
research capacity, user-controlled
    organizations 219
research conscience 89–90
research findings, working together on
    216–17
research process 82–3
    Good Times Bad Times 95–108
    Living Safer Sexual Lives 109–25
research topics 139–40
researchers
    as advocates 49–50, 203–6
    challenge imposed by emancipatory
        research 59–60
    co-researching 214–16
    as consultants 211–14
    distinctive voice 178–9, 201–3
    ethical dilemmas 185
    as expert advisors 50–1
    legitimization of research focus 88
    Living Safer Sexual lives 116–18
    polarity amongst 26
    respondents' perceptions of 71
    self-reflection 38–41, 71, 202
    sympathetic 66–7
    as teacher and coach 208–10
    tension between reputable and
        helpful research 9–10
    see also non-disabled researchers
'Researching Together' 176
resistance, to colonization 86
resistance texts 36
'Risk, Resilience and Competence' 168
roles
    clarification of 209–10
    non-disabled researchers 58,
        159–61, 192–8

Scandinavian model, normalization 45
Scottish Home and Health Department
  72
self advocacy 54–9
  co-research 151–2
  finding a voice through 60
  groups
    Bristol 129–30, 153, 172, 184
    finding participants for research
      157
    Norton 139, 141–2, 154, 172,
      184
  movement 70
  research 184–5
    initiation of 129–30, 137
  service-centred perspective 180
'Self Advocacy: Speaking Up for
  Ourselves and Each Other' 171
self-consciousness 40
self-criticism 148
self-distancing 72
self-identification 72
self-reflection 38–41, 71, 202
self-representation 67–9
semi-structured interviews 136–7,
  139–40
service evaluation
  by learning disabled 137–8
  co-research 150–1
service evaluators 70
service provision
  people with learning disabilities
    45–6
  self advocacy agenda 180
  see also quality of services
sexual abuse 110
short accessible method 173–4
'Shouting the Loudest' 142, 171
silences, important questions emerging
  from 91
skills, learning disabled 114
Skills for People Newcastle 165
snowballing method, finding
  participants 157

social care, participation 189–90
social change
  commitment to 29–32
  research as tool for 60
social justice 31
social model, disability 50–4, 169, 183
social relations, research production
  212, 221
social role valorization 44–50, 59, 74
societal discrimination 37, 39, 87
societal injustice 88
societal values 50
Stegley Foundation 13
stereotypical victim category 166
stereotyping, inclusion 81
Sticking up for Yourself 137
stigma 68–9, 156
'Still Family' 168
story analysis, Living Safer Sexual Lives
  119–20
story tellers, Living Safer Sexual Lives
  118–19
students, learning disabled as 208–10
substituted judgement 50
support workers 209
symbols, accessible information 53, 174
sympathetic researcher 66–7
sympathy, through auto/biographical
  accounts 167

taking charge, of research 152–4, 184
teachers, researchers as 208–10
'Telling People What You Think' 153,
  197
terminology 19–20
  erasure of difference 160
  intellectual disability 51
  non-disabled researchers 192–4
theorizing 217–18
  abstract 186
  by learning disabled 56, 141–2
'Theory and Experience' 186
traditional research, learning disability
  empirical model 64–5

qualitative studies 65–6
training 218
'Trying to Get it Right' 53, 147

United States
    early instances of self-representation
        68
    model of normalization 45
    self advocacy movement 70
user involvement
    service evaluation 180
    social care 189–90
    violation of rights to control life
        stories 177–8
user-controlled organizations, research
    capacity 219

value base, normalization 47–8
valued others, association with 48
valued social role 49
values
    inclusive research 221
    societal 50
Values and Visions 171
Valuing People 180, 183, 211
Venus on Wheels 202–3
victim message, in research 165–6
video 175
'Voices of People with Learning
    Difficulties' 165–6

We Can Speak for Ourselves 70
Wells Road service 47
western discourse, Orient as Other 81
whole life approaches, initiation of
    research 131–6
'Woman to Woman' 171
women
    in research process 35
    see also feminist research
Women First 96–7
Working Together for Welcoming
    Communities 174
"writing hand" technique 102, 197

Author Index

Abbott, P. and Sapsford, R. 66
Anderson, I. 83, 84
Andrews, J. (with Rolph, S.) 57, 133, 168
Armstrong, D. 36
Aspis, S. 16, 52, 57, 58, 60, 141, 142, 180, 208
Atkinson, D. 12, 48, 49, 57, 63, 70, 71, 103, 104, 135, 149, 160, 181, 195
Atkinson, D. and Cooper, M. 150, 171, 195
Atkinson, D., Jackson, M. and Walmsley, J. 102, 149
Atkinson, D., McCarthy, M., Walmsley, J. et al. 15, 95, 101, 132, 143, 165, 175, 192, 194
Atkinson, D. and Walmsley, J. 67, 131
Atkinson, D. and Williams, F. 12, 49, 61, 73, 74, 75, 76, 178
Aull Davies, C. and Jenkins, R. 72, 136
Ayer, S. and Alaszewski, A. 66

Baddou, F. 31
Baldwin, S. and Glendinning, C. 66
Bank-Mikkelson, N.E. 45
Barnes, C. 62, 176, 203
Barron, D. 57, 132, 133
Bayley, M. 11, 66
Benmayor, R. 30
Benn, C. 34
Beresford, P. 43, 53, 62
Bersani, H. 12, 56, 179
Blunden, R. 46
Bogdan, R. and Biklen, S. 80
Bogdan, R. and Taylor, S. 12, 68, 69, 133
Booth, T. and Booth, W. 12, 49, 87, 133, 134, 160, 161, 168, 170, 178

Booth, T., Simons, K. and Booth, W. 87
Booth, W. 161
Braye, S. 189, 190
Brechin, A. and Sidell, M. 26, 80
Brown, H. and Thomsom, D. 140, 204
Brown, H. and Turk, V. 110
Brown, S., Johnson, K., Jackson, A. and Wyn, J. 14
Brown, S., Johnson, K. and Wyn, J. 14
Brydon-Miller, M. 31
Butler, K., Carr, S. and Sullivan, F. 49

Campbell, J. and Oliver, M. 52
Caplan, P. 40
Carr, W. and Kemmis, S. 31
Carroll, L. 23
Carson, D. 110
Cattermole, M., Jahoda, A. and Markova, I. 72
Central England People First 57, 129, 185, 213, 214
Chamberlain, M. 166
CHANGE 174
Chapman, R. and Carlisle People First Research Group 130, 157
Chappell, A. 46, 47, 48, 52, 62, 63, 67, 135, 159, 164, 179, 184
Chappell, A., Goodley, D. and Lawthorn, R. 51, 66, 169
Chenoweth, L. 87
Clark, D., Fry, T. and Rodgers, J. 171
Cocks, E. and Cockram, J. 62
Colin, T. and Garrow, A. 32
Commonwealth Government 87
Cooper, J. and Vernon, S. 46
Cooper, M. 57, 67, 102, 132, 133, 143, 149, 172, 195, 208
Cooper, M., Ferris, G., Coventry, M. and Atkinson, D. 150
Corker, M. 186
Cosier, J. and Glennie, S. 31
Coventry, M. 133

Daly, J. 35
Danziger, K. 126
David 109
Deacon, J. 12, 67, 132
Denzin, N.K. and Lincoln, Y.S. 26, 80
Department of Health 180, 183
Department of Human Services 81, 87
Di Terlizzi 133

Edgerton, R. 61, 68
Edgerton, R. and Bercovici, S. 61, 68
Edgerton, R., Bollinger, M. and Herr, B. 61, 68
Emerson, E. 45
Evans, G., Todd, S., Blunden, R., Porterfield, J. and Agar, A. 46

Ferguson, P.M., Ferguson, D.C. and Taylor, S.J. 80
Ferris, G. 133
Fine, M. 39
Fine, M. and Gordon, S. 39
Finkelstein, V. 38, 54, 167, 180
Flynn, M. 12, 49, 70, 71
Flynn, M., Griffiths, S., Byne, L. and Hynes, K. 167, 178
Foster, M. 27
Frank, G. 202
Frawley, P., Johnson, K., Hillier, L. and Harrison, L. 120
Freire, P. 10, 25, 28, 85
French, S. 47
French, S. and Swain, J. 63

Gerber, D.A. 69
Gillman, M., Swain, J. and Heyman, B. 149
Gluck, S.B. 30
Gluck, S.B. and Patai, D. 27, 30, 35, 36
Goffman, E. 68
Goode, D. 183, 205
Goodley, D. 55, 56, 135, 179, 181

Grant, G., Ramcharan, P. and McGrath, M. 135, 136
Gray, B. and Jackson, R. 208
Greenwood, D. and Levin, M. 31, 80
Gridley, H., Moore, S., Higgins, J. and Johnson, K. 14

Harrison, L., Johnson, K., Hillier, L. and Strong, R. 16, 114, 119, 121, 123, 125
Hevey, D. 50
Hiscoe 55
Hollingsworth, S., Dadds, M. and Miller, J. 82
Holman, A. and Collins, J. 137
hooks, b. 27, 36, 186, 210, 220
Horton, B. 32
Humphrey, S., Evans, G. and Todd, S. 46
Hunt, N. 67, 132

Jackson, M. 143–4
Jackson, T. 31
Jahoda, A., Markova, I. and Cattermole, M. 12, 72
Johnson, K. 40, 49, 84, 117, 134, 157, 192, 194, 202, 204
Johnson, K., Frawley, P., Hillier, L. and Harrison, L. 109, 120
Johnson, K., Frawley, P., Holopainen, D., Hillier, L. and Harrison, L. 134
Johnson, K., Hillier, L., Harrison, L. and Frawley, P. 87, 110, 120, 136, 157
Johnson, K. and McIntyre, D. 40
Johnson, K. and Tait, S. 51
Johnson, K., Topp, V. and Andrew, R. 46, 70, 71, 110
Johnson, K. and Traustadottir, R. 131

Kaplan, S.J. and Alsup, R. 27
Keith, L. 50
Kellett, M. and Nind, M. 144, 179, 205
Kiernan, C. 64–5, 66, 69, 164
King's Fund 48

Knox, M., Mok, M. and Parmenter, T. 159, 160, 193
Krech, D. 31
Kristiansen, K. 133

Lather, P. 26
Lewin, K. 25, 31
Liffman, M. 34
Lyons, J.F. and Heaton Ward, W.A. 11

McCarthy, M. 87, 136, 140, 158, 167, 178, 196, 205, 210
McClimens, A. 164
McTaggart, R. 31
Maguire, P. 31, 38
Mairs, N. 56
Mansell, J., Felce, D., Jenkins, J., de Kock, U. and Toogood, S. 46
March, J., Steingold, B., Justice, S. and Mitchell, P. 57
Markova, I., Jahoda, A. and Cattermole, M. 72
Marris, P. and Rein, M. 9
Mercer, J.R. 69
Millard, L. 110
Millear, A. (with Johnson, K.) 15, 37
Mitchell, P. 151, 152, 157, 160, 176, 179, 181, 192
Mittler, P. 66–7
Mohammed, J. 84
Moore, S., Gridley, H. and Johnson, K. 14
Morris, J. 66
Mulholland, V. 109

Nicholls, R. and Andrew, R. 46
Nind, M. and Johnson, K. 126
Nirje, B. 45

Oakley, A. 25, 26, 27, 32, 35, 36, 39, 202
O'Brien, S. and Johnson, K. 33, 46, 71, 72

Oliver, M. 38, 47, 50, 51, 184, 212
Open University 15, 55, 97, 103, 175, 175, 197
Osman, L. 46

Palmer, N., Peacock, C., Turner, F. and Vasey, B. Supported by V. Williams 136, 153, 169, 172, 184, 186, 197
Park, P. 28, 31
Patai, D. 35
Pecket Well College 103, 197
Philpot, T. and Ward, L. 171
Plummer, K. 25, 36, 68, 177, 195
Potts, M. and Fido, R. 49, 134, 135, 143
Priestley, M. 38, 184, 221

Race, D. 47
Ramazanaglou, C. 91
Ramcharan, P., Roberts, G., Grant, G. and Borland, J. 81, 87
Rapoport, R.N. 27
Reason, P. 10
Reinforce 57
Richards, S. 64
Riddell, S., Wilkinson, H. and Baron, S. 16
Ristock and Pennell 166
Roberts, H. 36
Rodgers, J. 53, 60, 147, 148, 167
Rolph, S. 57, 98, 133, 134, 135, 143, 147, 152, 157, 158, 160, 170, 176, 181, 192, 195
Rose, N. 126
Russell, F. 25

Said, E. 81
Sanderson, H. 170
Saxe, J.G. 79
Saxton, M. and Howe, F. 52
Senn, C. 110

Shakespeare, P., Atkinson, D. and
    French, S. 40
Shakespeare, T. 176
Sheldon, A. 184, 186
Sigelman, C.K., Budd, E.C., Spanhel,
    C.L. and Schoenrock, C.J. 70
Simons, K. 50, 130, 136, 137, 160,
    173
Sinason, V. 40, 160, 198
Slattery, J. (with Johnson, K.) 15, 67,
    132, 133
Souza, A. (with Ramcharan, P.) 57, 103
Spedding, F., Harkness, E., Townson, L.,
    Docherty, A., McNulty, N. and
    Chapman, R. 143, 208, 209
Spelman, E. 27
Stainton 183
Stalker, K. 141, 167
Stancliffe, R. and Lakin, K. 65
Steier, F. 40
Sutcliffe, J. 136
Swantz, M.L. and Vainio-Mattila, A. 31
Swindon People First Research Team
    130, 172

Taylor, S.J., Bogdan, R. and Lutfiyya, Z.
    47, 81, 87, 201
Todd, S. and Shearn, J. 142
Townsley, R. 53, 60, 62, 173, 216
Townsley, R. and Macadam, M. 137,
    180
Traustadottir, R. 39
Traustadottir, R. and Johnson, K. 132,
    173, 175, 178, 184, 197
Traylen, H. 31
Tredgold, A.F. 11
Treleaven, L. 31
Tuhiwai Smith, L. 86
Turk, V. and Brown, H. 110
Tuttleby, A. (with Johnson, K.) 57, 133

Van Hove, G. 155, 160, 193
Veck, W. 217

Vernon, A. 38, 184
Vichealth Koori Research and
    Community Development Unit 85
Victorian Government 46

Wadsworth, Y. 32, 38
Wadsworth, Y. and Epstein, M. 32, 34
Walmsley, J. 14, 41, 51, 52, 53, 57, 60,
    66, 72, 73, 78, 96, 97, 98, 134, 147,
    149, 151, 156, 157, 164, 169, 173,
    174
Walmsley, J. (with Downer, J.) 15, 55,
    57, 58, 103, 142, 143, 171
Ward, K. and Trigler, J.S. 184, 209
Ward, L. 47, 171
Ward, L. and Simons, K. 126, 147, 176
Webb, P. 166
Welsh Office 46
Whittaker, A. 57, 137, 150, 151, 180
Whittell, B., Ramcharan, P. and
    members of People First Cardiff and
    the Vale 130, 171
Wickham, P. 197
Wilkinson, J. 49
Williams, P. and Schoultz, B. 55, 70,
    137
Williams, V. 57, 62, 130, 136, 139,
    141, 153, 154, 155, 159, 160, 172,
    176, 179, 181, 184, 186, 191, 192,
    194
Wolfensberger, W. 45, 47, 55
Wolfensberger, W. and Thomas, S. 45
Wolfensberger, W. and Tullman, S. 45

Zarb, G. 38, 50, 63, 156, 176, 184,
    212, 219, 221
Zuber-Skerritt, O. 31